"Richard Twiss's legacy is to challenge th
to explore how a more faithful life on tł
important not only for cowboys and Indians but for all who are committed to the
cause of the gospel in our twenty-first century global context."
Amos Yong, professor of theology and mission, Fuller Theological Seminary

"Richard Twiss's *Rescuing the Gospel from the Cowboys* provokes and challenges while
leading readers into a Native American understanding of the 'Jesus Way.' The reader
is confronted directly with racism, oppression and pain in Twiss's own personal
narrative as he sought to express a contextualized indigenous Christian theology
that extended far beyond the limitations of 'white man's religion.' This indigenous
account of decolonization of the gospel presents profound truths about the person
of Christ and significant historical lessons from indigenous believers."
Mae Elise Cannon, author of *Just Spirituality* and *Social Justice Handbook* and coauthor of
Forgive Us

"Dr. Richard Twiss is an irreplaceable voice for all peoples. His work is academically
astute. His prose is inspiring and articulate. This work stimulates the mind, woos
the heart and ultimately transforms faith."
Tony Kriz, author of *Aloof: Figuring Out Life with a God Who Hides*

"I wish I had this book a decade ago when I started in Native ministry, desiring to create
a fellowship where Native American students could meet Jesus without being required
to cross cultures. Twiss challenges those who long to see an indigenous Native
American church that contextualization must go beyond initial changes in music and
language and 'address economic, political, legal, health, agricultural, etc., issues as well.'
I can't wait to have the conversations Twiss starts in this book with my coworkers and
others who long to see Jesus' church thrive in the Native community."
Megan Krischke, co-coordinator of Native Ministries, InterVarsity Christian Fellowship

"Having sat at the feet of Richard Twiss, known the warmth of his friendship and
grieved his passing, I was thrilled to learn of this volume we now hold. *Rescuing the
Gospel from the Cowboys* is a significant book for all who seek to live in the way of
Jesus. Speaking honestly and respectfully in the face of oppression and violence
perpetrated in the name of the good news, Twiss invites fresh and real ways of following in the way of Jesus without preference to any one cultural frame, and
therefore opens the way to be who you are, as a particular person, of a particular
culture, and to do so in the shambolic way of the Creator. This book accomplishes
a vital task that should be self-evident: a person can be fully Lakota and fully
Christian—in fact, there is no other way to be fully Christian. Twiss throws open
the door for all indigenous churches to wrestle afresh with the fact that the gospel
is at home in every culture and simultaneously alien to every culture."
Dwight J. Friesen, Seattle School of Theology & Psychology, coauthor of *The New Parish*
and author of *Thy Kingdom Connected*

RESCUING THE GOSPEL FROM THE COWBOYS

A NATIVE AMERICAN EXPRESSION OF THE JESUS WAY

RICHARD TWISS

EDITED BY **RAY MARTELL**
AND **SUE MARTELL**

IVP Books

An imprint of InterVarsity Press
Downers Grove, Illinois

InterVarsity Press
P.O. Box 1400, Downers Grove, IL 60515-1426
ivpress.com
email@ivpress.com

InterVarsity Press® is the book-publishing division of InterVarsity Christian Fellowship/USA®, a movement of
students and faculty active on campus at hundreds of universities, colleges and schools of nursing in the United
States of America, and a member movement of the International Fellowship of Evangelical Students. For
information about local and regional activities, visit intervarsity.org.

Unless otherwise indicated, all Scripture quotations are taken from the Holy Bible, New Living Translation,
copyright ©1996, 2004, 2007. Used by permission of Tyndale House Publishers, Inc., Carol Stream, Illinois 60188.
All rights reserved.

In Memoriam is used by permission of Terry LeBlanc.

While all stories in this book are true, some names and identifying information may have been changed to protect
the privacy of individuals.

Cover design: Cindy Kiple
Interior design: Beth McGill
Images: Lakota Trinity by Father John Giuliani

ISBN 978-0-8308-4423-4 (print)
ISBN 978-0-8308-9853-4 (digital)

Printed in the United States of America ∞

Library of Congress Cataloging-in-Publication Data

Twiss, Richard, 1954-2013.
  Rescuing the Gospel from the cowboys : a Native American expression of the Jesus way / Richard Twiss ; edited by
Ray Martell and Sue Martell.
     pages cm
  Includes bibliographical references.
  ISBN 978-0-8308-4423-4 (pbk. : alk. paper)
  1. Indians of North America--Missions--History. 2. Indians of North America--Religion. 3. Indians of North
America--Canada--Religion. 4. Christianity--United States. 5. Christianity--Canada. I. Title.
  E98.M6T95 2015
  971.004'97--dc23
                                                                                        2015013537

P   24   23   22   21   20   19   18   17   16   15   14   13   12   11   10   9   8   7   6   5   4

Y   35   34   33   32   31   30   29   28   27   26   25   24   23   22   21   20   19   18   17

To Katherine . . . my lifelong friend, partner and love of my life. We continue to learn to walk side by side as we figure out how to be the best human beings we can be for one another, our children, grandchildren and *Tiyospaye*, "extended family."

I am deeply grateful for you and what we have forged together.

CONTENTS

IN MEMORIAM

RICHARD LEO TWISS

June 11, 1954–February 9, 2013

Richard Leo Twiss, Taoyate Ob Najin, "He Stands with His People," passed from this life and into the next on February 9, 2013, in Washington, D.C., encircled by his wife, Katherine, and sons Andrew, Phillip, Ian and Daniel. Richard was fifty-eight.

Richard was born on the Rosebud Reservation, South Dakota, among his mother Winona (Larvie) LaPointe's people, the Sicangu Band of the Rosebud Lakota/Sioux. Richard's father, Franklin (Buster) Twiss (deceased), was Oglala from the Pine Ridge Lakota/Sioux Reservation, also in South Dakota.

Until age seven Richard lived in Rosebud, a town of six hundred, on the reservation. In 1961 Richard's mom moved the family from the reservation to Denver, then to Klamath Falls, Oregon, and eventually to Silverton, Oregon, where Richard attended the third through twelfth grades. Richard's mom ensured they made regular summer visits back home in order to stay connected with family and culture.

After graduating from high school in 1972, Richard moved back to Rosebud to attend *Sinte Gleska*, "Spotted Tail," College. It was here that he became involved in the American Indian Movement (AIM). During this tumultuous time, Richard strengthened his connection with relatives and deepened his appreciation for Lakota culture.

Richard wandered for a while, ending up on the island of Maui in

Hawaii, where late one night, alone on a deserted beach, Creator responded to Richard's desperate prayer, making himself known to him. From that night in 1974 until his passing, Richard was on a spiritual journey to live a meaningful life as a Lakota follower of the Jesus Way.

Richard met and fell in love with Katherine Kroshus, of Vancouver, Washington, and married her in 1976. Richard's proudest legacy is his four boys, Andrew (Diana), Phillip, Ian (Toni), and Daniel; and his grandsons, Ezra, Leo and Jude.

In February 1997 Richard and Katherine founded the nonprofit ministry of Wiconi International. Through Wiconi, Richard and Katherine touched the lives of many thousands of people. Richard also cofounded NAIITS (North American Institute for Indigenous Theological Studies); he was chairman of the board for My People International, a member of the CCDA (Christian Community Development Association) and cofounder of Evangelicals for Justice. In 2011 Richard earned his doctorate in missiology from Asbury Theological Seminary. Until his passing, Richard continued his teaching career through the NAIITS program, Portland State University and other institutions of higher education.

Richard authored a number of books, pamphlets and articles over the years. His first book, *One Church, Many Tribes*, reached many people with the message of an inculturated faith in Jesus.

Richard's mother, Winona LaPointe, sisters Elaine and Laurie LaPointe, nieces Stacy (Mark), Melissa (Tony), Jana and their children remain to continue his memory. His brother Tom passed before Richard in 2010.

Composed by Terry LeBlanc, with assistance from Richard's family

FOREWORD

Each of us met Richard Twiss at different times, yet each of us met when our own journeys (and Richard's) needed additional lift to go forward on our common trail. Whether our first meeting was at a conference, through an introduction, while studying together, or just hanging out and taking a retrospective look at our Creator's thoughts, all of us became fast friends with Richard.

We all reflect very similarly on the fact that Richard had the astounding ability to absorb what he read or heard from others, transforming and then seamlessly integrating it into his own thinking. While each of us does somewhat the same thing as a function of our Indigenous communal approach to knowledge, Richard was a master.

It was in Spokane, Washington in 1995 where Richard hit his stride. He had convened a Christ, Culture, and the Kingdom seminar for pastors to present our "new" ideas about culture and faith. When the conference ended and all the attendees had departed, we turned to one another amazed that non-Indigenous pastors were keenly interested in what we had to say. It was the start of a new era for Indigenous followers of the Jesus Way.

Our individual and collective encounters forged links of deep and unbreakable friendship. Our camaraderie was truly symbiotic—an idea from one transformed by the other, complete with escalating humor. Our journey together depended so much on humor that after a number of years of tag-team conferences, Richard's mom referred to us as a stand-up comedy team. There was never any doubt that Terry was the straight man!

When Richard was provided the opportunity for doctoral studies at Asbury Theological Seminary, he was more than a bit reluctant to attempt such a lofty goal. Moreover, we were all frustrated that advanced degrees seemed necessary to further our efforts to bring an Indigenous voice to the wider public. In Richard's first week of school we had no fewer than seven serious discussions about him quitting the program. Yet, in the end, the experience brought us closer together.

The Indigenous message we brought to class discussions became such a dominant decolonizing voice that we were concerned about being too great an influence—but the professors encouraged us, pointing out how we were empowering international students to speak up. Following a welcome event that we hosted—where Richard spoke words of affirmation for those in attendance—seventy students from around the world expressed that for the first time, they felt welcomed to this country.

Passionate argument often highlighted our close friendship. Yet, while so engaged, we never expressed animosity or ill will—only deep commitment to one another. Just before his passing, for example, an argument raged over Richard's attempt to nuance the definition of syncretism in this, his last book. He used the descriptor *counteractive* to modify the word *syncretism*, attempting a new definition with this two-word phrase: *counteractive syncretism*. We told him it was needless confusion—this hybrid phrase just didn't correspond to the simple definition of syncretism. A lot of food for thought like this came to him in deep discussions over many lattes.

That he took our viewpoints seriously was always evident because later on we would hear people say, "Richard says . . ." and in their words we would hear our own words being repeated—the ones we had previously discussed, even argued over. In our Indigenous communal way, he took our thoughts—those that were different from his—and made them his own. Two different things, his thoughts and our thoughts, became one new thing—*his* new thought. Now, that is the definition of syncretism! His nuancing of the word *syncretism* is still not what we might agree with, but we think he would just laugh at this *nonendorsement* endorsement of one of our best and deepest friends.

Richard was enigmatic. On the one hand, as he made clear in the closing years of his life, he was a common man. Yet undoubtedly, in many ways he was not. He became, for many in the wider Indigenous community, "the voice of one crying in the wilderness," inviting believers to make straight paths for people to find Jesus. Denominational and doctrinal competition that encroached on his early experience of faith set Richard up to return to the simple message of Jesus—a highly-energized story of a Jesus stripped of colonial baggage. And Richard used his unique style and affable sense of humor to communicate this like no one else ever could.

Richard was a foil to anyone who encumbered the message of Jesus with culturally-bound prejudice. He presented a simple path to faith— inviting people to be all they could be through a renewed relationship with Creator's son. He welcomed everyone to be a part of what Creator was doing among us, making everyone feel special in the process. We hope you will sense his generous spirit as he welcomes you to broaden your horizons—to come to understand a world where, in Richard's words, "The Gospel is being rescued from the cowboys!"

Terry LeBlanc (Gitpu), Mi'kmaq/Acadian, Listuguj First Nation/Campbellton; founding chair, director, NAIITS: An Indigenous Learning Community; executive director, Indigenous Pathways

Randy S. Woodley, PhD, Keetoowah descendant; Distinguished Professor of Faith and Culture, George Fox Seminary; author of Shalom and the Community of Creation: An Indigenous Vision *(Eerdmans) and* Living in Color: Embracing God's Passion for Ethnic Diversity *(InterVarsity Press)*

Adrian Jacobs (Ganosono), Turtle Clan, Cayuga Nation, Six Nations Haudenosaunee Confederacy; Keeper of the Circle (principal), Sandy-Saulteaux Spiritual Centre

Ray Aldred (Neyihaw), Cree, Treaty 8; assistant professor of theology, Ambrose University and Seminary; chair, NAIITS: An Indigenous Learning Community

YOU JUST GHOSTED

You didn't say goodbye you just ghosted
We turned around and you just weren't there
A thousand miles away from home you fell
You left for heaven and plunged us all in hell

You didn't give us a hug you just ghosted
In the middle of winter the cold breeze blew
Stranded and poor we had no way to get to you
A month later we finally showed softened and blue

You left without a word you just ghosted
Words only partially typed and a messy pile
Now we're sweeping things up and tying a bow
Finishing your story with "this is what we know"

You left without a signature you just ghosted
Outstanding heart accounts that'll never be paid
But we're carrying on doing the best we surmise

Dealing with your quick exit and total surprise

Adrian Jacobs

PREFACE

H*au kola,* "Hello friend."
This manuscript, *Rescuing the Gospel from the Cowboys*, is based on my reflections, experiences and intense research over the past twenty-four years. It is the story of many of us Native and Indigenous leaders who have been finding our way out of neocolonialism into a new liberty as we've walked this Jesus Road together since the late 1980s.

This book began as a doctoral dissertation to research whether or not there is, or has been, an Indigenous contextualized expression of the Christian faith among the tribes of the United States and, to a lesser degree, Canada. The purpose of my research was to identify in what ways Native leaders were reframing the gospel narrative as part of a larger narrative of postcolonial decolonization in their own unique cultural contexts. The specific focus will be on the years 1989–2009.

As I think about it these days, contextualization is not a principle, formula or evangelistic strategy. Contextualization is a relational process of theological and cultural reflection within a community—seeking to incorporate traditional symbols, music, dance, ceremony and ritual to make faith in Jesus a truly local expression. There is an honest recognition of the guidance of Creator's Spirit behind the widening critique and correction to the hegemonic assumptions of modernity and colonization/decolonization. Critical thinking and retraditionalization are key to the good contextualization efforts arising among Indigenous communities.

In the radically-changing ethnic demographics of American culture and the global community, followers of Jesus are presented with great opportunities and challenges for good. We must genuinely appreciate all cultures as being capable of reflecting biblical faith. We must move away from "American Christian mythology," which undergirds colonization and its resulting paternalism in Indigenous communities. We must embrace new theological perspectives emerging from Native leaders as being "equal." These perspectives provide new pathways for the contextualization process. These pathways identify Indigenous cultural values, spirituality and ceremony as central to the new approaches to discipleship and leadership development which occur within the community. No longer are such "new approaches" brought in by the cultural outsider.

THE CREATOR'S PRESENCE AMONG NATIVE PEOPLE

There is only one Creator of heaven and earth. There are not "many" Creators. Just one! *All* of human and nonhuman creation comes out of this one Creator. There is not a Creator who created Africa and Africans, or Asia and Asians, or Europe and Europeans, and so forth. Who can create something from nothing or bring into existence something that was previously nonexistent? It is only this one Creator and there is none like him/her.[1] That being said, this one Creator self-reveals in and through a myriad of cultural realities in human and nonhuman persons throughout *Unci Maka,* our "Mother Earth."[2]

There are world religions that present names for this one Creator. These religions provide creation stories and explanations for heaven, earth and humans, and supply wisdom and doctrines to help humanity resolve its existential dilemma. There are world religions that have a sacred text to reference their beliefs, and there are thousands of "folk religions" with oral traditions that do the same through story, yet—there is still just *one* Creator.

For us First Nations people, following Creator-Jesus within our Indigenous cultural ways without submitting to the hegemonic cultural assumptions of today's conservative evangelicals is tough. I am reminded weekly of these neocolonial and ignorant assumptions as they show up on the radar of my life. The following email conversation I had in 2012 typifies these "pings."

A group of my First Nations friends and I were looking for a facility to host a weekend planning retreat. We looked at a few of them and decided on one I knew about from past experience. The negotiations to book the facility took an unexpected but not totally surprising turn as the registration person reacted to the "heathen Indians" once again:

Hello Mr. Twiss,

Whenever we have a new group register with our facility we take the time and effort to research their beliefs and methods, etc. I have been doing that with your group and we must CANCEL your retreat with us. In your effort to "restore culture" you are taking the indigenous people back into paganism, shamanism, false gods and the occult. You are leading them away from the Gospel message of the Bible. We pray you will rethink what you are doing to the very people you love so much. I will return your deposit.

Thank you. "Jane Doe."

Greetings Jane Doe,

Thank you for your response. I have many years of involvement and friendship with people in your center. I look forward to continuing this conversation and still keeping our reservation to host our retreat there. While a few may have some narrow and misinformed ideas about our faith in Jesus and the scriptures, please be assured our group is as remarkable a group of Christ-followers as you will meet! Please feel free to give me a call on my cell phone today.

Thank you, Richard

Hello Richard,

Thank you so much for your email. I am aware of your history. We do not doubt your sincere heart and desires. But some of the teachings of your group and/or its speakers seem to be steering people away from the solid Gospel and taking people toward other gods. It may be subtle, and it may not be your intent, but if one person leaves our facility compromised in their Christian walk then we have failed in our mission. It is a hard thing we have to do but the Lord has asked us to take a very strong stand and we can do nothing less. I have returned the deposit and have still canceled the retreat. We pray the Lord will continue to guide you carefully in your efforts.

Jane Doe

Greetings Jane,

Thanks for your response, which honestly surprises me. It is certainly not the spirit that I have felt from the organization's beginning as its founders poured their lives into creating a space for people to wrestle with the deep issues of life and spiritual growth. So many of us were in our early twenties when we first journeyed there, struggling to make sense of this new faith and life we found in Jesus.

The accusations you make against us—"biblical compromise [falsehood/heresy], steering people away from the Gospel into idolatry [rejecting Christ]," clothed in the notion of protecting the true Gospel from Native cultural ways of our Native Christian community—are plainly offensive, theologically arrogant and judgmental at best—perhaps culturally racist at worst. Your language of "the Lord has asked us to take a very strong stand" against people like us and the way we express our faith in Jesus, biblically, culturally and theologically, reveals the kind of cultural oppression our people face from an idealized and racialized view of scripture. If the goal is to turn your center into a bastion of biblical protectionism, theological control and cultural judgmentalism, your words well reflect that direction.

Peace and grace—Richard

Richard,

The answer is still "NO." I hear what you are saying, but we still cannot support what your group and the Indigenous People Movement are teaching. No retreat at our facility.

Jane Doe

While this person may represent a more extreme point of view, it nonetheless is what the majority of Euro-American evangelicals believe about our Native cultural and ceremonial ways. Ignorance, suspicion and fear of Native ways run deep in the soul of the American church. I will show later how this has been (and remains) the American church's attitude toward our Native ways for centuries now. The tragedy is that it is not just we who suffer. Because we suffer so deeply, the entire church and nation does too!

However, suspicion and fear run both ways. Indigenous people have a lot to fear about the "white man's religion"! Conquest, racism, hatred, prejudice, exclusion, forced assimilation and ongoing institutional injustices are just a few of the fears that come to mind.

"EVEN WHEN WE GET IT RIGHT, WE GET IT WRONG"
—SPOKANE GARRY

When my wife and I lived on the Coeur d'Alene Reservation in Northern Idaho in 1996, I was introduced to a life-changing story about a remarkable Native leader named Chief Spokane Garry. He is one of my heroes of faith and culture. Creator used Chief Garry (1811–1892) as a "messenger" who had a profound spiritual impact by spreading the gospel (along with his friend and co-worker Kootenai Pelly) among his people and numerous other tribes in Washington, Idaho, Oregon and southward.[3]

I have been to the cemetery in Spokane, Washington where Chief Garry was buried. It was an honor and a privilege to be standing there and I was deeply touched. He was a tribal leader, husband, father and advocate for justice and Christian values. While his efforts appeared to have no lasting impact and did not bring the white settlers to an understanding of justice, nevertheless—throughout it all—he remained true to his faith in Jesus. He died rejected and impoverished.

While we were living on the "Rez" (reservation), we did not know of one Native man who regularly attended any of the six Protestant evangelical churches—despite Garry's life work. Barely half a dozen women attended. This was true as well for the neighboring Nez Perce and Kalispel reservations. This fact stood in stark contrast to the amazing spiritual movement inspired by Chief Garry in this region that occurred *prior* to an established colonial presence.

There were other instances of divine intervention in "preparing the way of the Lord" (Isaiah 40:3) for mission work among the tribes of this area, including prophecies among the Middle Spokane and Kalispel tribes.

Yuree-rachen. *Yuree-rachen*, "Circling Raven," was a shaman from the Middle Spokane tribe in the late 1700s. He had a personal crisis of faith in Creator after his son's untimely death, so he went to Mt. Spokane for a time of fasting and prayer. During this worship time, he received a vision from Creator, whom they called *Quilent-sat-men*, "He-Made-Us." In the vision, *Yuree-rachen* saw white men dressed strangely, carrying bundles of leaves fastened together. He was told that the people were to learn from the teachings inscribed on the leaves.[4]

Shining Shirt. A similar vision, in about the same time period, was given to "Shining Shirt," said to be both a chief and a shaman of the Kalispel tribe. Ethnologist Harry Holbert Turney-High writes that Shining Shirt was granted a vision in which he was told that there is a Creator, and that fair-skinned men in black robes would come and teach them how to live in a new way, according to a moral law. During the vision Shining Shirt was given a metal object engraved with a cross. White men were *unknown* to these tribal people at that time.[5]

Creator had been at work preparing the Native people for the arrival of the gospel of Jesus. The Christian revival among those tribes evangelized by Spokane Garry and Kootenai Pelly was noted by white settlers and explorers. For example, Washington Irving, in "The Adventures of Captain Bonneville," further documents the spread of Christianity throughout the tribes of that region. During the winter of 1832, Bonneville camped with the Nez Perce on the upper Salmon River in Oregon and observed:

Simply to call these people religious . . . would convey but a faint idea of the deep hue of piety and devotion which pervades their whole conduct. Their honesty is immaculate, and their purity of purpose, and their observance of the rites of their religion, are most uniform and remarkable. They are, certainly, more like a nation of saints than a horde of savages.[6]

I think the purity and genuine faith mentioned by Bonneville and others was a result of a faith birthed from the witness of Jesus-following Indigenous people to their own tribes. They spoke the contextual gospel from their hearts among their people. This was not simply the "white man's gospel"![7]

During the time frame of 1835 to 1850, European-American missionaries arrived in Washington and Oregon. They communicated the gospel from their own cultural viewpoints. The truth is that the gospel of Christ *already* had a foothold among the tribes of these areas.

With the arrival of the white missionaries and their brand of Christianity, the story takes a predictable and unfortunate turn. Just as Catholic missionaries insisted on Roman control over earlier Celtic Christian areas,[8] so these Anglo missionaries insisted on Euro-American (Western-style) Christian worship as well as doctrine. What is worse, their paternalism, ethnocentrism, colonial collusion and modernism soon "civilized" this Indigenous movement of the gospel story and thus blinded these Christians to the already existing work of Creator among the Native nations of the land. Today, throughout the entire region, except for the history books, there is but a remnant of that remarkable outpouring of Creator's story of grace, spirituality and community renewal.

Unfortunately this negative legacy of Christian mission among the Coeur d'Alene, Spokane, Nez Perce and other tribes is not exceptional. After four centuries, First Nations peoples' cultural expressions are still marginalized or oppressed across North America. Native leadership in the wider church is absent in the evangelical mainstream. These early missionaries, "people of their times," found little reason to regard Native believers as coequals because they perceived their own cultural ways as superior. Thus, the majority of these missionaries denounced and demonized Native cultural ways, part and parcel, as pagan, idolatrous, evil and sinful.

As a result, an authentic Native American cultural or Indigenous expression of following Jesus was never allowed to develop—the very idea being rejected as syncretistic and incongruous with "biblical" faith. This kind of colonial missionary mindset is, sadly, not a thing of the past, but is still the prevailing perspective (in both Native and non-Native Christian leaders) among those working in our tribal communities today. Instead of embracing Jesus as the Creator, the majority of Native Americans blame American Christianity and the church for the loss of their own culture and identity. Is it any wonder that the vast majority of Native people today reject Christianity as the "white man's religion"?

The headline of a 2007 article from the CBC News Network in Canada read, "Winnipeg Church Nixes Native Dancing at Habitat for Humanity Event." The article went on to say:

> A Winnipeg church prevented aboriginal dancers from performing at a Habitat for Humanity event this week, saying the performance was not an expression of Christian faith.... "Native spiritual dancing has its roots in a different spiritual belief system that is incongruent with traditional Christian worship."—Pastor Mark Hughes.[9]

This pastor and his church staff, though professing a vision for creating a multiethnic congregation, are not exceptional in their ethnocentric views and attitudes toward First Nations people and their cultural expressions. This church averages 2,500 people in Sunday attendance, is one of the largest in Canada, and is considered a leading "Christian voice" in the province and city.

Because of colonial missionaries' attitudes of cultural superiority, a Native American cultural expression of following Jesus didn't develop at the time. Another powerful factor contributing to the cultural oppression brought with the gospel was that Native people were, many times, first introduced to Jesus as part of American territorialism, treaty enforcement, educational programs, economic hegemony and social disintegration through assimilation. For a period of time beginning in 1869, "Indian agencies were assigned to religious societies." Those assigned were "duly subordinate and responsible" in these of-

BOARDING SCHOOLS

Perhaps the most devastating blow to the lives of Native Americans was the forced removal of thousands of their children from their homes, the goal being assimilation into American or Canadian society.

My grandparents, parents, aunties, uncles and numerous cousins were all required and/or forced to attend either a Bureau of Indian Affairs (BIA) or Catholic-run boarding school on the Pine Ridge or Rosebud Lakota/Sioux Reservations. I have heard heartbreaking stories of many of their traumatic experiences. As children my relatives endured such cruelties as: being forced to work in the fields, dairy, bakery and shops as free laborers; eating onion sandwiches while watching the priests and nuns dine lavishly by comparison; and being severely punished for speaking so much as one word in their own language. It was not unusual for children to suffer nervous breakdowns as a result of various abuses.

While my mother and her siblings grew up speaking Lakota in their home, they chose not to teach us, their children, in order to protect us from the kind of racism and prejudice they had experienced. In part too, they wanted us to be successful in the white man's world, and speaking Lakota was a hindrance to that. The boarding school experience was a major factor in their decision.

The effects of the Boarding School era have steadily flowed down through the generations to my relatives, and, to a lesser degree, to me, and now my wife and sons. We see the results of this policy on the Rosebud Reservation today.

An article in the New York Times titled "Indian Reservation Reeling in Wave of Youth Suicides and Attempts" tells the story of the traumatic results of these boarding schools.[10] The young people attempting and/or committing suicide are the children and grandchildren of those forced to attend the boarding schools on the Rosebud Reservation.

David Wallace Adams, in his book *Education for Extinction: American Indians and the Boarding School Experience, 1875–1928*, goes into great detail about the history of the Boarding School Era.[11]

ficial capacities as Indian agents to the United States Department of the Interior, via their denominational structures. The Federal Government, along with denominational and missionary groups, believed this plan might improve the ability of government policies to stimulate "the slow growth of the savage beasts," leading to the "moral and religious advancement of the Indians." It was hoped that this collaboration between Christianity and government agencies would work to "assume charge of the intellectual and moral education of the Indians . . . within the reach of their influence."[12] The intention was to improve the well-being of the tribal people assigned to the care of these various church missionary societies.

WHAT HAPPENED TO THE GOOD NEWS?

My twenty years of observation and participation in mission activities among First Nations people has made it evident that rather than *good* news, the "Good News" story remains highly ineffective among Native people, and for many, it means *bad* news. After hundreds of years of missionary efforts, an extremely low number of Native people are actively engaged in a life of faith in Jesus and participation in some Christian tradition. This is largely reflective of Euro-American colonial cultural forms, expressions and worldview values. The majority of Native evangelical church leaders and members today have little understanding or appreciation of the meaning and value of critical contextualization— at least in a ceremonial or "religious" setting. Little attempt has been made toward the establishment of a truly Indigenous church movement that occurs "within" the sociocultural, ceremonial and religious lifeways of the community.

While I am only briefly mentioning some points of historical oppression and trauma, there are volumes of texts that describe in great detail how a Eurocentric and "modern" worldview of early missionaries and church workers engendered a neocolonial hegemony in American missionary efforts toward the Indigenous tribes.[13] These modernist assumptions resulted in the church's inability to represent Jesus Christ appropriately to the host people of the land; thus came the failure to form

a biblical Indigenous faith among the tribes of North America. This hegemony has not dissolved or disappeared over time, but instead continues as a major problem plaguing the work of the church among First
Nations people. However, some Native ministry leaders have begun to
address this problem with vigor, wisdom and courage—and that is the
point of this book.

I have observed that Indigenous believers are increasingly disen-
chanted, disillusioned and dissatisfied with their traditional, evangelical,
mostly "white church" experience. This has served as the impetus for a
new decolonizing contextualization movement of the gospel. This
movement had multiple creative centers, each somewhat independent of
each other, and spread from those centers beginning in the late 1980s
and on into this century. The writings from African, South American
and Asian theologians, as well as conversations with Indigenous leaders
around the world, inspired a new generation of Indigenous leaders
within the wider Christian community to begin exploring other possibilities (i.e., "innovations"). As they freed themselves from colonial
Christianity and began a process of personal internal decolonization,
they sought to contextualize the gospel in their various cultural contexts.
In the past twenty years, this dissatisfaction has spread all across North
America as believers embrace a new and holistic view of their relationship with Jesus and their religious practice *within* their cultural ways.

So, Is There a Problem?

For over twenty years I have been a part of the growing international phenomenon of emerging Indigenous decolonizing contextualization initiatives. These initiatives are contextualizing the gospel and engaging in revitalization efforts in response to the prolonged paternalism and
marginalization of Native peoples. Various First Nations–led decolonizing
efforts are proactively challenging and offering alternative narratives to the
cultural hegemony of previous decades of Native missions. The paradigms
of mission and ecclesiology that are surfacing are biblically-informed alternatives to the current neocolonial models and practices of denominations, mission agencies and some Native Christian organizations.

I have used Everett Rogers's *Diffusion of Innovations* in my research.[14] I have identified the innovators, early adopters and opinion leaders and traced various networks and communication channels. Through interviews with the key leaders, I discovered the foundational ideologies and theologies that have inspired the various Native American Indigenous contextualization initiatives within the period from 1989 to 2009. Obviously these initiatives did not occur in a vacuum. The work and writings of others inspired the efforts of these innovators prior to 1989, and I will reference a few of them, but limit my study to the past twenty years. I gathered evidence illustrating how the prevailing attitude of existing Native church leaders and mission agencies toward these emerging contextualization efforts—which had been primarily negative—has changed over the past twenty years.

It is my great hope that this book will enhance the existing body of literature on First Nations decolonizing contextual efforts in North America. Because this wave of contextualization is so new, there is very little literature available. There have been many books written by Native thinkers and theologians on the negative impact of missionary efforts among Native people. While offering a helpful *critique*, they offer little help in creating a redemptive way *forward*.

I want to magnify the awareness and critical importance of innovative missiological paradigms emerging from the Native Christian community as viable biblical alternatives to existing models. A few Native leaders— representative of a "conservative evangelical" theological perspective— have written articles and materials that are highly critical of contextualization efforts.[15] Other Anglo writers have been very "fundamentalist" or "modernist" in their criticisms of the movement.

This book, as a broad analysis of these decolonizing initiatives, represents the significant possibility of restructuring missionary approaches and introducing new models for the encouragement of community development among our North American tribal people. This is not exclusively true for Native peoples. Our society as a whole is becoming more diverse culturally and in choice of religious faith. New mission and community development paradigms will be required for those cultures as well.

I have read volumes about the early accounts of missionary activities in the United States—primarily in the Protestant community, but with some reference to the work of Roman Catholics—in order to discover the primary influences that shaped Christian missions to Native Americans. I explored some American denominational missions' history literature—including material on First Nations people—to provide a more comprehensive understanding of the context in which these missionary activities occurred.[16] I focused on the people whose stories both informed and shaped my understanding of the ways in which Christian missions have affected them. I reviewed various Euro-American philosophical, ideological and sociopolitical influences that provided perspectives to make sense of America's role in the larger Western history of colonization.[17] Particular attention is paid to America's self-identification as a "Christian nation" and its policies of territorial expansion and dealing with the "Indian problem."

While this book is focused on North America, our colonial missions' history is fundamentally similar to that of all Indigenous communities around the world where European colonization occurred. In my travels I have talked at length with Indigenous friends in New Zealand, Australia, Peru, Argentina, South Africa, Samoa, Mexico, Hawaii, Rwanda, Micronesia, Mongolia, Korea and other countries. In reality the story of Native Americans is true of all Indigenous peoples' stories.

Syncretism & Westernism—All Mixed Up

Syncretism. What is syncretism? Basically it is the idea of mixing, combining or blending. In the ancient world it was the military alliance of Cretan cities in Greece that combined their armies to fight "the bad guys." It is related to synergy, which is a mutually advantageous combination of distinct leaders, organizations, ideas, elements, plans and designs working in unity. Synchronized swimmers coordinate their movements in the pool to swim as "one" unit.

Relative to this book, syncretism is a theological term that carries the idea of mixing religious beliefs together. For some this is a matter of critical concern because these are not just any beliefs, but what are perceived as incompatible or opposing beliefs—not just surface or behavioral beliefs, but essential worldview perspectives. Over the past two to three decades in North America, syncretism has become a topic of intense disagreement among those involved in Native American ministry. When it comes to Western systematic theology, syncretism is not seen as positive, but rather as antithetical to "sound doctrine." These perceptions of syncretism are particularly strident in Indian Country when it comes to the intersection of faith and culture. I acknowledge there are situations where mixing can blur or distort one's vision of Christ, which I think is the essential problem. We know that Christ is not distorted but people's perceptions certainly can be. "Now we see things imperfectly, like puzzling reflections in a mirror, but then we will see everything with perfect clarity. All that I know now is partial and incomplete, but then I will know everything completely, just as God now knows me completely" (1 Cor 13:12). If we can only, at best, see "puzzling reflections," then perhaps we can never totally escape distortion. I am suggesting in light of the arguable definitions of "what is and what isn't" syncretism, that mixing is a normative process of positive change and transformation— and not always so clear.

Without attempting to present a succinct definition of syncretism, I invite you to join me and briefly wrestle with the evolution and fluidity of meanings, applications and language. This means considering the sources or locations from which authoritative definitions originate. As Indigenous scholars, we acknowledge the need to speak to people in their own cultural languages—but there still exists the tension of remaining true to Creator's unique story of Jesus and Great Spirit's work among us while doing that.

While theologians and church leaders attempt to define syncretism with "relative objectivity," I don't see this being possible because the conversation is situated within, thus prejudiced by, Western reductionist categories. Native North American ministry leaders have never seriously studied its meaning outside these Western categories and are thus predisposed to consider syncretism to be synonymous with biblical heresy.[18] Ineffective ministry strategies continue unopposed when syncretism is confused with critical contextualization.

My friend Harold Roscher (Cree) invites us to widen this discourse to include "How we as 'Indians' thought about syncretism. What was our word for that idea?" He says, "I suggest we use our Indigenous eyes to look at the concept of syncretism not only as comparison, but to show the broader world we struggled with these issues before Christian missionaries showed up." He explains it this way:

> For example let's say you were a spiritual leader from the Pine Ridge Sioux Reservation in South Dakota and you moved into our territory here in Northern Alberta (Canada) Cree country. After arriving you began sharing your Lakota teachings among the Cree. After a while, you might mix in some Cree teachings to make it more palatable for us Crees. Our Cree Elders are not opposed in principle to your being a cultural teacher; however, as a Lakota elder you must follow our protocols for teaching. In the old days you as a Lakota elder would sit with four different Cree elders and discuss your teachings, and these four elders would eventually get together to discuss/discern your teachings. If they felt your teachings were trustworthy, you would be given permission, even the blessing, to conduct your Lakota ceremonies in Cree Country. I believe each tribe had its way of dealing with false teachings and the blending of teachings. It is because of these cultural safeguards the teachings in our original languages stayed purer. Translation into English has been difficult for tribal rituals and ceremonies to remain as exact to the traditional teachings. So, is translation another component to syncretism?[19]

As followers of Christ we share a common belief in a Ghost. Jesus said he had to leave this world so that "The Helper" would come in his place. Our Spirit Guide—our Helper—is a Ghost. Fundamental to my discourse about syncretism is a great confidence in the presence, power and persuasion of the Holy Spirit to help keep us from going off the deep end on this journey of personal and spiritual transformation when it comes to cultural appropriation in light of biblical revelation.

Globally, contemporary definitions and concerns about syncretism must be rescued from "the Cowboys" or "Western cultural captivity." While I feel compelled to use existing terminology on the topic, we desperately need to relocate the discourse about syncretism from its Western epistemological hegemony to an Indigenous worldview framework. For many evangelicals this hegemony is understood as biblically rooted in the concern for "converting the lost." Thus syncretism is threatening because it encroaches on the gospel message as *the* saving message by differentiating good from evil, sacred from profane, heaven from hell, and, in our instance, Native from non-Native.

As a beginning point for this rescue operation, while I acknowledge the word *syncretism* cannot be rehabilitated because of its theologically political nature, I do hope to dull its edge. To some degree at least, I hope to reduce its culturally demonizing power in our Indigenous communities by widening the context of the conversation. I am proposing, based on biblical research by reputable scholars, that a transitional process of syncretism is a normal part of our spiritual growth—yes, normal! It might even be thought of as "transitional" syncretism or a syncretistic process of transformation.

People move in and out of syncretism as they embrace, reject, modify, learn and grow toward spiritual maturity as sociocultural persons following Jesus. Syncretism is not the undisputed end of the process, although it might end up that way. Contemporary evangelical thought has been inclined to see syncretism in a dualistic interpretive context—as a final and unchangeable state of being. It is seen as the consequence of combining good and evil, right and wrong, correct and false, biblical and heretical, godly and demonic, enlightened and deceived beliefs or practices resulting in falsehood, heresy or ultimate deception. This cultural "deception" is identified by contrasting it to the theological standards for the "true faith," which is firmly embedded in a Western polemic.

Peter van der Veer suggests that the term *syncretism* refers to a "politics of difference and identity and that as such the notion of power is crucial in its understanding. At stake is the power to identify true religion and to authorize some practices as 'truthful' and others as 'false.'" *Syncretism* came to be used by defenders of "the true faith" as a protection against illicit contamination—"a sign of religious decadence," "betrayal of principles" or the "corruption of the Truth." "What it attempted to do was to establish itself as the single source of authentication."[20]

A group of Native evangelical leaders (CHIEF—Christian Hope Indian Eskimo Fellowship) offers this definition of culture and syncretism:

> By native culture, we mean the dynamic learned life-ways, beliefs, and values of our people as revealed in our languages, customs, relationships, arts and rituals. In native culture, religion permeates all aspects of life and is often identified as being the culture, even though it is only an aspect of it.
>
> By syncretism, we refer specifically to the subtle attempt to integrate Biblical truth and faith in Christ with non-Biblical Native religious beliefs, practices, and forms. The result is an adulteration of Biblical truth and the birth of "another gospel" (Gal 1:6-9).[21]

In 2000 the Native American District of the Christian and Missionary Alliance (C&MA) Church produced a position paper titled "Boundary Lines." In the preamble they write their purpose:

> [T]o assist pastors and lay people to protect [them] from unbiblical teaching and to promote the proper use of culture in the Native American evangelical Christian context. Over the years, there seems to have been a consensus among the evangelical denominations, mission organizations and independent Native Christian churches that true believers should break completely with all animistic practices. Recently, there has been introduced in the Native evangelical church community the concept that drums, rattles, and other sacred paraphernalia formerly used in animistic worship can be "redeemed" for use in Christian worship. This position does not enjoy consensus among Native evangelical church leaders. The Paper addresses the fundamental issues relating to the concept of redeeming/transforming animistic objects for Christian worship. Legitimate definitions of the terms "Culture," "World view," "Syncretism," "Cultural

Form and Meaning," "Sacred Objects," and "Critical Contextual-ization" as they relate to this study have been provided.[22]

Both of these Native-produced documents attempt to establish their views as the standards for biblical authenticity or "the official" Native positions. They are quoted as authoritative sources of biblical scholarship within our wider Native evangelical community. Their use of the phrases "adulteration of Biblical truth," "birth of another gospel," "true believers," "unbiblical teaching," "proper use of culture," and "legitimate definitions of terms" implies control. It is again what van der Veer describes as "the power to identify true religion and to authorize some practices as 'truthful' and others as 'false' . . . as the single source of authentication."[23] It is not good hermeneutics.

It would appear that theology needs not only to be rescued from the cowboys and the Crown, but perhaps the Indians (Indigenous leaders) too! Rather than creating categories of true and false, I think we would be better served if we considered syncretism to be the exploration of the synthesis of faith, belief and practice in a dynamic process of blending, adding, subtracting, changing, testing and working things out. This process does not take anything away from the authority of Scripture or orthodoxy. The critical dynamic for this process of pro-ducing loving and mature followers of Jesus, however, is that it is not an individualistic venture. It is thoroughly rooted in a community of fellow seekers. This is where safety and balance are found. That being said, however, conversations between the conservative and less-conservative Native leadership have not occurred with any regularity, and relationships remain estranged.

Because we're frail human beings, the dynamics of personal spiritual growth over time cannot be easily, cleanly identified and quantified, or categorized for accuracy. Jesus told his early disciples that after new seeds were planted and weeds began to grow up alongside them, they couldn't distinguish the difference between the weeds and the wheat growing in the field. So he advised them not to pull up the weeds be-cause they'd be pulling up the wheat too (Mt 13:24-30). Jesus said, "Yes, just as you can identify a tree by its fruit, so you can identify people by their actions" (Matt 7:20). The fruit of the Spirit is love, joy, peace, patience, kindness, goodness, faithfulness, gentleness and self-control (Gal 5:22). While these fruits, qualities, values or characteristics are universally true for all people, how do they find expression, uniquely, in each local culture?

Charles Kraft notes the question faced by Christian witnesses is, however, "whether any given undesirable state is but a step in a continuing process or whether the changes have virtually come to an end and the people are settled in their present beliefs and behavior."[24] Is someone simply passing through on his or her journey, or have they decided to settle in and dwell there? Is settling for an hour too long? How about a week, month, year or decade? What is actually at stake with syncretism? Salvation? Eternal acceptance in heaven or rejection in hell? Judgment? Or how about power, control, position, status and authority?

Syncretism implies mixing. As cultural beings, we have nothing but syncretism in the church, and rightly so, since the gospel always gets inside culture (parable of the yeast and the dough, parable of the mustard seed, parable of the wheat and the tares). We mix music, ceremony, language, art, symbols, vocabulary, fashion, ideologies, nationalism and cultural metaphors constantly.

So the question is, is this a step or the end product? And, is this a kind of mixing that respects Creator and culture, or the kind that contradicts or eliminates either a particular view of Creator (what most people mean by syncretism) or culture (what the conservatives end up doing)?

True conversion—becoming transformed, and over a lifetime *conformed* to the person of Jesus—is a gradual and erratic process of sociocultural change or acculturation. It is not regulated or predictable, nor is it an evenly paced process of change and transformation, but quite the opposite. It is uneven, variable, messy, irregular and fluctuating. It is an organic process of spiritual transformation as we engage the sacred ways of our Creator, bound by the limitations of our existence as finite human beings.

As a "syncretist" I have a core allegiance to Jesus as Creator that is enriched, further informed and inspired by traditional Lakota ceremonial ways and beliefs. I am able to hold the "exclusive" claims of Christ in tension with the religious claims of other Indigenous ways that I embrace, and lose nothing of my faith in Jesus in the process. This is part of the contrast of confidence between Western dualistic categories as the container for "true knowledge of God" and Indigenous ambiguity for embracing Creator "all around." This ambiguity is normative syncretistic process, not counteractive syncretism.

Counteractive syncretism. A legitimate concern exists about a kind of mixing that I will call "counteractive syncretism." Counteractive syncretism conveys the idea of a kind of mixing of core religious beliefs that ultimately diminish, fully resist, or finally stop—*counteract*—one's personal faith journey as a follower of Jesus and his ways. As I alluded to earlier, I believe that any of these three conditions—diminish, resist or stop—can be temporary realities in a person's journey. As the adage goes, however, "It's one thing if a bird lands on your head. It's another thing if you let it build a nest."

Does blending or mixing cultural ways/beliefs complement or mutually and positively inform varying faith perspectives, or does it result in the rejection of the centrality of the biblical, historical Jesus Christ as Creator—the incarnation of Creator among us? Does this rejection stem from assumptions that other religious beliefs/spiritual practices are equally dynamic in fulfilling Creator's intended purposes for creation through Jesus? Adrian Jacobs (Cayuga from the Handsome Lake Longhouse of the Six Nations Iroquois Confederacy) sees the essential problem with syncretism as "taking two things that are not the same and in the process of syncretism making them the same." He would appeal to the apostle Paul's positive reference to the belief of the Mars Hill devotees before the altar to the Unknown God as being equivalent to (and thus syncretized with) Paul's declaration of Jesus (Acts 17:22-34). He asserts that if all non-Christian religious beliefs are wrong—antithetical to biblical truth—then Paul was promoting counteractive syncretism in his message to the Mars Hill people.

Conversely then, does embracing Christ require that one reject all other cultural and religious ways of being, thinking, expressing and living out our faith in Jesus as Cree, Lakota, Maori, Navajo, Hawaiian, Aborigine, and so forth?

Counteractive syncretism might be experienced as an uncritical, open-ended or naive embrace of religious pluralism. Additionally, there might not be any acknowledgment of the evil, dark, malevolent forces that frequently find expression in some religious practices. Counteractive syncretism would direct one's "primary allegiance" to someone/something other than Jesus Christ by reason of a person's participation in a new religious system. As my Cree friend and biblical scholar Ray Aldred would say, "Syncretism is not good when it takes away from the real message of communion—the redemptive death and resurrection of Christ which produces life from above, liberating all of human and non-human creation to find and experience the beauty of Creator's love."[25]

It seems that Western-trained theologians and the theologies rooted in them are quite concerned about protecting the Bible from a kind of imagined "Indigenous cultural invasion." The Roman Empire had a huge military force to protect its land claims and authority from hostile enemies. The United States of America has a similar force in place and is not afraid to use it to protect its national borders and international interests.

It isn't unusual for influential church leaders to perceive any new movement as a threat to a "genuine" expression of Christian faith. Because these new ideas often originate in the margins of power and end up outside the culturally-formed religious "boxes" of these leaders, their authority as representatives of correct biblical truth is threatened. Their belief systems (or they often believe, God's perspective) are under attack. They become intent on protecting God's reputation, authority and sacred text from being compromised by being too closely linked or combined with Indigenous ways of being, believing and living.

As you have read, this has happened in Indigenous communities all over North America and among the Maori of New Zealand, Aborigine of Australia, Hawaiians, Quechua of Peru and around the world. The extensive mission history of the past, not biblical study, has prompted an intense fear of counteractive syncretism—*instead* of it being considered a part of the normal process of adaptation.[26]

American nationalism—counteractive syncretism. I want to suggest that openly displaying the American flag alongside the "Christian flag" on each side of the stage or pulpit is an example of counteractive syncretism. It is blending the ideology of nationhood and the Christian religion. It presupposes an idealized national exceptionalism of God's chosenness, blessing and approval of America. The result is a unique Americanized version of Christianity that directs attention away from identity in Christ and his kingdom. It redirects allegiance to a kind of "Christian patriotism" that demands a deep-seated loyalty, reverence, trust and faith in political, military and economic might. It inspires national pride and the assumptions of Creator's divine favor. Why don't Canadian churches place Canadian flags in their churches?

The mixing of Euro-American culture with the gospel—from Plato to Andrew Jackson to Ronald Reagan—is considered permissible and orthodox. Brian McLaren sees counteractive syncretism, when used in typical ways by white Euro-American male theologians, as intended to attack the mixing of any cultural heritage (other than their own) with the gospel. For him the result "is the mixing of Platonic categories with the biblical witness (as the creeds exemplify—dependent as they are on terms like 'homoousios' and 'hypostasis') without claims of syncretism, but Native American stories and culture cannot" do the same.[27]

The 2008 pre-election rhetoric voiced the fears of many conservative American Christian leaders, who believed that the election of President Barack Obama would signal the "end times" and the return of Jesus. Why didn't the presidential elections of Brazil, the Philippines, Russia, and so on, cause similar anxieties? Because American ethnocentrism is constructed and fueled by theologically informed nationalism. In my view this politico-religious syncretism results in a "compromise of Scripture" that has and does suppress Indigenous cultural identity. It oppresses Native intellectual thought and resists desperately needed wisdom located in the Indigenous "knowledge traditions" that Western Christianity lacks. This does not take into account the dehumanizing enslavement of tribal people from Africa, utilizing a biblical narrative that identifies them as "descendants of Ham" and "cursed by God" and thus not fully human. Nor does it account for the elevation of male over female and the unjust oppression of women, particularly in church matters.

Counteractive syncretism is not about playing a powwow drum in church on a Sunday morning, doing a Maori *Haka* dance or going on an Aborigine "Walkabout." Nor is it about burning sage or sweet grass in my prayers, or sitting in a sweat lodge ceremony helping young people make healthy life choices—helping couples to become more loving wives/husbands, mothers/fathers and community members!

This discourse on syncretism invites First Nations/Indigenous theologians and scholars to prophetically address what is an oppressive Eurocentric cultural syncretism in our countries.

While I am responding to this concern primarily as framed within the North American evangelical community, it is necessary to consider ongoing developments in global missions thinking to widen the conversation as Indigenous scholars worldwide find their voice in this emerging era of postcolonial Christianity.

Western(ism) culture. In *Christian Conversion or Cultural Conversion?* Charles Kraft finds it unfortunate that many missionaries have such a poor understanding of the cultural dynamics of crosscultural communication with "regard to culture in general and Western culture in particular." He states the obvious that people from Western cultures are most familiar with a Christianity that is highly adapted to Western cultural forms. He writes elsewhere, "Western Christianity is (ideally) God in Christ made relevant to members of Western culture, which is characterized by familiar forms of worship, music, organization, philosophy (theology) and moral standards."[28]

Without exception the many Native North American authors I have read and researched have wrestled, in their words, with the negative influences of Westernism, Western culture and Western-American and Euro-American cultural forces. Realizing the magnitude and history of these concepts, in this book I will nonetheless reference the more commonly understood meanings behind the concepts of colonialism and

Westernism. These meanings will be best understood in our North American context, yet woven into the fabric of a global postcolonial dialogue. I will frequently use these terms interchangeably or as synonyms.

Andrew Walls, in "America as the Ultimate Development of the West" (a section of his book *The Missionary Movement in Christian History*), offers this perspective on the unique American expression of Western culture:

> In so far as America stands for the West, America is the West writ large. Western characteristics are exemplified to the fullest extent. Americans themselves have always been aware that they represent the decisive and ultimate development of the West. Without plunging into such deep waters, we may still recognize a specifically American Christianity, an expression of Christian faith formed within and by American culture. Among the features that mark it out from other such Christian expressions are vigorous expansionism; readiness of invention; a willingness to make the fullest use of contemporary technology; finance, organization, and business methods; a mental separation of the spiritual and the political realms combined with the conviction of the superlative excellence, if not a universal relevance, of the historic constitution and values of the nation; and an approach to theology, evangelism, and church life in terms of addressing problems and finding solutions.[29]

While Walls's caricature of American Western culture is certainly debatable, it does provide a framework to help describe Westernism. Lesslie Newbigin, in *Foolishness to the Greeks: The Gospel and Western Culture*, also does excellent work identifying "the essential features of our modern Western culture."[30]

The argument made by William Reyburn in *The Missionary and Cultural Diffusion* is that essentially "the modern missionary's inherited view of the universe is an inseparable part of his own ethos (the distinctive point of view of his culture) with which means he comes to terms with Christianity. His thinking and action are cast in a framework which is for him necessary and meaningful, but which appears to the folk societies quite often as meaningless."[31] In other words, the missionary cannot help but be who he or she is culturally, whether German, American, Dutch or Korean, and this is true for all those who have come to our reservations and tribal lands for centuries.

This is a problematic feature of crosscultural communication—the spread of the gospel message from one people and place to another. Jesus said to go and communicate with all people in all places the good news of his coming. It is problematic when the culture of the foreigner becomes associated with "normative" biblical faith, as it occurred throughout North America. One of the features of Western thought has been a perceived dichotomy of natural and supernatural, which has rarely made sense to local Indigenous communities. Reyburn points to the fact that

> the missionary who disavows being a carrier of Western culture is denying himself the very structure of his thought into which he cradled his presentation of the gospel and life. The ordered view of the universe means that faith to believe must be placed in something which is not beneath that order but over and above it. The modern man does not sacrifice the ordered feeling for the universe when he finds faith to believe. He views his faith as finding its locus and the source of order.[32]

A short time ago I met with a non-Native colleague who is actively involved in full-time Native ministry as a Bible teacher for a Native Christian organization. While discussing the controversy and challenge of doing contextualization, he said to me, "I barely know my own white culture, let alone Native culture, so I am just going to stick to teaching the Word of God and you can teach about culture." His pejorative comment reflects a Western dichotomy that is problematic for us. Reyburn comments on a nearly identical comment made by a missionary in Africa who said, "We are here only to present the Gospel, not American or Western civilization."[33]

It is actually a ridiculous thing to say, yet again reflects Western dichotomous notions I will reference throughout this paper. From our First Nations experience, this "Westernism" is not a faceless, ethereal and abstract philosophical construct. Rather, it manifests itself daily in persons, ideologies, policies, institutions, structures and organizations. Reyburn describes this reality well:

> The introduction of Christianity in this century is heavily secularized and institutionalized. The creation of a new class or classes within the old society opens up new channels for the diffusion of Western culture. The process is that of making a copy, an imitation. A copy can only be partial, especially where there are barriers for intimate contact.[34]

Dale Kietzman and William Smalley in *The Missionary's Role in Culture Change* provide some analysis by pointing out that missionaries

> who declare that they are not going out to introduce Western culture, but only to preach the gospel, are no different in this respect from those with whom they contrast themselves. It is usually institutionalism (hospitalization, education, agricultural mission, etc.) which they are rejecting by such statements, not really their roles as agents of westernization.[35]

Lesslie Newbigin, and recently Soong-Chan Rah, have articulated the inherent bias of specific worldview assumptions and thought processes of Eurocentric people that I will refer to as "Western."[36] That being said, it is impossible to comprehensively define the ideas contained in the term *Western culture*. Throughout this book I will give specific detailed examples of how this Westernism has plagued the work of Jesus among the people and First Nations of North America, and continues to do so.

CROSSCULTURAL STORYTELLING OR DECOLONIZING CONTEXTUALIZATION

This question of how to do contextually appropriate work among Native American peoples is a centuries-old question. It is answered and practiced poorly by innumerable individuals, organizations, agencies, local churches and denominations operating from a colonial, paternalistic and hegemonic paradigm. While I will review this history, this book will focus on Indigenous contextualization initiatives of the past twenty years.

Though the phenomena of contextual work ranges throughout North and South America, my primary focus is on the Western United States and to a lesser degree Canada, although again it is equally applicable to Indigenous people and their struggles with neocolonialism globally. While it might make sense to include some detailed cases of Native ministry leaders who actively oppose or reject contextualization in Native ministry, their concerns are well represented in Native and white communities in speech and print.[37] The design of this book is to discover what initiatives are being made in the *direction* of contextualization.

The two theoretical frameworks I used as lenses to look at this are the Innovation Diffusion model of culture change and the Critical Contextualization model of crosscultural communication.

The Innovation Diffusion model. Everett Rogers's book *The Diffusion of Innovations* reviews all the research on the means and manner of the diffusion of innovative ideas and technologies. I found it a helpful model to examine the ways in which the contextualization movement of the gospel has emerged and spread. What are the organizational and relational "mechanisms" by which people come to know about a new idea or process? How do people make decisions about adopting or not adopting such an idea? According to Rogers, an innovation—which I propose is a holistic gospel or contextual Native ministry for many people—is "an idea, practice or object that is perceived as new by another individual or unit of adoption."[38] Rogers defines diffusion as "the process by which an innovation is communicated through certain channels over time among the members of a social system."[39]

Diffusion as process. Diffusion is any process through which ideas are dispersed. Knowledge of the innovation is communicated through mass media and interpersonal channels at different times and for different purposes. An innovation becomes more acceptable as potential adopters have more experience with it. They then begin to know that it is compatible with their culture, understand it because it is not too complex, try it out, and discover that the innovation has a relative advantage over existing products or practices.

The spread of an innovation takes time because people do not adopt the innovation at the same rate. In fact, the rate of adoption accumulates over time into an S-shaped curve model. Initially there is rejection, then openness, some small acceptance, wider acceptance and then the acceptance of the idea/innovation as normative. The takeoff point, what Malcolm Gladwell calls the "Tipping Point," occurs when more than just the innovators and early adopters begin to adopt, often when knowledge becomes personal and opinion leaders begin to recommend the innovation.[40] Diffusion takes place through groups and networks already defined in the social system; thus, boundaries and barriers to diffusion differ for every system. This is particularly true for diffusion among Indigenous peoples, given there are some five hundred tribes spread across the continental United States with some two hundred languages. Also, there are tribal nations in various stages of assimilation, some with hundreds of years of European contact and missionization, starting from the east, moving west and continuing to the far north.

I have used Innovation Diffusion theory as a way to understand how contextualization has grown and been diffused across North America among Native American populations. Rogers was helpful in considering the need for new structural models of mission and community building for the emerging contextualization movement. Using these principles it became clear that new ways of considering how the gospel is communicated or "proclaimed" are needed, among them an honest, critical analysis of the positive and negative impacts various mission methods or models have had on families and communities. Do these versions of the gospel reflect and embrace an "authentic" Indigenous expression of Christian faith and not simply some superficial version of it? Rogers notes that "the innovation-decision process is essentially an information-seeking and information-processing activity"[41] driven by questions about the innovation, including its advantages and disadvantages. While I will use Rogers's principles as a theoretical framework, they are limited in that they were developed in the analysis of more traditional technological scientific settings, not in theological, anthropological or philosophical settings.

"Reinvention" as described in the innovation process, speaks to the issue of indigenization as an integral part of the formation of new mission strategies. According to Rogers, "Most re-invention occurs at the implementation stage of the innovation-decision process."[42] Thus, reinvention is really about "making the thing your own." When applied to the gospel and spiritual transformation, encouraging new disciples to "make the faith their own" should be at the heart of the intentions of any missionary. Unfortunately, in crosscultural situations, worldview clashes have made it difficult for new ideas to naturally emerge—or to allow the living out of the gospel in a unique cultural context. This is often a reflection of a sense of superiority in the change agent (missionary), which, in social-change innovations, affects the adoption and the diffusion rate due to the perception that adoption will alienate people from their traditional knowledge entirely.[43] Tinker would assert, however, that today "an Indian pastor is more likely than a white missionary to criticize the paganism of traditional spirituality" because of a kind of "internalized oppression."[44] These would be individuals identified in Rogers's paradigm as rejecters of contextualization as a legitimate biblical model of innovation.[45]

Rogers's principles will provide the theory to help understand the "perpetual liminality" faced by First Nations people today, their relationship to the dynamic sociocultural and religious shifts occurring within the First Nations Christian community, and the acceptance or opposition to the growing contextualization movement. These principles can help us anticipate where we might be headed and what actions or structures are needed to fulfill our sense of calling and prophetic destiny as First Nations leaders.

A careful analysis of why people make decisions to adopt innovation (the theme of much of this book) might offer us an identifiable pattern for behavior on which to build a mission strategy for contextualization efforts. In the "life" of an idea or movement, an obvious, discernible, critical threshold might appear, which may require one or one hundred people for a new innovation to be adopted. I hope to discover if and where we may be on this continuum toward developing critical mass in the acceptance of critical contextualization as being "normative."

THE MAIN ROLES OF A CHANGE AGENT

One of the "main roles of a change agent" is to facilitate the communication of an innovation from a person or place to an intended audience.[46] Rogers identifies a seven-stage process that I use to explain ways in which this Native-led movement spreads a contextualized gospel as innovation:

1. "Develop a need for change." The gospel story can be introduced at the point of need or as the idea that creates the need, depending on the person and culture. Looking at the social, medical, economic and other categories of contemporary Native life—in light of over four centuries of Christian missions—makes the need for change painfully obvious.

2. "Establish an information-exchange relationship." All the early innovators were members of existing relational or organizational networks and denominations. They had credibility and were able to build on their relationships early on to engage in authentic listening and reflection with "fellow" seekers.

3. "Diagnose problems." The traditional method for problem solving has been to ask yourself why what you are currently doing does not work. A more helpful modality would use an asset-based approach to describe life at its best. As they met over time, innovators were able to assist and complement one another in diagnosing the problem much more comprehensively across Indian Country, not just within their local contexts.

4. "Create intent to change in the client." The disparity between what they know and feel with what they are doing creates the decision potential. Through honest inquiry, dialogue and acknowledgment of the problem and potential solution, contextualization leaders began formulating ways to introduce these changes as solutions.

5. "Translate intent into action." Influence the person or group for change in appropriate ways. Many of these leaders began writing, creating, teaching seminars and speaking to a wider audience of Native ministry pastors and workers in order to influence decisions that incorporate the innovations being introduced.

6. "Stabilize adoption and prevent discontinuance." This translates into culturally relevant discipleship with new traditions and rituals rooted in the culture. Through ongoing conferences

and gatherings and ongoing access and availability to these new
ideas, the innovations spread quickly and widely, gathering gradual
and continual acceptance.

7. "Achieve a terminal relationship—initiate self-renewing behavior."
The apostle Paul made it clear to Timothy that he must train others
in the ways he was trained. As innovations were accepted and adopted by a larger number of people, soon new innovators emerged
who then started new networks aside from those established by the
early innovators.

While the field of innovation-diffusion research was a helpful "interpretive lens"—because Rogers's theories are drawn almost exclusively
from research and development efforts in the fields of technology, biology,
telecommunications, marketing, health and medicine and primarily ag-
riculture—I had to add to his applications. He identifies anthropological
research as a cultural outsider who is primarily "concerned with the
transfer of technological innovations from one society to another as com-
pared to the diffusion of a new idea within a society or system."[47] His use
of the term *intercultural diffusion* deals with, for example, the introduction of the ax and other types of technology, and the introduction of
the horse to Indian tribes. Conversely, the knowledge of corn cultivation
was transferred from First Nations to European settlers.[48]

These principles do help in anticipating where these contextualization
efforts may be headed and what actions or structures are needed to assist in
the work of decolonizing the gospel. We must progress beyond the narrative
of Euro-American imperialism, conquest and assimilation via Christian
missions—and move forward as prophetic advocates seeking guidance from
our very present Creator made known among us in Jesus, who is the Christ.

Critical contextualization. In the history of Christian mission, crosscultural communication has always been a cause of critical reflection and
great concern. At the advent of the first-century Church, the Mediter-
ranean world was a familiar world. From there Christ-followers headed
out to the ends of the earth, from India to Russia to the Far East, to strange
and exotic lands filled with strange people and exotic customs. These

Jewish storytellers told the story of Jesus to their foreign neighbors across national, ethnic, cultural, linguistic and religious differences. They were simply Jewish messengers of the "good news" of freedom and salvation in Jesus the Christ. They didn't even have a Bible to use or denominations or organizations to provide oversight, training or guidance. This process is referred to as contextualization—the attempt to communicate ideas across cultural differences in ways that make sense to a particular audience.

These Jewish storytellers had no intention to politically, economically or militarily colonize the people in these other countries. They were genuine ambassadors of "the good news" as best as they could understand what Jesus meant when he said "Go into all the world" and tell others about what happened to them.

People attempting to communicate the gospel of Jesus across cultural settings have, by the very nature of crosscultural communication, been doing contextualization since Jesus encouraged his early Jewish followers to do so. This notion of "crosscultural communication" can be seen in the Old Testament where Creator comes to people in ways and forms they can understand. The New Testament as well bears witness to this process, notes Dean Flemming:

> It provides "stories of contextualization"—particularly in the Gospels and Acts—in which Jesus and the apostles tailor the gospel message to address different groups of people. The journey of the church from its beginnings as a Jewish sect to becoming a largely Gentile body that proclaimed a universal faith required the gospel to engage new cultural groups and circumstances at each point along the way.[49]

In his article "Contextualization: The Theory, The Gap, The Challenge," Darrell Whiteman echoes this perspective saying, "The concern of contextualization is ancient—going back to the early church as it struggled to break loose from its Jewish cultural trappings and enter the Greco-Roman world of the Gentiles."[50] Noting the evolution of the concept, or at least the terminology, he sees it as a part of an

> evolving stream of thought that relates the Gospel and church to a local context. In the past we have used words such as "adap-

tation," "accommodation," and "indigenization" to describe this
relationship between Gospel, church and culture, but "contextualization," introduced in 1971, and a companion term, "enculturation" that emerged in the literature in 1974, are deeper, more
dynamic, and more adequate terms to describe what we are about
in mission today.

Having arrived at a point where he sees *contextualization* as a better term,
Whiteman describes *good* contextualization as

> attempts to communicate the Gospel in word and deed and to
> establish the church in ways that make sense to people within
> their local cultural context, presenting Christianity in such a way
> that it meets people's deepest needs and penetrates their worldview,
> thus allowing them to follow Christ and remain within their own
> culture.[51]

Essentially, contextualization addresses the challenge of framing the
gospel message culturally as either a sacred story or a myth of divine
proportions, so that it makes sense to people "on the ground" where they
live every day. Its challenge is avoiding the foreignness of a story confined
to a singular culture (that of the teller, historically dressed in Western
clothes) that characterizes the era of noncontextualization. It seeks to
overcome the ethnocentrism of a monocultural approach by taking cultural differences seriously, and by affirming the good in all cultures.[52]

In particular, "critical contextualization" leads us to see contextualization as an ongoing process.[53] Critical contextualization allows us
to trust the Holy Spirit to direct us in this erratic, courageous and
faithful process of discovery. We are free to make mistakes, trusting
in the Holy Spirit to provide correction and guidance. Here, old beliefs and customs are neither rejected nor accepted without careful
examination in light of biblical and cultural humility.[54] A good place
to start is the premise that *all* things are possible and work our way
back from there.

Indigenous expressions of Christian faith must be firmly rooted in
Scripture and the historical/living Christ. From this "root," local Indig-

enous forms, structures and practices can be fearlessly considered an integral part of the process of making Christianity one's own—personally and collectively. An Indigenous faith thus flows out of critical contextualization. Here the local cultures are examined phenomenologically to understand their beliefs, the things upon which people act. "Studying a culture means understanding the categories, assumptions and logic the people use to construct their world," not just using the hegemonic categories of the outside observer.[55]

Samuel Escobar in *The New Global Mission* presents an overview of a theology of mission citing Andrew Walls's description of the dramatic and "massive southward shift of the center of gravity of the Christian world," and the dynamism of "missions from below" as the gospel travels from southern to northern nations.[56] As a South American who has worked in North America for many years, he provides American evangelicals with a different lens with which to view the various realities of globalization, colonialism, pluralism, secularism and westernization—and their impact on shaping the future of Christian mission.

He is aware, as a Latin American theologian, of Indigenous peoples' experiences with Spanish and European colonialism throughout Central and South America—experiences which are nearly identical to ours in the North. I have included some of his thoughts regarding the need for a wider postcolonial theological conversation. He sees Creator's mission as a seamless unfolding of Creator's heart and his redemptive plan for creation that is all-encompassing and inclusive of every sphere of creation's activity. I see Escobar's book as offering a helpful critique of the assumptions of North American missions to help us better understand the need to be more holistic and/or contextual in our future missions endeavors among the tribes of North America.

The central theme that Escobar weaves throughout his book is "Christian mission in the twenty-first century has become the responsibility of a global church."[57] For him this entails embracing a holistic approach. I share his concern that if a theology of mission is to emerge that effectively meets the challenges of reaching today's postmodern global community, it must break free of Western theological provincialism. For this to happen, non-Western theologians must exegete their own culture in light of Scripture in order to articulate new biblical understandings of the fundamental gospel narrative.

American evangelicals must discontinue propagating their erroneous dichotomization of the gospel narrative because "the message of Jesus Christ is 'translatable,'" writes Escobar. He further states that

> this means that the gospel dignifies every culture as a valid vehicle for God's revelation. Conversely, this also revitalizes every culture: no "sacred" culture or language is the exclusive vehicle that God might use.[58]

Escobar provides a theoretical perspective from which to examine the Indigenous contextualization or revitalization endeavors I have identified as expressions of "holistic missions." These efforts are occurring around the world. Are these North American movements part of a larger movement of decolonizing the gospel narrative? If so, Creator is moving in powerful and unique ways.

Native believers are straining to break free from the shackles of a deeply oppressive doctrinal framework in order to incorporate their First Nations worldview values into what it means to be Jesus-followers. This framework is the result of the recent modernist blend of fundamentalism and its first cousin, conservative evangelicalism. Good contextualization is the appropriation of Indigenous beliefs and practices in the process of making Christianity one's own. This is being accomplished by Indigenous theologians, often in the face of hostile opposition from missionaries and Native Christians raised in a fundamentalist or conservative evangelical way of thinking. If the Christian tradition is to become relevant to North American Indigenous people, theology must be conducted in the context of local cultural settings. "Today, Indigenous churches around the world are formulating their own theologies."[59] However, attempts to force the Native church to adopt and preserve Western or Euro-American theologies of missions and ecclesiology continue. This illustrates the tragic tale of colonial Christianity.

While much could be included on this subject, one such problem described by Hiebert and Meneses is, "On the cultural level, many missionaries unconsciously took with them the western worldview that makes a sharp distinction between natural and supernatural realities."[60] Additionally, on the social level, "Western leaders have a culturally-shaped drive to create formal, highly-organized institutions."[61] This Westernism is overlooked because these "foreign" Western missionaries were people who got in their cars and drove many hours away from their living rooms to our Indigenous homelands in South Dakota, Arizona, Oklahoma and so on, never leaving "their country," thus assuming our people were just like them, only a brown version. Consequently they had no need to reflect critically on their worldview assumptions as Westerners, because they were simply Americans ministering to other Americans.

There is also a need for missionaries to reflect critically when considering the various forms of Native artistic expression. Traditional Native musical constructs, sounds, dances and ceremonies are being developed and are now found within worshiping communities. The Indigenous church is using principles of critical contextualization to incorporate signs, symbolism, imagery and sculpture as part of the indigenization process that speaks of the transcendence and mystery of the Christian faith.[62] Andrew Walls dedicates a chapter in his book, *The Missionary Movement in Christian History*, titled "The Western Discovery of Non-Western Art," to the conversation of how Christian faith should be and is incorporating localized art, architecture and religious symbolism. Commenting on how early Catholic missionaries coming out of Europe were struggling not to view "local art as a threat to Christian integrity," Walls notes that there was an admonition within missionary movements "to return to the . . . three vital principles: evangelize, not colonize; respect the art and culture of the country; and remove foreign forms from sacred art."[63]

Indigenous expressions of Christian community. For years missiologists have said a truly Indigenous church would be like a three-legged stool—self-governing, self-supporting and self-propagating—not just a Western missions church attended by Indigenous people.[64] William A. Smalley debunks the notion of the three-legged stool, calling it a false diagnosis and axiomatic in much missionary thinking.[65] Kraft agrees with this westernized notion of the Indigenous church: "The mere fact of self-government, self-support, and self-propagation does not ensure that the church in question is 'Indigenous.' The indigeneity (if present at all) lies in the manner in which such selfhood is expressed." This selfhood speaks of the ability of the local Indigenous members and leaders to move away from Euro-American cultural expectations and begin defining faith within their spiritual and cosmic world. This especially means to begin interpreting the biblical text and creating their hermeneutical community process. Kraft notes that more often than not—which is true of the majority of reservation churches—when the missionary is long gone, and there may be a Native pastor in charge, what they essentially do is "maintain the foreign forms, imposing them on new generations." They end up with little regard for the fact that the forms they impose convey very different meanings to the new generations.[66] Smalley, going further, explains and emphasizes this perspective:

> I very strongly suspect that the three "selfs" are really projections of our American value system into the idealization of the church, and that they are in their very nature Western concepts based upon Western ideas of individualism and power. By forcing them on other people we may at times have been making it impossible for a truly Indigenous pattern to develop. We have been Westernizing with all our talk about indigenizing.[67]

His critique is germane to the discussion of contextualization in that we are seeking the establishment of truly Indigenous churches as a result of genuine critical contextualization. Smalley suggests an Indigenous church might be viewed as

> a group of believers who live out their life, including their socialized Christian activity, in the patterns of the local society, and for whom any transformation of that society comes out of their felt needs under the guidance of the Holy Spirit and the Scriptures. . . . For one thing, the church is a *society*. . . . If other patterns are forced upon a church by missionaries, consciously or unconsciously, such a church will not be an Indigenous one.[68]

So then a gathering of Navajo, Lakota, Ojibway, Cree, Yupik, Maori, Aborigine, Saami, and so on, followers of Jesus, would develop theologies and practices of worship, prayer, ceremony, music, liturgy and leadership that were rooted in their local tribal histories and stories. It would look, act, sound and behave "Indigenous." People often say if something looks like a duck, walks like a duck and quacks like a duck, it's probably a duck. In the same way, if it looks white, sounds white and behaves white, it's probably the "white man's religion." This book is an attempt to tell the story of how the colonial Native church is slowly reclaiming its own sense of tribal identity—through decolonization and retraditional-ization—and becoming an Indigenous expression of the Christian tradition. This is critical contextualization.

Being a Story Collector

In pursuit of this larger story, I collected many dozens of personal stories to gain a broader understanding of the nature, scope, impact and viability of these intercultural efforts. I used a variety of sources including historical documents, literature, archival records, personal interviews, direct observations, participant observations, internet surveys and questionnaires.

For roughly fourteen months, beginning in November of 2007, I studied the active contextualization efforts of numerous leaders across the United States and Canada. All of the participants were invited through my personal and shared social networks.

Invitations to participate in the web-based or mailed questionnaires were sent to about 250 people. They were selected from a variety of denominations and regions of the country listed in *Polished Arrow*, a North American–wide First Nations ministry directory produced by Dee Toney.[69] Additionally, invitations to participate in my web-based survey were sent to an existing email subscriber database of 4,700 people, which included an unknown number of Native Americans.

In the end, 415 Native and non-Native people chose to take part. I interviewed more than fifty Native people, either one-on-one, or in a group or over the phone. There were 380 people who responded to the email invitation to participate in the web-based survey, and 315 of these completed it. Of these 315 respondents, 132 (or 34 percent) identified themselves as a Native person, with 248 (or 65 percent) indicating they were non-Native. The 250 study invitations that were mailed to selected Native and non-Native organizers or leaders listed in *Polished Arrow* elicited a much lower response rate, with only thirty-six agreeing to participate.

THE SELECTION PROCESS

The fifty-plus people I personally interviewed were members of different tribes living across the western United States and working among several different tribal groups, ranging from the traditional (reservation) to the urban. The participants' roles in their respective church, ministry or denominational agency; their location (urban or reservation); and their linguistic, cultural background (e.g., raised in a traditional community), age, occupation, clergy/laity roles, mother-tongue speaker or recent tribal-identity discoverer were all taken into consideration. These characteristics and circumstances enabled me to identify where these contextual endeavors were finding their greatest audience, supporters, impact and opposition. As the writer, observer and participant, I took into account the various characteristics and roles I embody, such as insider and competitor, along with my gender, age, tribal identity, economic status, education, language, location, status in the national Native Christian community, and so on.

Some individuals I considered but did not include for a variety of reasons, such as distance, availability, distrust or lack of relationship. Those that I did select for personal, in-depth interviews were chosen based on several criteria. First, I knew them all in some capacity, from deeply-trusted family friends, good friends and casual acquaintances to nominal acquaintances. Second, I knew them all to be followers of Jesus, though from a wide variety of church traditions. Third, in principle I supported and agreed with their work (though not always with their methodologies or doctrine). Fourth, they were sincerely and sacrificially engaged in legitimate contextualization efforts because of a genuine love and concern for the well-being of Native people in their communities. Fifth, they were all innovators or adapters (at some stage) in their respective contextualization activities.

In addition to my research, I was (and still am) a regular participant in our local/national Native community and culture, taking part in sweat lodge ceremonies, dancing in powwows and praying with my sweet grass and sage. After two years of hanging out with my friends and listening to their stories, I gathered even more stories beyond the surveys, interviews and questionnaires—discovering hundreds of people fully engaged in contextual endeavors.

It's a deeply enriching and fulfilling journey of discovery to see ever-increasing numbers of leaders engaging in a wide range of contextualization practices. There are encouraging, heartening signs. Many of these practices are unique to specific tribes and their own tribal practitioners. In the urban areas, many types of tribal contextual practices are being used by a broad range of intertribal practitioners.

I am excited about how these new contextualization practices are being used in "advocacy-for-action" agendas and for the reform of sociopolitical, economic, educational and family issues facing our Native communities.

INDIGENOUS ETHICAL AWARENESS AND PROTOCOLS

Throughout this book, I have sought to remember that these stories are entrusted to my care and ultimately belong to the people who shared them with me. They have only been loaned to me and will need to be returned in some fashion when the time comes. In addition to researching Indigenous contextualization efforts, I have chronicled my experience as an Indigenous researcher/participant and my discomfort with theological academic assumptions.

This means, as a Native writer and researcher, I am mindful to "not further marginalize or disempower" the people, communities and histories from which I "borrow" stories. I am aware of offense or criticism I could create toward participants because many of them are attempting to figure out how to contextualize current practices and views of rituals and ceremonies still practiced by traditionalists. Thus, the possibility for misappropriation and misunderstanding is high.

I am also mindful of an Indigenous morality and ethic of research and writing, and while meeting academic standards of "good scholarship," internally I push against the hegemony of Western academic expectations. I resist getting overly burdened by the categorical reductionism of Western research methodologies and theory as described by the Maori scholar Linda Smith in *Decolonizing Methodologies*. I hope this "scholarship in a good way" leads to the discovery of new ways that research can be used to benefit those from whom data is collected.

I readily identify with Lakota scholar Dr. Beatrice Medicine's struggle in this area when she describes her dilemma in *Learning to Be an Anthropologist and Remaining "Native."* Dr. Medicine writes, "How much could I write that would pass my own peoples' scrutiny without casting me in their eyes as an 'informant' to anthropologists?"[70] Expanding this quandary, she notes, "Native populations are wary of others' interpretations of their behaviors, even when they are dealing with 'one of their own.'"[71] At the same time, however, I also concur with her conclusion that, as a Native writer, my research can be "applied to benefit colonized people" and also be informative and beneficial, with "meaning for others" as well.[72]

Donald Fixico calls for a respectful and professional set of ethics and scholarly responsibilities when it comes to the "researching, writing and teaching of American Indian history." One point he makes that is relevant to this book is that "American Indian history is not just one history of all Indian people. Actually, it is a field of many tribal histories, complicated by their relations with the United States." As he aptly points out, "there are 547 federally-recognized tribes and Native communities in the United States." He spells out the obvious though often-overlooked perspective that "interpreting research data and writing to take into account the Indian viewpoint is a most important ethic."[73] For me this study is reflective of Fixico's concern for the "need for ethics and responsibilities in teaching and writing American Indian history" as more people become interested and engaged in our history at an academic level.[74] Karen Swisher echoes these concerns stating, "The words, voices, stories and perspectives [of Native American researchers] are prevalent in recent reports of research and typify the intent of educational researchers to present more accurate interpretations of the qualitative research experience."[75]

Linda Smith (Maori), in *Decolonizing Methodologies—Research and Indigenous People*, encourages us to be wary of allowing ourselves (Indigenous academics) to be co-opted by the modernist epistemological assumptions concerning "data and research."[76] We must think critically about the categorical frameworks that originate in Western scholarship and would determine the ways in which we understand ourselves through the "foreign eyes" of "objective" empirical research. The hegemony of this propensity reduces us to reading about and studying ourselves in the textbooks, while little value is given to what we have to say about ourselves—because it is not reflective of the kind of categorical language of the academy.

Smith chronicles the conflict in academia between the epistemological assumptions of Western modernity and historically oral cultures. The tensions and points of conflict she identifies are equally applicable in Western theological educational institutions. In addition to revealing hegemonic Western missions and academic predilection, I want to incorporate her caution and admonition to the research phase of my dissertation, which is why I have cited her book. She writes:

> The ways in which scientific research is implicated in the worst excesses of colonialism remains a powerful remembered history for many of the world's colonized peoples. It is a history that still offends the deepest sense of our humanity. . . . The term "research" is inextricably linked to European imperialism and colonialism. . . . It appalls us that the West can desire, extract, and claim ownership of our ways of knowing, our imagery, the things we create and produce, and then simultaneously reject the people who created and developed those ideas.[77]

In certain respects, this is doubtless true for the several dozen international theological students that I have conversed with who are studying in American seminaries. As Indigenous peoples, we come to discover the categories that a Western-formed anthropology and missiology have created and defined for us so we can better understand ourselves. Meanwhile, when reading about and studying ourselves in the textbooks, little value is given to what we have to say about ourselves because it is not reflective of the kind of reductionist categorical language of the academy.

Smith highlights a critically important feature of doing research within our own tribal communities: following local cultural protocols.[78] In First Nations communities there are protocols of being respectful, of showing or accepting respect and reciprocating respectful behaviors, which also develop membership, credibility and reputation.

Lobo and Peters in *American Indians and the Urban Experience* (Contemporary Native American Communities series), identify a kind of "social science inquiry" created by the link between anthropology and research and writing. It has to do with the "traditional anthropological stance emphasizing the static model of the 'ethnographic present.'"[79] Here, First Nations people still live somewhere in the 1800s in some isolated reality:

> This model often has been criticized for its idealized frozen-in-time effect. The ethnographic present, almost exclusively rural in context, created a mindset, generated by anthropologists and historians, but embraced by the general public, that has been very difficult to set aside.[80]

Taiaiake Alfred thinks of "indigenizing the academy" as "working to change universities so that they become places where the values, principles and modes of organization and behavior of our people are respected in, and hopefully even integrated into, the larger system of structures and processes that make up the university itself." He challenges me as an Indigenous researcher to "come into confrontation with the fact that universities are intolerant of and resistant to any meaningful indigenizing." While seeking to conduct research deserving of the highest grades and standards academically, I find myself in agreement with Alfred when he explains that "our experiences in universities reflect the tensions and dynamics of our relationships as Indigenous peoples interacting with people and institutions in society as a whole: an existence of constant and pervasive struggle to resist assimilation to the values and culture of the larger society."[81] I find myself in this research process easily identifying with his assessment of "the academy"—that is,

> places we as academics work—they are our sites of colonialism. And, they are our responsibility. Like all Indigenous people, if we are accountable to our nations and truly cognizant and respectful of our cultures, we have a responsibility to do what we can where we are to ensure the survival of our culture and our nations. Being in the university, we as Indigenous academics have the responsibility to work to defeat the operation of colonialism within the university and to reorder academe.[82]

Because the school I received my degree from is a theological institution, my struggle with the hegemony of Western epistemological assumptions was magnified because we were at times studying God—theology. Our Creator was reduced to a systematized set of propositional truth statements that were assigned authority as the ultimate divine opinions regarding creation as we know it. In many evangelical circles this is known as "absolute truth." A current neo-Calvinist or evangelical notion of absolute truth is considered to be free from human prejudice and is understood to be "pure God." Its proponents can be heard to say, "If you have a problem with what I've said, take your issue to God because I am just telling you what the Word of God says" (that is, pure God = pure reductionist baloney).

I found Western theology was wed to a Western pedagogy that often required cultural compromise or compliance in order to produce "good" scholarly work. It is the hegemonic cultural bias of Western theological educational pedagogy that unnecessarily "bends people culturally" in order to succeed. I am committed to Alfred's invitation to work "to ensure the survival of our culture and nations" as we pursue higher education for future generations as a means of creating a collaborative independence as coinhabitants in the land and establishing our place in a modern world.

As a Native person doing research among Native people, it was my desire to produce a paper informed and supported by the finding of "appropriate" research that will serve to benefit our people in a real and practical way. Smith, Fixico and Medicine have helped provide a kind of "Indigenous ethic" or ethnomethodological "voice" for my research and writing.

SUMMARY

Christian missions among Native North Americans have become a very complex and distorted chapter in American history. I have introduced some early missionary attitudes, practices and terminology. In the following chapters I will develop the points I've introduced to demonstrate and articulate why the gospel has been regarded as the "white man's religion," one that lacks acceptance among Native North American people.

I have set the background for my study to discover in what ways Native people in North America are initiating cultural revitalization efforts while holding on to a faith in Jesus. Creator was already working among the tribes in North America (Rom 1:19-20), revealing Creator's divine attributes through the beauty and splendor of creation. Creator was revealing Creator's self in the life of Spokane Garry and others to give evidence to the fact that Creator's Spirit was already here long before the Europeans came. I am encouraged to find many Indigenous leaders deconstructing neocolonial paternalism in their lives, organizations and ministries as they pursue better ways to serve their respective communities.

DISCUSSION QUESTIONS

1. Describe how early Native American prophecies prepared the way for the gospel.

2. In the section titled "What Happened to the Good News?" Dr. Twiss reveals "the point of this book." What is it?

3. Dr. Twiss asks, "Is syncretism a step or the end product?" What do you think?

4. How has your own cultural background shaped your views on mission work—or on syncretism?

5. Discuss the need for "indigenizing the academy."

THE COLONIZATION, EVANGELIZATION AND ASSIMILATION OF FIRST NATIONS PEOPLE

As I searched deeper into the early European missionary history of the 1600s, which set the stage for missionary efforts among our Native people, I became extremely disillusioned and even more skeptical of current missionary endeavors among First Nations people. Scot Mc-Knight, in his book *A Community Called Atonement,* finds the source of this tension to be

> the conglomeration of Euro-American scholars, ministers and lay folk who have, over the centuries, used their economic, academic, religious and political dominance to create the illusion that the Bible, read through their experience, is the Bible read correctly.[1]

If self-revelation is the work of Creator and Creator's engagement with people and nations, then crosscultural communication never occurs in isolation, in a cultural vacuum, but by definition occurs in a crosscultural context. Human messengers are never free from the prevailing cultural influences of their upbringing, worldview values and sociocultural/political attitudes of their day.

In 2012 I sat with some friends and acquaintances for their weekly luncheon discussion. They were all white Christian businessmen. We had been discussing "white privilege" for a few weeks, and I had been sharing a bit about bad missions theology, genocide, boarding schools and the devastating effect of colonization in our communities. A gentleman I have known for several years, a highly successful businessman and supporter of missionary work in Mexico, said, "Well Richard, don't you think it's better for your people that we, a Christian democracy, conquered your people? After all, it could have been the Nazis, Russians or Japanese. Somebody was going to eventually conquer you, so don't you think your people are better off that it was us rather than someone else?"

Pure shock rattled my whole being. I and several others couldn't believe he actually said that. It took a few seconds for what he had just said to fully register. Then I was angry and these words came like a flood. I clearly, carefully and precisely said, "So let me get this straight. Are you saying we should be grateful that your people came here and brutally sodomized us? Are you saying we are better off for being sodomized by you and we should be grateful for it? And we should be glad that you used the Bible as a lubricant to brutally sodomize us? Is this what you are saying to me!?" After a few moments of dead silence in the room, I then said, "The vulgarity of my words pales in comparison to the vulgarity of your words."

The images I saw when I said those words had, as a backdrop, pregnant Native women being cut open and their babies' heads smashed with rifle butts; entire villages of old men, women and children being bludgeoned to death after the women were defiled in the worst imaginable ways; forced starvation, violent imprisonment and torture; tens of thousands of little Indian boys and girls being hauled off to boarding schools where they were plagued with sexual, physical and psychological abuse of immeasurable cruelty and enduring devastation. The gross inhumanity that crushed our people was of the most horrific and vulgar in Western history.

This guy is not a bad person. He has been a church-attending man for decades and faithfully served in his church. While incredulous that someone I know, and who knows me, could hold that belief, it should not surprise me. But it did. So, old history lives on.

The missionary views the world, including the people he or she walks among, through a set of deeply embedded, culturally conditioned lenses or realities, both at a conscious and subconscious level. Starting with the missionaries who arrived to work among the Eastern tribes in the 1600s through the present, this has not changed.

What hindered or prevented the early missionaries from contextualizing the gospel? What still hinders Anglo-Christian workers and missionaries from contextualizing on our reservations today? I contend a major reason is the hegemony of Western culturally informed theologies that remain intact within religious institutions and structures. They have a commitment to produce results. There is a functional pragmatism connected to the gospel that results in the need for quantifiable conversions, economic viability and church growth in ways that make sense to them culturally, or, they might say, "biblically." A man recently said to me that his organization supported a worker who was able to show them a "convert to dollar" ratio or track record.

We are entering the era of postcolonial Christianity. This is making it possible for young leaders to experience wisdom, empowerment and knowledge resulting from increased cultural integrity, access to the emerging global hermeneutical community and a reframed narrative for life in Christ as an Indigenous story among Indigenous people. It's as I heard a man say from an Indigenous framework, "Wisdom is knowledge experienced relationally."

THE MANY FACES OF COLONIZATION

Christianity and Christendom. Honestly, any sense of biblical justice I have is shattered by reading early mission history, and I work hard to not emerge an utter cynic, harshly critical of Christianity. To make some sense of early missionary endeavors and this troubled history, I am compelled to make distinctions between following Jesus, Christianity and Christendom. Christendom is described by professor Peter d'Errico "as an alliance of princes and priestly authorities that culminates in the doctrine of divine right of kings and popes."[2]

Lamin Sanneh sees the same important distinctions but chooses to nuance them a bit differently, arguing that

"World Christianity" is the movement of Christianity as it takes form and shape in societies that previously were not Christian, so-cieties that had no bureaucratic tradition with which to domes-ticate the gospel. In these societies Christianity was received and expressed through the cultures, customs and traditions of the people affected. World Christianity is not one thing, but a variety of Indigenous responses through more or less effective local idioms, but in any case without necessarily the European Enlightenment frame. "Global Christianity," on the other hand, is the faithful rep-lication of Christian forms and patterns developed in Europe. It echoes Hilaire Belloc's famous statement, "Europe is the faith." It is, in fact, religious establishment and the cultural captivity of faith.[3]

Tite Tiénou comments that, in our day, one should be able to take for granted that Christianity is not just the religion of white people. He writes, "Polycentric Christianity is Christian faith with many cultural homes. The fact that Christianity is at home in a multiplicity of cultures, without being permanently wedded to any one of them, presents for Christians everywhere a unique opportunity for examining Christian identity and Christian theology."[4]

Philip Jenkins, while acknowledging that we are undergoing the greatest shift in the history of Christianity, sees

the story of Christianity being inextricably bound up with Europe and European-derived civilizations overseas, above all in North America. Until recently, the overwhelming majority of Christians have lived in White nations, allowing theorists to speak smugly, arrogantly, of "European Christian" civilization. Conversely, radical writers have seen Christianity as an ideological arm of Western imperialism. Over the past century, however, the center of gravity in the Christian world has shifted inexorably southward, to Africa, Asia and Latin America.[5]

"When we make these important distinctions," writes d'Errico, "we can begin to understand the possibility of differences between the teaching of Jesus and the political and legal doctrines of a church-state complex operating in his name."[6] While these distinctions help make some sense of things philosophically and ideologically, I remain somewhat bewildered. It was men and women professing faith in Jesus Christ and a commitment to the Scriptures who perpetrated these oppressive, unjust and sometimes horrific acts against Native people. Sadly, in many cases they still do.

Liminality—caught in-between. For Indigenous communities, identity and land are closely connected, often inseparable. Colonialism's pursuit of natural resources, land, power and control impacts tribal people at deeply fundamental psychological, cultural and social levels. The loss of land, beyond dirt, relates to "losing sacred space and place" and its influence in shaping personhood, being and identity. Land provides a sense of being from and belonging to a place. Many First Nations peoples have lost their land completely. Their self-identities, which are tied up with place (their land), have diminished along with the loss of land. Other Nations have retained their physical lands, but many individuals no longer have a strong connection to their land as a sacred place.

One result of prolonged colonization is that our peoples have fallen into a state of liminality wherein transition has become our enduring reality. I am using the term liminality as referenced by A. H. Mathias Zahniser to describe the second of a three-phase rite-of-passage ceremony, "Separation, Liminality, and Reintegration":

> The second phase, liminality, is from a Latin word meaning "threshold," because it is transitional. This liminal phase provides initiates with a chaotic limbo condition of transition "betwixt and between" the clearly defined statuses and roles of childhood and adulthood in their society. This phase . . . involves ordeals causing physical and mental weakening as though initiates were to forget their childhood.[7]

As Native people, we are in between the worlds of yesterday and where we will be; between traditional worldviews and Western rationalism; between community and individuality; between spirituality and religion. We are not what we used to be and we are still becoming what we are not yet. In this in-between time we experience confusion, deep loss, fear, the unknown, searching and despair. In Native terms, "our circle is broken." Our identity is constantly being stressed, reshaped, redefined or altered as we regain our balance in the hegemonic, modernist world where we live as Indigenous peoples. This process of adaptation is now often referred to as "retraditionalization."

Many of us, particularly those of us living in urban centers, carry the burden of having to live in two very different worlds. As the decades go by, we better understand how critical it is for Native people to live biculturally. In Portland, Oregon, I serve on the board of the Native American Youth and Family Association (NAYA). We provide a wide range of community services that address the social, cultural, healthcare and educational needs/concerns of our members.

Lobo and Peters chronicle the effort to force Native people—through legislative means—to assimilate into the mainstream "melting pot" of America as good citizens. Moving into the twentieth century, the tribes were militarily conquered, treaties were established and peoples settled under "government care" on reservations. The next step the Federal government took to solve the Indian problem was a grossly misinformed attempt at social engineering—that is, "relocation."[8]

Assimilation was deemed the best way to handle the embarrassing "Indian problem," assuming that once in the cities, Native people would eventually become absorbed into the dominant culture as productive members of American society. In 1953 Congress passed the Termination Resolution that called for Indian equality under the law. From 1954 to 1962, Congress terminated sixty-one tribes, bands and communities. This meant they no longer existed as tribes, they were now subject to state laws, and their lands were sold off. These policy decisions were presented to them as "freedom" from further federal intervention. In addition, in 1952 Congress established a "Voluntary Relocation Program." Indians were enticed to leave the reservation through promises of jobs, education and housing.[9] Thus began a steady migration from the reservation to the city:

> The "Voluntary Relocation Program," through which thousands of
> Native people moved from their reservation homes to cities, did

not result from any specific piece of legislation. Nevertheless, the program, officially inaugurated in 1952, was at least as important as termination policy in its long-term effects on Native people. Along with land dispossession, the growing influence of wage, labor and wartime experiences and the relocation program contributed to the urbanization of Native people during the latter half of the twentieth century.[10]

The fact that 78 percent (or more) of the Native population live in cities today presents a significant opportunity for the gospel. Table 2.1 shows the steady pattern of urban migration in the past century.[11]

Table 2.1. Urban Indian Migration

Year	Indian Population	% Urban
1900	237,000	0
1910	277,000	4
1920	244,000	6
1930	343,000	10
1940	345,000	7
1950	357,000	13
1960	524,000	28
1970	793,000	44
1980	1,364,000	49
1990	1,959,000	65
2000	2,476,000	78

Source: American Indian Facts of Life (2004:57). See endnote 11 for 2010 US census figures.

With the arrival in the cities of Native people from numerous reservations and tribal memberships, the "urban Indian" as a subculture came into existence. Feeling lost and overwhelmed in the strange world, they found solace and meaning as part of a new "pan-Indian" identity. Here some of the distinct tribal edges were rounded away, and in the city being

Native became as important as being Navajo, Kiowa, Apache, Lakota, and so on. The hegemonic social and cultural forces faced by this new pan-Indian community created huge levels of distress or liminality for the people who were simply, *earnestly*, in search of sources of spiritual, economic, medical and cultural assistance.

The challenges faced by the urban Native gave rise to a new brand of Indian social and political activity. Urban Indian centers—with programs and services designed to ease the transition to city life and encourage a sense of "Indian-ness" and belonging—sprang up in cities containing large populations of Native people.[12]

Having lived off the reservation most of my adult life, I agree with the statement that "urban is not a kind of Indian, but is instead a kind of experience many Native people have."[13] Because of the constant migration of Native people between cities and their reservation communities, there exists today a living connection to home with a strong and growing sense of being reservation-centered.[14] Lobo and Peters note that on a practical basis, individuated themes and approaches within the domain of social welfare are problematic because they create "static generalized categories that fail to recognize the unique Diasporas of the Indigenous population."[15] It is worth noting the fact that many Native urban dwellers now "visualize" their place in the city as an "extension of home territory," or as one person said, "our urban encampment out here."[16]

To better understand contextualization and revitalizaton movements, we must view neocolonial missionary enterprises as dynamic contributors to the new "urban Indian reality." Organizations like ours (Wiconi International) and the Native American Youth and Family Center (NAYA) assist Native people in returning to a lifestyle—at least in a quasi-traditional form—that embraces, promotes and supports positive change in a holistic way for our people. This is the core of retraditionalization and the renewal of Native communities.

COLONIZATION, EVANGELIZATION AND ASSIMILATION

The history of mission outreach to Native North American people is a story that ranges from dismal failure causing extreme grief to bright possibilities of hope for the future. There was potential in that the people had a prevalent belief and faith in a monotheistic Creator—the Spirit of the Lord was already here revealing the Creator of Abraham, Isaac and Jacob to them. (If there is only one Creator of this one earth and this one humanity, why is there such gross failure to recognize the *pervasive presence* of Creator—regardless of time and space—among biblically informed followers of the ways of Jesus?) Sadly, many missionaries from the past couldn't see the people they were sent to serve as fellow children of Creator, created in his image and precious in his sight. Their perception was obscured by their worldview.

American attitudes toward its Indian problem. Philip Jenkins, in *Dream Catchers*, gives a detailed historical overview of the evolution of sweeping social and anthropological "scientific" theories that influenced the attitudes of Americans throughout the twentieth century toward the religious beliefs and practices of Native peoples. In addition to Jenkins, others who have written insightful and helpful books on this subject are K. Tsianina Lomawaima and Teresa L. McCarty, *"To Remain an Indian": Lessons in Democracy from a Century of Native American Education*; Daniel M. Cobb, *Native Activism in Cold War America: The Struggle for Sovereignty*; Hilary E. Wyss, *Writing Indians: Literacy, Christianity and Native Community in Early America*; and Amos Yong and Barbara Brown Zikmund, *Remembering Jamestown: Hard Questions About Christian Mission*.[17]

One of the great values of *Dream Catchers* is its exhaustive research of historical documents. From these, Jenkins paints a picture of an evolution of thought and attitudes in American history that, among other things, clearly reveals the collaboration of church and state in dealing with "the Indian problem."[18] Officially it was the responsibility of the Bureau of Indian Affairs (BIA) to formulate a policy of dealing with the Indian problem. Always cautious of Native ceremonies, in 1902 BIA Commissioner William Jones identified "a few customs among the Indians which . . . should be modified." Among these he listed long hair, body paint, Native dress, dances and feasts. Although not "objectionable in themselves," they did however constitute to Jones "a badge of servitude to savage ways and traditions which are effectual barriers to the uplifting of the race." The Court of Indian Offenses placed ever-increasing restrictions on Indian dances, including laws forbidding their usage.[19] This empowered and encouraged missionaries to then forbid the use of Native cultural expressions for any purpose, but especially for churchly use.

These lawmakers made missionary workers unwitting partners with the Federal government to provide humane and "Christian" ways of solving the problem. *Dream Catchers* reveals the deep-rooted ethnocentrism of the day, "which similarly consigned primitive peoples to a kind of racial childhood . . . as the world's primitive and 'savage' races."[20] The different approaches had far-reaching policy consequences, since the developmental view was that Indians could and should progress toward civilization. Those who held the separate origin theory rejected this prospect. But in either case, whether Indians were children or quasi-animals, they stood at a much lower stage of human development.

This Spencerian evolutionary view meshed well with contemporary hegemonic scientific theories, which similarly consigned primitive peoples to a kind of racial childhood. Jenkins chronicles the nineteenth-century debate among several anthropological schools divided partly by how they explained the world's primitive and "savage" races.[21] The view of polygenesis suggested that different human groups in fact had separate origins, so that primitive people were only loosely related to the higher races. Indians might thus be, literally, animalistic. Others accepted a common human origin, but believed the different human races stood at different developmental stages, corresponding roughly to phases of human growth. Jenkins cites Lewis Henry Morgan, an American lawyer who was an amateur anthropologist on the side. Morgan's book *Ancient Society* (1877) told the story of "human progress from Savagery through Barbarism to Civilization." Higher races were adult and mature; lesser breeds were children.[22]

Contemporary writers of the day were alarmed that the ancient Indian peoples would literally become extinct before they could exercise the benefits of their full cultural influence on the American mainstream, and that this would come to pass within a few decades. In 1896, Julian Ralph described Indians as "a dead but unburied race."[23]

EARLY MISSIONARY ATTITUDES

Biblical narratives were interpreted in such a way as to justify the "civilizing" of the New World and create the American myth of "chosenness" and destiny. This was clearly obvious with the striking of the Great Seal of the Massachusetts Bay Colony, as Puritans prepared to depart England for America in 1629. The seal's central figure is an Indian man holding a bow in one hand and an arrow in the other, naked but for a girdle of leaves. From his mouth issues a ribbon with the words "come over here and help us."[24] This reference to the apostle Paul's "Macedonian call" thus invoked a sense of Creator's leading them to evangelize the inhabitants of the new world.

Around this time in England there were speculations that Indians were part of the lost tribes of Israel:

> The discussion in the 1640s and 1650s depended on the belief that conversion of Jews would precede universal Christianity. Thus if Indians were gentiles, their conversion to Christianity could not signal the initiation of end-time events but was rather a taste of the massed conversions to come. If, however, Indians were members of the lost tribes of Israel, their conversion to Christianity could indicate Christ's imminent return.[25]

For Puritan writers, connecting biblical eschatological implications for Indian converts depended on uncovering biblical types. They found in Ezekiel's vision of dry bones coming back to life a comparative application to Christian Indians, people who English writers asserted had been "dead" in their sin before hearing the Word:[26]

> Truly the work [of evangelism] is honorable [wrote a Puritan missionary] . . . it tending so much to be of good for the soules of these poor wild creatures, multitudes of them being under the power of Satan, and going up and downe with the chains of darkness rattling at their heels. [Another missionary wrote of the Native communities]: " . . . miserable captives—slaves to the devil from birth—poor soules captive to Satan."[27]

Jenkins' detailed account of American attitudes toward Native people, including both public and government attitudes, again helps to create the context for the past twenty years. The past two decades did not occur in a vacuum, but are the result of the religious, social and political forces that shaped the American attitude and policy that is alive and powerfully active today.

George Tinker addresses the process of Christianization as "the internalization of the larger illusion of Indian inferiority and the idealization of white culture and religion." He fundamentally describes the historic missions community as seeing its purpose through a lens of ethnic superiority and control with the end result being that "oppressed peoples internalize their oppression" and come to believe the imposed stereotypes of the oppressor, thus leading to "internalized racism or self-hatred."[28]

I would agree with Tinker's overarching analysis that "by and large Indian people have not found liberation in the gospel of Jesus Christ, but rather continued bondage to a culture that is both alien and alienating, and even genocidal against American Indian peoples." What he calls "cultural genocide" is most predominantly something that occurs subliminally at a systemic level, though a high incidence of conscious, intentional genocide has occurred. The problem is that good people often are responsible for terrible things that happen to others as a result of misguided actions. He sees that good intentions can become so "mired in unrecognized systemic structures" that many well-intentioned Christian workers actually wreak havoc and "destruction that results from those good intentions."[29]

At the core of Tinker's critique of missions among First Nations people is his definition of cultural genocide: "The effective destruction of a people by systematically or *systemically* (intentionally or unintentionally in order to achieve other goals) destroying, eroding or undermining the integrity of the cultural system of values that defines a people and gives them life." He then nuances his definition with four interrelated implications: (1) Political aspects (2) Economic aspects (3) Religious aspects (4) Social aspects.[30]

He examines the work and periods of John Eliot, a Puritan from New

England; Junipero Serra, a Catholic missionary to California; Pierre-Jean De Smet, a Catholic missionary to the Midwestern United States; and Henry Benjamin Whipple, first Episcopal bishop of Minnesota.[31]

Tinker examines these individuals and eras in social, political and economic detail and identifies, among other things, the negative effects of systemic causation, economic privilege, political ideologies and manifest destiny. Such negative effects were to varying degrees embedded in the efforts of these influential missionary figures; these he sees as generally reflective of most all missions' endeavors. Perhaps Tinker's most indicting commentary is that the resultant:

> Cultural myopia of the missionaries functioned to facilitate the exploitation of Indian people by both government and the private sector or by land-hungry immigrant farmers. Identifying their actions as well-intentioned but misguided certainly does not exonerate the missionaries. It was impossible for any missionary to avoid complicity in the genocide of Native American people.[32]

In support of his notion of internalized oppression, he cites the fact that today "an Indian pastor is more likely than a white missionary to criticize the paganism of traditional spirituality." As social commentary on this predicament, he sees the systemic problems of power and control in Christian organizations taking their toll in Native people who likewise become "stuck in the affirmation of white power and white structures, even to the point of strongly articulating self-criticism of traditional culture."[33]

An example of this is found in a Native leadership training manual that has circulated in some Native ministry networks in recent years. In 2004 Native pastors and Bible teachers Jim (Chippewa) and Faith (Crow) Chosa wrote a biblical training manual, *Thy Kingdom Come Thy Will Be Done In Earth*. In the appendix the Chosas serve an indictment against the traditional Native drum, stating:

> We also are aware of many cultural elements which are distinctly in contradiction to the Word and unredeemable such as the use of drums as the sole musical instrument for worship of God. In many

regions of America, ancient people established drum cults, which worshipped the drum and established religious ceremonies centered on the use and sound of the drum.[34]

Another example is found in the book *Muddy Waters: An Insider's View of North American Native Spirituality* by Native author Nanci Des Gerlaise (Cree). She attempts to discredit the efforts of retraditionalization by Indigenous believers by saying they are of the devil:

> Many Native American or First Nations tribes are exploring the renewal of their ancient spiritual traditions and reinstituting ancestral and mystical practices. Natives involving themselves in this pursuit see this as an opportunity to bring recognition to the forgotten and once persecuted Native American religion. They failed to realize that they are actually participating in a mass deception spreading throughout the world in the days prior to Christ's return. . . .
>
> In his book, *One Church Many Tribes*, Twiss states: ". . . Around the globe among Indigenous Christians, cultural identity is surfacing as the key dynamic in this emerging new Native ministry paradigm. . . . Christians are debating the use of Native American drums, gourds, rattles and dances as legitimate expressions of godly faith. In the next decade or so, this controversy will also subside, and we will hear and see Indigenous sounds and movements in church services across the land."
>
> What Twiss is saying is very scary because a lot of people will be deceived into thinking that what he is proposing is a good thing. . . . Native spirituality is surging forward, ultimately forsaking the purity of the Gospel.[35]

These critical, reactionary Native Christians still demonize the efforts of those bringing together faith and culture. I agree with Tinker who sees postcolonial First Nations people in a social, political, economic and psychological framework.[36] It may be that the psychological and religious aspects are the most important factors in the recovery of Native people and their communities.

Sociological influences and attitudes. Early missionary John Sergeant, while serving as pastor of a Christian Native community, "emphasized to his converts their cultural inadequacy and their personal responsibility for overcoming that inadequacy. . . . Only through a complete sense of their own inadequacy can Natives be properly Christianized." His goal was the "total eradication of all that marks them as native . . . to root out their vicious habits, and to change their whole way of living."[37]

Craig Storti explains this blindness as a process in which our minds or worldviews interpret what we see, then ascribe meaning and value to what is observed or experienced. When it is something unknown, it can only be interpreted through the lens of previous "non-experience," an empty vacuum, and is typically misunderstood. I believe it is primarily for this reason that we have not yet experienced the birth of a North American Indigenous church.

Ethnocentrism. At the root of this problem is a clash of fundamental worldview assumptions. The result of these misunderstandings is that today the vast majority of Native people reject Christianity as the "white man's religion." The gospel message of liberation in Jesus and redemption from our brokenness has been lost to us in the fog of American colonial Christianity.

These modern assumptions produced a deep-rooted case of ethnocentrism in American Christianity. Storti refers to this as "the ethnocentric impulse" or "phenomenon of cultural conditioning."[38] There was a European expectation that these Native people would act, think and behave like them because that is how "real" or "normal" people are. Though it was not logical for Europeans to assume that these people would act like them—because they were not operating at a logical level, but instead at an instinctive level—logic lost its fight with instinct.[39] When Native people exhibited local behavior that violated values so fundamental to European identity and sense of self-esteem, missionaries were left with no choice but to reject what they had encountered.[40] New negative categories had to be created.

Paul Hiebert describes the "White Man's Burden" as his supposed responsibility to teach and civilize the rest of the world.[41] People today are

as immersed in the attitudes of their societies as were the first missionaries to the Native people of North America. Those missionaries saw
themselves and their British/European "Christian" cultures as superior
to the cultures and people they encountered. This belief was based on
the idea that science, industrialization and the European style of com-
merce made societies "civilized." In their eyes, only the West was "civilized." All other cultures were considered "primitive." Hiebert describes
how this pattern was established early on:

> The seventeenth century New England Puritan missionaries largely
> set the course for modern missions. They defined their task as
> preaching the gospel so that Native Americans would be converted
> and receive personal salvation. But early in their missionary expe-
> rience these New Englanders concluded that Indian converts could
> only be Christians if they were "civilized." The model by which they
> measured their converts was English Puritan civilization. The mis-
> sionaries felt compassion and responsibility for their converts.
> They gathered these new Christians into churches for nurture and
> discipline and set up programs to transform Christian Indians into
> English Puritans.[42]

Philosophical influences. Albert Borgmann notes that among early
colonization efforts, the first arrivals to the American continent "never
wore the fabric of medieval life, yet the early settlers brought late medieval practices and institutions with them."[43]

In the early years, the hardness of life and the hurriedness of conquering the land prevented people from recreating the communal
charms of Britain in the New World, but even in the most challenging of
circumstances they quickly built their church and school as powerful
focuses of common life.

Throughout United States history there has been a nationalized connection between America's growth and Creator's favor or blessing.

Modernism. "Francis Bacon, along with René Descartes and John
Locke, laid the theoretical foundations for the project [that Borgmann
calls] modernism."[44] It builds the framework for modernity specifically

around three foundational documents of modernism: Bacon's *New Atlantis* (1627), Descartes's *Discourse on Method* (1637) and Locke's *Second Treatise of Civil Government* (1690). Borgmann sees these treatises as pleas as much as proclamations:

> They plead for a new order and derive much energy from their indictment of medieval disorder, the duress of daily life, the deadwood of tradition and the oppression of hierarchy and community. They urge a new fundamental agreement, one that razes the tottering and constricting medieval structures and begins anew on a solid fundament.[45]

Synthesizing these three documents, Borgmann invites us to consider "modernism as the conjunction of Bacon's, Descartes's and Locke's projects, as the fusion of the domination of nature with the primacy of method and the sovereignty of the individual."[46] I want to highlight two constructs to help us better understand what might be considered as philosophical underpinnings to the resistance and opposition of critical contextualization among Native evangelical leaders today: aggressive realism and methodological universalism.

Aggressive realism. This is the idea that nature, no matter how mysterious, grand or impossible, could and should be conquered for the good of humanity. Borgmann sees that "the modern domination of nature was not an aristocratic assumption of the reins of power but a violent campaign of conquest."[47] Whatever limitations existed that might hinder the spread of civilization—land, sea, air, people, politics, and so on—were obstacles only until the necessary technology, ideology, philosophy or political imperative could be found to overcome them. With the invention of gunpowder, guns, ocean-going ships, steam engines and steel, along with the right of discovery, revolution and "The Enlightenment," it was only a matter of time before the wave of European colonization would stretch out over the world.

Methodological universalism. As the era of modernism grew "in its initial stages, the campaign to subdue nature was a war of thousands of relatively limited and isolated forays" carried out by many disconnected individual efforts. Soon the discovery of new lands, new technology and access to new resources fueled the "spirit of domination." From this point emerged formalized scientific research to "uncover and articulate the universal and lawful relations between heat and energy, between the pressure and volume of gases, and so illuminated, confirmed and advanced rigorously what the inventions and improvements of the steam engines" could achieve. With enough scientific research, humans could discover methods to unlock every secret of the universe and overcome nature to create a "new" world.[48]

Underlying the "modernist" worldview assumptions that informed and shaped the 1500s and 1600s missionaries' view of Scripture and mission were, as Peter L. Berger and Thomas Luckmann describe it, "conceptual machineries of universe maintenance" and the idea of a "symbolic universe" where "ideas, concepts, and experiences become objectivated."[49] They become the definable building blocks from which societies and institutions are constructed. In both cases there is a kind of legitimated "norm" for which underlying meanings emerge. However, Berger and Luckmann write, "There is no such thing as a harmonious, self-enclosed, perfectly functioning 'system.'" Every society has problems. When deviant problems arise—those in contradiction to the status quo—a crisis of definition of reality is provoked.[50]

When the first European Christians arrived in North America, the Christianity they introduced had the devastating effect of a hostile pandemic-like religion—an aberrant representation of Jesus and a gross misrepresentation of the gospel. It was a Christianity so thoroughly contextualized to European civilization that the mixture of the values of the culture with the values of Christianity made it aberrant in terms of its net impact on the tribes here. They were perhaps well-intentioned people with noble aspirations, yet they were possessed of worldview assumptions infected with hegemonic presuppositions fueled by modernism, humanism and rationalism. This viral strain surfaced when their reality was threatened by the "deviant realities"[51] of the Host People of the land; the response of the European missionaries was to legitimate their own "official universe" by demonizing the foreign reality as "heretical."[52] These socially constructed realities filtered their reading of Scripture and justified their ethnocentric attitudes and genocidal tendencies toward the Host People.

SOCIOCULTURAL INFLUENCES

An early missionary, Timothy Woodbridge (1709–1774), observed some of the newly-converted Natives "conducting a powwow" in worship to their new Christian Creator. It was their attempt to bring Christianity fully into their lives, keeping with their own traditions of worship. This horrified Woodbridge and he approached them to "inform them that God was not to be worship'd in such a manner." But some Natives protested, saying "they knew no harm in it—they made their application to the great God and to no other." Woodbridge then reported, "When I had instructed them as well as I could, they resolv'd never to do so any more." Furthermore, and much to his satisfaction, "Those of them who had been best taught were much troubled, that they had taken so wrong a step." Both John Sergeant and Woodbridge condemned the Natives for making Christianity "unfamiliar to their English sensibilities."[53]

Mungo Park was an English explorer in Africa during this era. Like those who traveled to North America, he was nonetheless a product of the social and philosophical shifts of his day. He is quoted as saying that he could not imagine that a country so beautiful and abundantly gifted with natural resources should remain in its savage and neglected state. Similarly, another explorer describing the vast lands that he saw considered them to be suffering from the appearance of a kind of nakedness. His solution was to fence these lands, thereby rendering them sufficiently beautiful, improving on what nature had already done.[54]

Colonialism and ideology. Germane to our discussion is the work of John and Jean Comaroff who describe British colonial efforts among the Tswana people of South Africa. They demonstrate that woven throughout the "philosophical construct" of colonialism are two dynamic realities: hegemony and ideology. They define and reveal the roles that hegemony and ideology played in the colonial campaigns of Europe, in particular the unique variety manifested by the British and Dutch in South Africa.

During the 1600s, the British penchant for discovery, expansionism, and evangelistic fervor marked an unparalleled period in global history.[55]

The Comaroffs hypothesize that the final objective or target of colonization is consciousness: to establish control and rule by replacing one way of seeing and being with the axioms, images and aesthetics of a foreign culture.[56] The epistemological assumptions of the period shaped the development of the social, philosophical, scientific and economic ideologies, as well as the evangelistic efforts of the missionaries. African scholar Ngũgĩ wa Thiong'o describes this reality from his point of view, the colonized one:

> But the biggest weapon wielded and actually daily unleashed by imperialism . . . is the cultural bomb. The effect of a cultural bomb is to annihilate a people's belief in their names, in their languages, in their environment, in their heritage of struggle, in their unity, in their capacities and ultimately in themselves. It makes them see their past as one wasteland of non-achievement and it makes them want to distance themselves from that wasteland. It makes them want to identify with that which is furthest removed from themselves; for instance, with other peoples' languages rather than their own. . . . Possibilities of triumph or victory are seen as remote, ridiculous dreams. The intended results are despair, despondency and a collective death-wish.[57]

While declaring that "the real aim of colonialism was to control the people's wealth, what they produced, how they produced it," Thiong'o sees the way that control was introduced and managed was to deconstruct the people's sense of self and replace it with that of the colonizer. This would occur when a people's perception of themselves and their world was overthrown.

> Colonialism imposed its control of the social production of wealth through military conquest and subsequent political dictatorship. But its most important area of domination was the mental universe of the colonized, the control, through culture, of how people perceived themselves and their relationship to the world. To control a people's culture is to control their tools of self-definition in rela-

tionship to others. For colonialism this involved two aspects of the same process: the destruction or the deliberate undervaluing of a people's culture, their art, dances, religions, history, geography, education, orature and literature and the conscious elevation of the language of the colonizer. The domination of a people's language by the languages of the colonizing nations was crucial to the domination of the mental universe of the colonized.[58]

As we examine Christian missions among the tribal people of North America, a valid question to ask is, Was it possible for the missionizing of the tribes carried out by British, French, Spanish, Dutch and later "American" people to be free from the goals of imperialism and colonization that Thiong'o identifies in the African context? I will say no. I will not attempt to quantify to what extent that is true, but when examining contextualization endeavors, I find they are being done to correct the syncretism of colonization and evangelization in American missionary efforts. How is it that well-meaning and genuinely Christian people could consciously and intentionally engage in such culturally hegemonic, oppressive and later genocidal activities in the name of biblical truth—as followers of Jesus, lovers of Creator and as led by the Holy Spirit?

Having read British views of the kingdom of heaven, civilization, conversion and redemption, and finding them so infused with the assumption of divine mandate and chosen-ness, the Comaroffs posit the theory behind their research of the Tswana people. The authors demonstrate and then differentiate the "colonization of consciousness" from the Tswana's "consciousness of colonization."[59] Pertinent to their theory is the discussion of conversion. The European missionaries' language of ethical and cultural universalism pressed on the Native people their notion of "difference." In their rhetoric of contrast they attempted to devalue the unique qualities and things that made Native people and their world distinct and inferior in European eyes. African scholar John S. Mbiti describes this reality:

> Christianity from Western Europe and North America has come to Africa, not simply carrying the Gospel of the New Testament, but as

RESISTING COLONIZATION IN MY LIFE

In 2002 Jerry Yellowhawk (Sans Arc Lakota) prayed over me in a Lakota naming ceremony where I was given the name Taoyate Ob Najin: "He Stands with His People." Vincent Yellow Old Woman (Siksika) gifted me with his eagle feather war bonnet to confirm the name and Creator's gifting in my life. It was a defining moment in my journey as a Lakota follower of Jesus that further clarified and enforced the need for a contextualized approach to life and faith. To understand why critical contextualization has not been the fundamental approach to missions among Native people, it is important to understand what philosophies and ideologies shaped the thinking of early American history.

In the summer of 2008, I asked twenty-six seminary and other students—who were participating in a crosscultural immersion course I was coleading on my reservation in South Dakota—to attend nine churches on Sunday morning and report back what they experienced. Without exception they said they could have been sitting in any suburban white church in America (except for two churches with some Native symbols). The music, order of service, language and church culture were completely Anglo, although most congregants were Native. Only two of the nine had Native pastors. Some of these churches had been on the Rosebud Sioux Reservation for seventy-five years. This section will explain how they got that way.

In my first fourteen years of embracing Jesus, I conformed to the expectation to accept interpretations of the Bible that said "old things had passed away and all things had become white"—regarding my following Jesus in the context of Native ways of music, dance, drumming, ceremony and culture. In reference to my Native culture, I was informed that the Bible said, "Touch not the unclean thing," or "come out from among them and be separate," or "what fellowship does light have with darkness?" This meant I needed to leave my Indian ways behind me because I had a new identity in Christ and it *was not* Indian! The Bible was used to demonize just about everything important to our cultural sense of being one with Creator and creation. As the years went by and I visited my reservation to attend the funerals of relatives, my heart began to remember how I felt during my American Indian Movement (AIM) days and how good it felt to "be home." Soon Jesus began to enter those areas of my identity that had been sitting idle. My internal journey of self-discovery was beginning as I pondered how my faith in Jesus fit with my Lakota culture, long before I heard the word "contextualization."

a complex phenomenon made of western culture, politics, science, technology, medicine, schools, and new methods of conquering nature. It is necessary to draw a distinction between the Gospel and Christianity, which are not synonymous at certain points.[60]

Conversion, the ultimate goal, was a process of removing these differences and distinctives and assimilating them into the moral economy and civilization as measured against a single value of absolute truth. Over time this process would not efface human differences but would slowly try to absorb them into a kind of homogenized European system: a single scale of social, spiritual and material inequality.[61] For the Puritans, the Pauline model of conversion had become deeply enshrined in modern Western thought.

This compelling sense of responsibility to civilize and Christianize the world then became fuel for the evangelistic fire that was growing in Britain, and mission associations were formed to dispatch missionaries. However, it was in this climate of technical optimism and rational idealism that the stage was set for what they perceived in their own eyes as "humane imperialism."[62]

These observations made by the Comaroffs about far-off Africa are, in fact, for First Nations people, the same ones experienced then and today: the hegemonic realities of colonialism are deeply embedded in the ethos of American Christianity. Only now they are carefully cloaked in neocolonial "constructs of modernity" and the ideologies of fundamentalism or conservative evangelicalism.

EUROPEAN DOCTRINES OF DISCOVERY IN THE NEW WORLD

Upon Christopher Columbus's return from discovering the New World, Spain sent emissaries to Rome to seek official and legal recognition of their claim to these new lands. In response to their request in 1493, Pope Alexander VI issued four papal bulls confirming Spain's title.[63] In *Inter caetera II*, "The pope (Alexander) now drew a line of demarcation from the North Pole to the South Pole, 100 leagues west of the Azores Islands off the coast of Europe, and granted Spain title under the authority of

God to all the lands discovered or to be discovered west of the line." Portugal was granted the same rights east of the line. This bull also declared the Pope's desire that "'barbarous' nations be overthrown or subjugated and brought to the Catholic faith and Christian religion 'for the honor of God himself and for the spread of the Christian Empire.'"[64]

Doctrine of Discovery. England and France, along with the rest of Northern Europe, were not going to be left out when it came to claiming their fair share of the lands and riches the New World had to offer. England and France both claimed "the rights and powers of first discovery in North America." They based their territorial claims on the "Doctrine of Discovery." In 1493, France, England and Spain were all Catholic countries. The kings of France and England would risk excommunication if they violated Spain's rights—rights granted them by papal bull under the rule of Alexander VI.[65]

In order to avoid excommunication and retain the favor of the Pope, Henry VII, England's king, had to devise a way to legally claim land already given to Portugal and Spain. They decided that if the land in question had not already been "discovered" by an explorer sent by any other "Christian Prince," then England was free to explore and colonize that land. That meant that Catholic King Henry VII would not violate the 1493 papal bull. Queen Elizabeth I stretched the boundaries of the "Doctrine of Discovery" even further by determining that European countries must actually occupy and be in possession of any desired territories.[66]

Terra nullius. "Consequently, Henry VII, his granddaughter Elizabeth I, and James I . . . repeatedly instructed their explorers to discover and colonize lands 'unknown to all Christians' and 'not actually possessed of any Christian prince.'"[67] This policy of exploration and territorial expansion was called the principle of *terra nullius*: "lands that were not occupied by any person or nation, or which were occupied but not being used in a fashion that European legal systems approved, were considered to be empty and waste and available for Discovery."[68]

The English Crown utilized Christianity as its moral and ethical rational to justify its claims to lands in the New World. Henry VII ordered the Cabots "to seek out and discover all . . . provinces whatsoever that may belong to heathens and infidels" and "to subdue, occupy, and possess these territories." Elizabeth I granted Sir Humphrey Gilbert the right to "discover such remote heathen and barbarous lands, counties, and territories, not actually possessed by any Christian prince or people, and to hold, occupy and enjoy the same, with all . . . jurisdictions." James I went further and granted his colonists property rights because the lands were "not now actually possessed by any *Christian* Prince or People" and "there is noe other the Subjects of any Christian King or State . . . actually in Possession . . . whereby any Right, Claim, Interest, or Title, may . . . by that Meanes accrue." James I also ordered his colonists to take Christianity and civilization to American Indians to "propagate *Christian* Religion to those [who] as yet live in Darkness and miserable Ignorance of the true Knowledge and Worship of God, and [to] bring the Infidels and Savages, living in those Parts, to human civility, and to a settled and quiet Government."[69]

AMERICAN BIBLICAL THEMES FOR TERRITORIAL EXPANSION

After the Revolutionary War, various states in the newly formed United States of America immediately began adopting constitutions and enacting statutes in which they asserted their superiority over Indians. In 1813 the Pennsylvania Supreme Court stated that Indians could not own real property since "not being Christians, but mere heathens [they are] unworthy of the earth."[70]

Manifest Destiny. The phrase *Manifest Destiny* was first coined by journalist John O'Sullivan in 1845 in a very influential editorial about the Oregon Territory called "The True Title." The term came to signify the mission of the United States "to overspread the continent allotted by Providence," with its pointed identification to Christianity as the principal ideological impetus for territorial expansion, and America's quest to control a continent and then an empire.[71] Anders Stephanson, in *Manifest Destiny: American Expansionism and the Empire of Right*, paints a concise yet comprehensive picture of the history of the theological underpinnings of the "doctrine" of Manifest Destiny and its evolution as a distinct aspect of America's self-identity as a "Christian" nation.[72]

This phrase articulated the national consciousness of America's divine right and quickly became a kind of social policy that justified American expansion. Interestingly, O'Sullivan expressly utilized the ideologies of civilization and divine providence to argue that the United States already owned Oregon:

> Our *legal title* to Oregon, so far as law exists for such rights, is perfect. . . . Our claim to Oregon . . . is by the right of our *manifest destiny to overspread and to possess the whole of the continent* which *Providence has given us* for the development of the great experiment of liberty and federated self-government entrusted to us. The *God of nature and of nations* has marked it for our own; and with His blessing we will firmly maintain the incontestable rights He has given, and fearlessly perform the high duties He has imposed.[73]

In 1854, Senator Stephen Douglass stated that the US would "expand, and grow, and increase, and extend civilization, Christianity, and liberal principles." Secretary of State James Buchanan also foresaw America's "glorious mission . . . [of] extending the blessings of Christianity and of civil and religious liberty over the whole of the North American continent."[74]

The two periods Stephanson examines closely are the 1840s and 1890s, quoting extensively from historical records. To comprehend the "justified" horrific and inhumane mistreatment, oppression and genocide of First Nations people in American history, understanding Manifest Destiny is of "signal importance": It is how "the United States came to understand itself in the world and still does," with all its "determinate effects." "Manifest destiny, like all ideological power, worked in practical ways and was always institutionally embedded. Historically, it could become a force only in combination with other forces and in changing ways. Not a mere rationalization, it appeared in the guise of common sense."[75]

Manifest Destiny had become "heavily suffused with religious overtones."[76] Stephanson notes the American sentiment of "the world as God's 'manifestation' and history as predetermined 'destiny.'"[77] This was the mindset which strongly influenced the first wave of immigrants arriving in New England from 1620 to 1660.

Lending a philosophical framework for Manifest Destiny were certain worldview assumptions about land. "For Europeans, land not occupied by recognized members of Christendom was theoretically land free to be taken. When practically possible, they did so. The Christian colonizers of the Americas . . . conceived the territory itself as sacred."[78] As so many have noted, this was "the New Canaan—a land promised, to be reconquered and reworked for the glory of God by His select forces, the saving remnant in the wilderness."[79]

> The Bible and natural law served as the two basic, partly overlapping authorities. The fundamental message, as it was understood at any rate, was to possess, multiply and fructify at the expense of the heathens.

> Treaties with Indians, as the governor of Georgia unflinchingly put it, "were expedients by which ignorant, intractable, and savage people were induced without bloodshed to yield up what civilized peoples had a right to possess."[80]

In his book, Stephanson creates a context in which we can understand that the current conditions among First Nations people are part of the evolution of American history over the past few decades. Understanding "Manifest Destiny" as a pervasive religio-political ideology is particularly relevant and crucial to my research of these movements as responsive or reactionary to the hegemony of American missionary methodologies and philosophies among Native communities.

A few of the many authors who have made significant contributions to the specific topics and issues raised by Stephanson, as well as notions of Manifest Destiny, are Anthony F. C. Wallace, *Jefferson and the Indians: The Tragic Fate of the First Nations*; Robert J. Miller, *Native America, Discovered and Conquered: Thomas Jefferson, Lewis and Clark and Manifest Destiny*; Steven T. Newcomb, *Pagans in the Promised Land: Decoding the Doctrine of Christian Discovery*; and Bernd C. Peyer, *The Tutor'd Mind: Indian Missionary-Writers in Antebellum America*.[81] Newcomb, in particular, offers an enlightening, interpretive paradigm—"cognitive theory"—as a way to explain, "not only the operations of the human mind, but also how U.S. government officials have sometimes consciously, but more often unconsciously, used certain doctrines of Christendom against American Indians."[82]

Biblical themes of colonization. The British, French and Dutch Christian colonizers of the Americas—as well as the Spanish and Portuguese—understood their endeavors as "sacred enterprises." As Anders Stephanson points out, "A primary theme for the Puritan missionaries was a reenactment of the Exodus narrative revolved around a powerful

---

WHAT ARE WE SAYING TO OUR CHILDREN?

I remember reading about Manifest Destiny in grade school, and the narrative only contributed more to the conflict in my soul. I was the Native guy in that painting being crushed under the lady angel's foot as she blessed wagonloads of pioneers flooding from St. Louis to settle the Wild West and kill Indians, the bad guys. Manifest Destiny, as a pseudobiblical ideology, carried the weight of providence and privilege. It became thoroughly institutionally embedded, politically and religiously—part of America's self-identity as a Christian nation. That myth has supported notions of America being founded by Christian leaders under the guidance of the Spirit of Creator, upon biblical truth and the sense of divine calling to establish the kingdom of Creator.

---

theology of chosenness that was to be decisive for the course of colonization as well as for the later American self-concept." He summarizes this in four fundamental biblical themes: "(1) election and covenant; (2) choice and apostasy; (3) prophecy, revelation and the end of history; (4) territory, mission and community."[83]

The first Christian missionaries in America used the Old Testament Exodus narrative to rationalize the decimation of Native populations by viral epidemics that had devastated the inhabitants of coastal communities before their arrival. "John Winthrop [1587–1649; four-term governor of Massachusetts Bay Colony] claimed in 1629 that 'God hath consumed the natives with a great plague in those parts,' and thus Puritan settlers had a 'warrant' to settle in New England." Another example of this type of thinking is revealed in this quote: "In Pequot War descriptions, Puritan victors exulted in the terrible deaths of their foes: 'But God was above them, who laughed at his Enemies and the Enemies of his People to Scorn, making them as a fiery Oven. . . . Thus did the Lord judge among the Heathen, filling the Place with dead Bodies.'"[84] Bross also writes, "The many who died from disease, they believed, had been willing occupants of the devil's territories and therefore merited death."[85]

Our American one-dollar bill reflects this view in the image of the Great Seal of the United States with the Latin phrase *Annuit Cœptis Novus Ordo Seclorum*—which translates roughly, "Providence has favored our beginnings," or "Providence has favored our undertakings."

Church and state partnership. Biblical themes served to inform governmental policy decisions about how best to handle the "Indian problem," when, beginning in 1869, "Indian agencies were assigned to religious societies." They served as "duly subordinate and responsible" Indian agents to the United States Department of the Interior. The Federal Government, along with denominational and missionary groups, believed this plan might improve the ability of government policies to stimulate "the slow growth of the savage beasts," leading to the "moral and religious advancement of the Indians."[86]

In 1882 then Commissioner of Indian Affairs, Hiram Price, reported on the positive effects of this ongoing partnership:

> One very important auxiliary in transforming men from savage to civilized life is the influence brought to bear upon them through the labors of Christian men and women as educators and missionaries. Civilization is a plant of exceeding slow growth, unless supplemented by Christian teaching and influence. I am decidedly of the opinion that a liberal encouragement by the government to all religious denominations to extend their educational missionary operations among the Indians would be of immense benefit.[87]

Hiram Price believed that the combined efforts of Federal policy and Christian teaching, as Steven Newcomb describes it, would facilitate "some huge Christian European reclamation project metaphorically conceiving American Indians as needing to be 'reclaimed' or 'recalled from wrong or improper conduct.'"[88]

Europeans viewed Native people through their own scriptural lens and found them to be lost in idolatry, deception, the worship of demons and on their way to hell. We have all sinned and have sin-stained cultures. "For all have sinned and come short of the glory of God" (Rom 3:23 KJV). We have all strayed from Creator's path. We all need to be reconciled with Creator through Jesus. Manifest Destiny, Scripture and Christian mission merged together and were perceived as one and the same for those entrenched in the European Enlightenment. This mindset led them to believe that they ". . . needed to lead the Indians to a moral way of life, which, from a Christian European perspective, was considered to be a 'civilized' and 'Christian' way of life."[89]

SUMMARY

Randy S. Woodley, PhD (Keetoowah descendant), in "A View of the Native North American Contextual Movement and Its Undecided Future," perhaps best sums up this chapter by telling his experience of living among the Kiowa people in Oklahoma:

> Today, the Kiowa, whom I love dearly and consider my relatives, may typify the dualistic results of the missionary influence and their penchant towards a colonized form of Christianity. Today, very few Kiowa Christians in the churches are able to express themselves spiritually with congruence. Instead, their faith has most often been expressed in one of three ways:
>
> 1. They have abandoned most of the religious and spiritual symbols of their Indian culture altogether and have, in most ways, with the exception of singing hymns in the Kiowa language (but with piano accompaniment) adopted the cultural faith expressions of the whites taught them by missionaries.
>
> 2. They express their faith in the culture of the dominant society at church meetings and then express their Kiowa cultural ways outside the church in ceremonies. For example, in church an eagle

feather and cedar smoke would be disallowed, but outside the church one might use it in a ceremonial way.

3. Their faith is expressed generally the same as those white Christians around them until a deeper faith is needed, such as during a crisis of faith like the need for healing a sick family member, at which time they revert to their Indian symbols and ceremonies for faith expression.

None of these alternatives offers much congruence of faith and culture, and as a result, a weak faith is oftentimes produced.[90]

Randy's story of the Kiowa church is the norm, not the exception, in Indian Country. It is equally true among the Navajo of Arizona, the Seminole of Florida, the Tlingit of Alaska, the Lakota of the Dakotas, and so on. Colonial Christianity is thoroughly impressed on the cultures of Native North America. While this is true, it is not the end of the story. Through the contextualization innovations being introduced across Indian Country, and reported in this book, winds of change are blowing.

DISCUSSION QUESTIONS

1. What hindered or prevented the early missionaries from contextualizing the gospel? What still does?

2. Discuss how biblical narratives were interpreted in such a way as to justify "civilizing" the New World?

3. Discuss "modernism" and how it influenced missionaries' views.

4. Describe how the concept of Manifest Destiny was used to justify American expansionism.

5. How is it that well-meaning and genuinely Christian people could consciously and intentionally engage in such culturally hegemonic, oppressive, and later genocidal activities, in the name of biblical truth—as followers of Jesus?

SWEATING WITH JESUS

Stories of the Native Experience

This chapter and the stories within it are a collection of real-life experiences of First Nations individuals and communities seeking a way out of the hegemony of American colonial Christianity in the hopes of finding a place longed for—for a long time. What we are seeking is a place where the gospel brings freedom and spiritual power to follow Jesus with all our hearts, souls, minds and strength, while still fully embracing our tribal identity, traditional customs, cultural forms, worldview and rituals. We seek a place where we are no longer seen as the perpetual mission field of the dominant culture church, but rather a place where we are honestly embraced as coequal participants in the life, work and community of Christ's followers—as Indigenous people.

NARRATIVES AND STORIES

This chapter is about my participation with and observation of some remarkable people and their stories. This narrative is the heart and soul of this book:

> Narrative is, after all, concerned with doings and goings-on, but somewhat like the alterations affected by wearing or removing stereoscopic glasses, narrative thinking alters what the observer observes. Behaviors, for example, were expressions of an individual's stories within a particular context at a particular time. It was important to consider the characters who were living the stories, the characters

who were telling the stories, the times at which stories were lived, the times stories were told, the places in which stories were lived.[1]

From an Indigenous worldview, these stories are sacred. Some sacred stories are not meant to be told to others, and some not fully explained. Some are not shared with cultural outsiders because they are held in trust by a tribal community or by an individual because the experience is deeply personal and thus private. In some cultures it is thought that telling stories will diminish their power, especially those that are only told during a specific season of the year.

These stories were entrusted to me to take care of as gifts. They are accounts of personal pain, oppression, faith and spiritual growth representing the parallel journeys of thousands of Native/Indigenous people in North America and around the world. Their pain is the direct result

CREDENTIALS VERSUS COMPETENCY

Whether my Native friends and colleagues and I like the academic tag or not, we are part of a growing community of First Nations intellectuals and theologians in North American Christianity, albeit "organic intellectuals." As a fifty-seven-year-old with only a high school diploma, I completed my two years of doctoral course work with all As. For more than fifteen years—and with no formal education beyond the twelfth grade—I lectured in colleges, universities and seminaries and became a published author and columnist. My story speaks to the hegemony of formal institutional educational systems, specifically the tension between "credentials" and "competency." My teaching and writings reflect my intellectual capacity, yet these achievements do not make me eligible for acceptance in a formal postgraduate study program—but I did complete the degree. In the world of academia in America, my participation as a faculty member is not permitted—disallowed for lack of a degree and limited to being a "guest lecturer." I am disturbed by this fact because in the course of this research I have met many "uneducated" yet highly competent, brilliant First Nations thinkers, scholars, theologians and "organic intellectuals" who are doing amazing work in terms of self-theologizing, missiology and contextualization. Far from the halls of formal theological institutions and seats of power in the Christian denominational world, their voices and contributions go unnoticed and unheard simply for lack of credentials.

I have found Elizabeth Cook-Lynn's observations regarding Native Americans in the intellectual world disturbing, especially in theological circles. Cook-Lynn aptly points out that

> The "American Indian Intellectual" is to many people a bizarre phrase, falling quaintly on the unaccustomed ears of those in the American mainstream. While there are images of Jewish intellectuals, European intellectuals, British scholars, African novelists, there is no image of an American Indian intellectual. There is only the primitive figure who crouches near the fire smoking a sacred pipe or, arms outstretched, calls for the Creator to look down upon his pitiful being.[2]

> The contributions First Nations anthropologists such as Francis LaFlesche, James Nason, Beatrice Medicine, Son of Many Beads and Curt Nimuendajú have made to the body of scholarly literature, as well other disciplines, are noteworthy. However, the same level of contribution has not, until recently, been true of theological literature.

of the colonialism, paternalism and ethnocentric theology I wrote about in previous chapters. My intention as a participant-observer researcher is to honestly recount them, having been given permission and encouragement to do so, in an honoring, respectful and inspirational way in order to help others on their spiritual journeys.

This research process has helped me identify my own internal journey toward decolonization. The academy's formal requirements for writing a doctoral dissertation created a high level of discomfort for me. I wrestled with not being found guilty of "using" our people's struggle for "identity," "place," and "self" as simply subject matter for my research. One of my strong objections to "revitalization theory"[3] is that it feels so dehumanizing to me as various peoples' struggles for survival become a category for analysis. I struggled with trying not to handle and retell my friends' and others' "story-gifts" as raw, exotic, empirical data used to fulfill the academic requirements for a doctoral dissertation with all of the accompanying theoretical frameworks, methodologies and structural requirements.

I listened to and participated in these stories and in social/religious ceremonies. As I did, new understandings emerged that altered and reshaped the way I recounted these stories and allowed them to tell themselves from Indigenous perspectives. While stressing the importance of the ethnohistorical approach to research, Donald Fixico cautions that an ethnohistory of Native people largely written from a Western perspective will continue to suppress the American Indian point of view.[4]

These stories from Lakota, Navajo, Paiute, Apache, Athabascan, Mohican, Keetoowah Cherokee, Arapahoe and dozens of other tribal communities are all part of a continuum of history, including those in the making, not yet told. Putting them on paper for others to enter into is a sacred trust because as Elizabeth Cook-Lynn says, "How the Indian narrative is told, how it is nourished, who tells it, who nourishes it, and the consequences of its telling are among the most fascinating—and at the same time, chilling—stories of our time."[5]

Liberating Our Stories

These First Nations stories must be considered in light of our particular context in a way similar to how Babacar Fall views African stories in the African context: "Life histories and other oral sources are an essential element of African historiography and ought to be integrated into the history curriculum of African institutions."[6] More than reciting thick narrative or coded data, I am telling these stories as a Lakota follower of the Jesus Way, in the hope that they can serve to deconstruct and belie the American missionary, government and, lately, conservative evangelical myths about our history and identity. Furthermore, and perhaps more importantly, I am especially hopeful that, on the redemptive side of the deconstruction equation, this book can and will contribute to the integration of First Nations worldview perspectives and the theological curriculum of North America and beyond.

This retelling of our history reorients it from a story of colonization to the liberation of people in the light of Jesus coming among us. It also talks about our resistance to oppression. We will struggle to tell our own story. Already we are accused of "revising" American Christian history and the socially constructed Euro-American myth of providential destiny and the racialization of the First Nations people of the land. Fall writes that for a long time

> [a]ll kinds of myths and prejudices concealed the true history of Africa from the world at large. African societies were looked upon as societies that could have no history. Today Africa is no longer denied a history, and African history has become a legitimate field of inquiry. African historiography however needs to continue to confront its construction as a historical discourse, which must "take apart a society in order to rediscover its ideals, values, and models for action." Reconstructed through multiple approaches, historical discourse follows the ebb and flow of cultural evolution, and is marked by various influences.[7]

In the same way that the African story is being regarded in a new light, my hope, at least in a small way, is that the stories in this research will provide a much-needed, fresh perspective as we tell our own stories. More and more, part of our work is that of being "historical correctionists."

My story. I was born on the Rosebud Reservation among my mother's people in June of 1954. My father was Oglala Lakota from the Pine Ridge Sioux Reservation in South Dakota, and my Mom is Sicangu Lakota from the Rosebud Sioux Reservation in South Dakota. They were both born and raised on their respective reservations, attended Catholic-run boarding schools, grew up speaking Lakota, and as young adults left the reservation to pursue careers. My parents were both *eyeska* or "mixed blood," meaning they also had European ancestry. Twiss is a common name from England, and my mother's maiden name, Larvie, is French. Her mother's maiden name was McLain. I am technically five-eighths Lakota with French, English and Scottish blood.

My parents met and got married, I was conceived, they got divorced, and my Mom moved back to Rosebud where I was then born. I only met my dad later in life and did not grow up around any of my Twiss side of the family. As a young boy growing up on the reservation in Rosebud, a town of several hundred where everyone was acquainted, life was a blast.

I have many fond memories of growing up on the reservation. My five-, six- and seven-year-old buddies and I walked around town, visited the local store, got into trouble, went swimming at the reservoir, explored the dump, stayed out late in the summers—a kid's paradise.

I especially loved attending the powwows. For a young boy it was a wonderful time of strengthening family relationships with my cousins and relatives, as well as participating in and observing the cultural activities of the tribe. The color and beauty of the traditional clothing (regalia) worn by the dancers was always an awesome thing to behold. The booming sound and rhythm of the drum and songs was very inspiring to my young heart. The amazing athleticism and grace of the dancers was something I really admired. All these memories left me with an indelible impression of the value and beauty of being Native American.

However, there was an underside of reservation life: alcoholism, poverty and violence. Not wanting us to grow up in that atmosphere and wanting us to learn to be successful in the white man's world, my mother eventually moved us from the reservation. We went to Denver, Colorado, then on to Klamath Falls, Oregon, and eventually to Silverton, a small town of 4,500 people near Salem, Oregon. I went from the third through twelfth grades in Silverton. During those years we made several summer visits back home in order to stay connected with relatives. On two different occasions during the 1960s, two of my Mom's sisters and their families lived with us for short periods of time.

During the 1950s and 60s, the US Federal Government was carrying out a policy of relocating Native people from their reservations to urban centers. The government subsidized the relocation of Native people to the cities through financial, housing and education incentives, with the goal of assimilating them into the mainstream of American society. Behind this policy was the underlying goal of making Native people less of a burden on US taxpayers. Akin to most of these attempts at legislated social engineering, the program was a dismal failure. It left Native people socially and culturally disenfranchised and devastated—and my family was no exception.

It was an ignoble scheme that created generations of hardships, broke up families, and created a subculture of Indian alcoholics for the skid rows of our major cities, such as Oakland, Cincinnati, Chicago, Dallas, Minneapolis and many others. The program moved the people to the city, put them through a "quickie training program," got them a cheap apartment, a short-term job, and then left them stranded and lost in the worst parts of town. The "skin" bars in those cities became famous and were the most troubled businesses of that type.

After settling in Silverton in 1962, my Mom never returned to the reservation to live, just visiting often, and as of this writing is eighty.

After leaving the reservation, my parents no longer spoke Lakota at home. They either did not consider the language important enough or did not have the time to teach it to us. None of my cousins learned the language, even those who spent their entire lives on the reservation. It was our parents' way of protecting us from the prejudice and discrimination they experienced and a way to help us succeed in the white man's world. I grew up speaking English only, except for a few Lakota phrases and words.

We did not keep Native religious or ceremonial practices in the home, in large part because my Mom was a faithful and staunch Catholic. We did listen to her many stories of growing up on the reservation that told of ghosts of the deceased appearing, the habitation of ghosts in homes, wild animals behaving in extraordinary ways, and various "paranormal" experiences that she, friends and family regularly experienced. We just called them "spook" stories and loved listening to her tell them to us. This led us to believe that spirits were a normal part of life, though frighteningly so. These stories enlarged our worldview to include a spirit world that helps shape *our* world and the lives of the people who live in this world.

My Mom talked about her childhood on the Rosebud Reservation. She lived in a small two-bedroom house in the country with no running water or electricity. She rode horses with her five brothers and sisters. She told us later of the painful and terrible things that happened to her brothers and sisters and other kids while they lived at the Catholic boarding school. She began attending the Bureau of Indian Affairs (BIA) boarding school on the reservation when she was five. At age six she moved to St. Francis Mission Boarding School, also on Rosebud, and graduated from twelfth grade there. Unlike her brothers and sisters who hated it and underwent some deeply wounding experiences that plagued them their entire lives, she grew and learned a lot from, as she would say, her mostly positive experience.

My uncle Leo was always running away from the boarding school. He was usually caught and taken back. One of his aunties gave him a Lakota nickname, *Gakenaya*, "There He Goes." I get my middle name from my uncle Leo. My son Phillip carries it as his middle name and one of my grandsons is named Leo.

I grew up always acknowledging being Native. I did not completely self-identify as Native until I left my nearly all-white high school and small-town social networks and returned to the reservation at the age of eighteen.

My mom is an amazing woman. During this time, as a single mother, she worked full-time as a nurse at nights, refusing to accept the aid of welfare or food stamps as she raised us four kids. My mom is the classic, strong, nonverbal type of lady. She is a beautiful and dignified woman. Unfortunately, after divorcing my dad, my mom married an abusive alcoholic from back home on "the Rez" (reservation). He used to beat my mom, and I can remember spending many frightening nights crying with my half-brother and sisters, listening to my mom and her husband fight. I can remember dreaming about the day when I would be big enough to beat the crap out of him. They divorced when I was about nine or ten, and Mom never remarried.

After graduating from high school in Silverton, Oregon, in 1972, I moved back to the Rosebud Reservation to attend Sinte Gleska (Spotted Tail) College. There I became involved in the American Indian Movement (AIM). It was during this time that I began to reconnect with my relatives and culture.

On a late November afternoon in 1972 I stood four stories up on the roof of the Bureau of Indian Affairs office building in Washington, D.C., watching nervously as some three hundred police arrived in full riot gear and surrounded the building. We had forced all the BIA employees to leave, chained the doors, and taken over the building. In the early evening several federal marshals were allowed in and they gave us an ultimatum: "Vacate the building in one hour or be removed by force."

I was part of AIM's "Trail of Broken Treaties" protest. We were expressing Indian peoples' frustration and anger over the United States government's unjust breaking of nearly all the hundreds of treaties with First Nations people.

The government threats to remove us forcefully only made us angrier. We reinforced the windows with duct tape and distributed water barrels with towels in anticipation of tear gas. We fashioned weapons of all kinds—spiked clubs, bows and arrows, spears, gas bombs and a small arsenal of guns—"articles of war." I later learned that there were several women who smuggled a large amount of dynamite into the building by taping it to their bodies. Throughout eight days, paper was scattered on almost every square inch of all four stories. At one point, along with several other people, I was given a dozen gas-filled light bulbs and instructed to start the building on fire, beginning on the top floor and working our way down to the bottom. Fortunately, the idea was scrapped.

The first couple of nights we experienced both fearful pandemonium and jubilation. In those days people used long-distance telephone calling cards. We confiscated hundreds of them and started calling our friends and relatives around North America. I called my pot-smoking pals in Oregon, telling them all about it. We talked for over an hour. I found out later the FBI called my pals and asked who it was that called them. My pals said they didn't know who it was. The FBI asked them why they talked for over an hour then. My pals said because whoever it was was a really interesting stranger. I never had any legal problems nor was arrested, though I likely had a "government eye" on me for a while after that.

After eight extremely intense days of threats, ultimatums and moments of mass hysteria, the siege ended. Fortunately, the marshals never did storm the building. Cooler heads prevailed because if they had stormed the building, many lives would have been lost. Many more would have suffered injury because this was part of the ongoing "Indian Wars" with the Federal Government, and the AIM leaders were serious.

Our siege resulted in our doing over two million dollars' worth of damage as we ransacked the entire building.

Although subsequently little changed politically, the Native American voice had exploded into the public eye. That voice empowered Native people to begin fighting with renewed faith and intensity for many local fishing, land and economic reform issues in our tribal communities.

Back in my aunt's home in Rosebud, the thrill of D.C. had worn off. I found myself both disillusioned and disappointed with AIM. I saw the same hypocrisy in the leaders of AIM that I had seen in the lives of other political and Catholic spiritual leaders. One night I watched one of the movement's most respected spiritual leaders come staggering out of a local reservation bar with a woman under each arm. I began drifting deeper into drug and alcohol abuse.

I left the reservation and traveled back to the Pacific Northwest to hook up with my old drinking and partying buds in Oregon. In November of 1973, while living out of my hippie/Indian van in a small lumber town, I had a brush with the law, resulting in a few days in jail for possession of marijuana and alcohol abuse. Because my alcohol content was so high when I was arrested, the judge concluded that I must have a severe drinking problem and decided to send me to a drug rehabilitation program as part of my release. But instead, I talked a friend into moving to Maui, Hawaii, with me.

Still searching, I was drawn into Eastern religions: Buddhism, Taoism and Hinduism. I practiced yoga, prayed mantric prayers and sought enlightenment. I traveled throughout the island of Maui and spent many nights praying and sleeping under the stars. The combination of hallucinogenic drugs, Eastern religions, my Catholic upbringing and Native spirituality only led to more confusion. This troubled me. I knew there had to be more meaning in life than what I was experiencing.

While I was hitchhiking to the other side of Maui one afternoon, a couple of guys picked me up. They began to talk to me about God, about Jesus Christ and his plan for my life. I thought they were narrow-minded, self-righteous Jesus freaks and Bible thumpers, and after giving them a piece of my mind I got out of the car. I had read about and understood the negative impact Christianity had worked among many of our Indian tribes historically. I saw it as nothing but the destructive religion of the white man. The last thing I wanted was to be a Christian.

There is a place on the coast of Maui called the Seven Sacred Pools where a small river cascades down a valley in a series of waterfalls. In a nearby meadow, psilocybin mushrooms (a very strong hallucinogenic) grew in great numbers. Often many of us spiritual seekers could be found there picking and eating them and "tripping out." On one of these days I had eaten numerous "magic mushrooms," and at two-thirty in the morning I found myself completely engulfed in paranoia and the fear of dying or losing my mind. I tried my Eastern meditations and prayers for relief, but to no avail. All I could imagine was going crazy and running down the beach with the men in white uniforms chasing me to lock me up. It was a horrible moment spiritually and psychologically.

At last, fearing the worst, I literally yelled at the top of my lungs, "Jesus, if you're real and you can do what those people said you could do, then I want you to come into my heart and life and forgive me for the wrong I've done." At that moment an incredible thing happened: *The effect of the drugs left, the fear disappeared, and a most awesome sensation of peace literally flooded my being from the top of my head to the bottom of my feet.* I felt clean, forgiven and filled with joy. It was there on that beach that the Creator revealed himself to me—in the person of Jesus Christ—and I became a follower of the Jesus Way. As I have reflected on this over the years, I am grateful that Jesus embraced me "outside" the church walls, not during an evangelistic crusade or through being led in "the sinner's prayer." The spirit of Jesus has walked with me through many difficult and trying seasons of my life, particularly with struggles in the Christian church world.

From Hawaii, I moved to Alaska to see a friend who had also become a follower of Christ. A few months after I had begun living at a Christian training center north of Anchorage, I began to wonder how my Lakota heritage could be part of my new Christian experience—especially after having recently come through the AIM experience. Six months earlier I hated white people and Christianity, and now I was a Christian and supposed to love them. So one afternoon I asked one of the pastoral leaders how I was supposed to relate to my Native culture as a Christian.

I distinctly remember him opening the Bible he was carrying. He read from Galatians 3:28 where Paul said, "There is neither Jew nor Greek, slave nor free, male nor female, for you are all one in Christ Jesus" (NIV). After reading it he commented how cultures should all blend together for us as Christians, and then concluded by saying, "So, Richard, don't worry about being Indian anymore—*just be like us.*"

Though he was unaware of it, essentially what he was saying was, "Forget your Indian-ness and embrace our white culture as the only Christian culture." Being young and naive as well as deeply grateful for Creator's love in setting me free from drug and alcohol abuse, and sincerely committed to becoming a wholehearted follower of Jesus, I believed that church leader. I really had no choice, being a new Christian, and he, being in a position of spiritual power/authority, gave an answer from the Bible about cultures. So for the next twelve years I lived the Christian life as it was culturally modeled for me by non-Native friends and Christian brethren—something I later found to be less than I am, and much less than the Lord Jesus wants me to be!

In 1976 I married my wife Katherine. Her mother was born and raised in Wales, and her dad was a second generation Norwegian from North Dakota. As a single man my only criterion in a potential wife was that she have a strong commitment to Christ. At the time the vast majority of the people at the Christian training center were Caucasian. Katherine and I met, fell in love and married. She was and remains the love of my life!

I left Alaska to serve as pastor at a predominantly white charismatic church in Vancouver, Washington, from 1982–1995. In 1987 I traveled back to Rosebud to attend the funeral of one of my aunties and to visit relatives. There had been a growing unrest in my soul about the dualistic gap Christianity had created for me. While in Rosebud I prayed that Creator would show me a sign about my future regarding my personal engagement with my Native culture. Creator gave me a sign: I met a man who was doing what I had asked to find. That was the point when I began some serious self-reflection and exploring of Native spirituality and its relationship to a biblical faith. I began to consciously choose the path of discovery as a Lakota man committed to following Jesus. As I look back on that time, I realize I was starting down the road of an internal, personal decolonization process and the deconstruction of my conservative evangelical introduction to biblical faith.

I made several summer trips to Rosebud with my family in the late 1980s and early 90s. Those visits affirmed and strengthened Creator's direction in my life. Reconnecting with my Larvie family members filled the vacuum of tribal identity in my soul. Participating in and observing the paternalism and near-total Anglicized way in which Native people on the reservation experienced Christianity was disheartening. Nevertheless, my heart and soul began moving toward a greater sense of wholeness and freedom as a human being walking in the light of Jesus.

I spent many years wrapped up in discovering how critical contextualization can help inform and improve our efforts at evangelism. I also believe critical contextualization must theologically—and specifically hermeneutically—include a view toward justice, notions of shalom, harmony, and spiritual well-being.

That being said, contextualization has inspired me to live out my faith in the day-to-day world of my Native community. During this time I became a Northern Traditional powwow dancer, participating in "sweat lodge ceremonies," praying while burning sage, sweet grass, tobacco and cedar, and attending various religious Native ceremonies—all things that I was not doing sixteen years before. Some of these things I had taken part in *before* choosing to follow Christ, but not for the next twenty years, from 1974 to 1994.

Contextualization and stories. In the introduction to Robert Atkinson's *The Life Story Interview,* his work is noted for making room for, even insisting upon, the "highly contextualized individual judgments on the part of the researcher," while engaging with the life stories of individuals and groups of individuals. It is both a nonstandardized and very personal approach with inherent flaws and challenges, yet it is considered a unique way of engaging life and story that allows the researcher to discover new

insights through the subjectivity of an unpredictable personal story. Atkinson finds it "difficult, if not impossible, to reduce these worlds to a few
representative dimensions."[8] As a research methodology, he notes,

> The life story is inherently interdisciplinary; its many research uses
> directly parallel the four classic functions of sacred stories. Telling
> a life story can help one to know one's self, others, the mystery of
> life, and the universe better than before and can also provide the
> researcher with a better understanding of how the teller sees him
> or herself within and in relation to these domains.[9]

SWEATING WITH JESUS

Sitting in the pitch-black sweat lodge—nearing 140 degrees (F) because
of the steam rising off the just-drenched, glowing hot rocks—the nine
Native men were bombarded with pain, confusion and doubts about
whether or not they had made a mistake. They were halfway through
their first traditional sweat lodge ceremony as followers of Jesus. Added
to the physical challenge was their spiritual concern as they listened to
the traditional spiritual leader. He was not a Christ-follower, and had
been asked to lead their prayer time.

Composite stories. I have created the hypothetical scenario of a shared
sweat-lodge ceremony experience as a way to tell the collective stories in
an orderly fashion. I have worked diligently not to change meanings.
With minimal structural revision, I have arranged the stories in the form
of a dialogic narrative. By recording these stories, I have invited readers
to join me in "listening in" on conversations commonly heard among
hundreds of First Nations Christ-followers scattered across North
America. I will insert some analysis in this chapter in order to highlight
the findings of my research and to demonstrate the power of story to
communicate "Indigenous self-theologizing."

Some of these stories are composites of numerous stories. Some are
biographical pieces. After reviewing all my research notes, interviews
and surveys, there emerged certain common themes, responses, reac-
tions and life experiences. All the events that are described or refer-

enced and all quotes from composite people actually occurred. These events may be found in stories from several different people, but not only did they happen—they are typical of hundreds of other stories I have listened to over the past fifteen years. My documented interviews, questionnaires and surveys are the sources of all the content in the following dialogues. The stories are written with minimal copyediting, except for context, conversational structuring and sequence. I have attempted, as Atkinson writes of the process, "to help people tell their stories in their own words."[10]

Composite man #1—Tony. He was born Native but raised in a non-Native Christian home and community. He was adopted by white parents from a white-run orphanage or foster home(s), or raised in a Caucasian community off the reservation in a mostly all-white world. He knew he was part Indian but considered himself Caucasian with some Native blood. Tony grew up going to church longing to know more of his Native past, but was never encouraged by family or circumstances to search things out because of their negative view of Native culture and religion. In time he began searching out his Native heritage and roots, eventually reconnecting with his Native family. In his forties he began to self-identify as a tribal person.

Composite man #2—Joseph. He grew up knowing he had some Native blood from one of his grandparents who was part Indian. He did not have any solid facts or details about that family story. He was not raised in Native cultural ways, but had heard some stories about them. He would occasionally identify himself as having a little bit of Native blood, but did not begin to identify with being part Indian until his thirties. His faith in Christ played a major role in his embrace of Native culture. He now self-identifies as a First Nations man and associates with the local Native community in his area. Joseph wears Native-style clothing and jewelry, has grown his hair long, attends powwows and listens to Native music. Some traditional people have taught him the values and practices of contemporary urban Indian culture and have mentored him. He is a powwow dancer, is regarded as a Christian spiritual leader in the Native community, and is active in local Native gatherings. People who knew him growing up would say, "I didn't know you were Native American." Joseph doesn't see much of a problem contextualizing his culture and faith.

Composite man #3—Russell. He grew up with Native parents on his reservation. A mixture of Christianity and traditional Native spirituality and ceremony was practiced in his household to varying degrees. He learned both ways but identified more with the traditional Indian ways and thought of Christianity as a "white man's religion." Russell always self-identified as a Native person. At the age of nineteen, he committed his life to following Jesus. For the next five years he was indoctrinated into a charismatic experience, and he left behind his cultural ways. His church leaders did not understand Native ways and considered most of it as fundamentally demonic. Often he heard from the pulpit that Natives must put away their Indian ways—that is, "the old man"—and follow Jesus. He went so far as to burn most of his Native ceremonial items. Later Russell reconciled these incongruities and is now firmly committed to contextualization as a way of life.

Biographical stories. Larry is sixty years old. He was raised in a non-Christian home on the reservation and has lived there his whole life. He came to follow Jesus later in life and readily made the connections between his faith and traditional cultural ways. Both his parents were Native and fluent in their language, and they taught Larry the language in their home. Larry's experience (or encounter) with Jesus was very personal, spiritual and mystical. Even though it occurred in an evangelical church service, it had very little to do with the service. He was taught in his church that his Native cultural ways were suspect at best and needed to be stopped at worst. Larry's worldview orientation allowed him to follow Jesus in the context of his experience of life. Though feeling misunderstood and being ignored by the leadership of his church, he grew in his faith, embrace of Scripture and love of Jesus. He has incorporated his cultural ways into his faith in Jesus in a very holistic and comprehensive way, with daily ceremonial prayer and participation in the ceremonial life of his tribe and community.

Bill is a mixed-blood Native man who was not raised on a reservation but rather in an urban, church-attending Christian home. His Native father was mostly absent due to alcoholism. His mother is Caucasian. Bill does not speak his language, was not raised with his cultural ways, and not until his late teens did he primarily self-identify as a Native man. Bill is now fifty and has been a follower of Jesus since he was twenty-three. He attended church, mostly embraced his Native identity growing up, and in his early twenties fully identified with his Nativeness as a Christ-follower. He did not have much encouragement and had to find his own way of following Jesus within his cultural ways. He often felt alone or like he was the only one thinking this way. Today he regularly participates in a wide range of Native cultural events.

Dale is a full-blood Native, born and raised on his reservation. His parents spoke the language, and he grew up speaking his language in his home. He was raised in a legalistic Pentecostal Christian home. This religious legalism taught that his culture was mostly demonic and had no place in Christianity. At one point this view created such internal conflict he stopped speaking his language for several years and tried to become the best "white man" he could be. In his twenties and thirties he began questioning some of his church's practices and started considering other ways of thinking about Creator and faith. Over time he diligently studied and listened to opinions on both sides of the issue. In his forties, he thoughtfully arrived at the conclusion that his experience of Christianity was incomplete because of the rejection of his culture. Not only that but, perhaps even more importantly, he was incomplete as a human being. He now is fully engaged with his tribal ceremonies and working out the theologies that provide biblical support to his beliefs and practices.

Robert grew up in a Native community without an official reservation. His community surrounded him with his cultural ways. This was not true in his home. One parent was Native and the other was not. He does not speak his language. He learned his tribal ways as best he could and as a young boy identified as a Native man. He came to faith in Jesus at the age of twenty-one at a church youth conference.

Will was born and raised in a traditional Alaskan village. His family later moved to Fairbanks. He was raised to hunt and survive in the wilderness of Alaska, and he learned the cultural and spiritual ways of his Athabascan people. After becoming a Christian, Will moved to Seattle for a time to attend a Bible school. Though misunderstood and often criticized in the church, he worked to maintain his cultural ways in an integrated way. He later served as the Grand Chief of the Athabascan Tanana Chiefs Association and as an advisor to the Governor of Alaska.

Listening In on Some Stories

"I want to thank you, my brothers, for praying with me today in this sweat," said Dale to the men sitting in the circle. "I felt Creator was here with us. I want to thank my relative here, Marshall, for leading us today. It is always good when we can join in a humble way like this to ask for Creator's help in our pitiful lives. It is a good thing to pray. Thank you too that some of us today prayed to Jesus and my relative prayed in his own traditional way to *Tunkasila*, our Grandfather."

Marshall said he was glad to help. Any time people want to pray he said he would gladly help. He then apologized because he said he had to leave to go help his cousin with his sweat. He said his cousin was troubled about his teenage children with all the suicides that had been happening among the young people and wanted some friends to join him in praying for them. Dale rose and slipped him some cash and a pouch of tobacco, thanking him again as he said goodbye.

The glistening men were comfortably sprawled in some lawn chairs outside the canvas covered domelike structure—the sweat lodge. The wood in the fire pit in front of the lodge opening had died down to glowing embers where the rocks had been heated.

As he was again wiping the perspiration from his forehead, Robert lifted his gaze with a small grimace/smile confessing, "I had no idea it would get so hot in there. Among our Apache tribe we don't have a sweat lodge ceremony, and in all my years of pastoring and seminary it certainly doesn't fit any of the theological categories I have, so this is all new to me."

"Wow," responded Joseph, "well, this was like déjà vu for me. About seven years ago I went to Russia and while I was there I went to a *Bania* that was a lot like this sweat lodge ceremony. There was no thermostat there either and when I stood up I about passed out because of the heat. Though it doesn't fit any of my Christian categories either, anything that our people did as a positive influence to our culture and our family was positive in the eyes of Jesus. This was very affirming of my faith in Jesus."

Nodding his head in quiet assent to both men, Larry admitted, "I kept wondering if I was going to faint from the heat. At my age, my endurance is not what it used to be. I have kept many of my Pueblo ceremonial practices as a follower of Jesus, so despite the heat, and the fact this sweat is new to me, I found it deeply spiritual."

After a moment of comfortable silence, Will spoke up, "For me, this brought back lots of really good memories of village life. Among our Athabascan people in Alaska, we do very similar sweats as a matter of routine in the long winter months for health and hygiene reasons. As a spiritual ceremony, however, I found it especially meaningful and was able to fully pray and worship Jesus."

Russell commented about how good it felt to be in there. "It was like coming home," he said. "I used to sweat all the time and pray with sage and sweet grass, pray with my pipe and dance my prayers at the powwows. But the church said I had to quit all that stuff because it was of the devil. I never really could understand that, but for about ten years I put it all away. Jesus was with me during those years, but I always felt a sadness, like a part of me was boxed up in the closet. One day I heard some guy talking about being Native and Christian so I began to pray and seek the Lord about these things again. As I studied the Bible and prayed, I believe the Holy Spirit made it clear to me that it was right to carry the pipe again. Then a cool thing happened. This guy came to me at a powwow and, just out of the blue, gave me a beautiful pipe. This sweat today touched my spirit just like when that guy gave me my pipe."

Across from Will, Tony laughed a little, sharing, "When they closed the flap and it got pitch black in there and then I heard the hissing of the water as it was poured on those hot rocks, and the first waves of steam filled the lodge and landed on me, I thought, this is okay. I can handle this. After it got hotter with the second, third and fourth pouring of water, I started wondering if I was going to have to get out, right now!"

"Well," Joseph agreed, "like I said, the physical discomfort was definitely tough, but when the medicine man told us he was going to call in all the spirits from the north, south, east and west to join us in there, I wondered what we had gotten ourselves into."

Tony and Dale chose to sit quietly and listen, nodding in agreement. They understood the various thoughts and perspectives of their friends—friends who had just endured their first traditional Lakota *Inipi*, "sweat lodge ceremony."

Taking a few moments to cool off, enjoy some rest and much-needed water, Dale broke the stillness with his own thoughts, "You know, I wondered too about inviting in all those spirits, so I was really on my guard trying to discern the presence of any evil or bad spirits. I gotta say, though, that I didn't sense anything like that. As a matter of fact, it was one of the most profound experiences I have ever had with Jesus in the past twenty years! It was weird, but awesome at the same time. What about the rest of you guys?"

Joseph answered, "You know, despite my categorical discomfort, the spirit of Jesus was definitely with me and with us in there."

Dale continued, saying, "It's experiences like this that mess with all my categories of what I was taught to believe about what it means to be a Native Christian. Since I was a boy, all I ever heard from the pulpit, whether it was a white or Native preacher, was that as Native believers, we had to get rid of all our eagle feathers, burn our regalia, stop attending powwows and other ceremonies and especially stop with all that 'pagan drumming' because it was all of the devil.

"Even now my pastor and church friends believe that attending this sweat is the beginning of me heading down a slippery slope away from Jesus back into the world of Indian religion and idolatry—backsliding. At the very least, though, they think what we did today is syncretism. You know, blending Christianity with Indian religion so that a false, compromised or distorted gospel results. Some even think this is some kind of biblical heresy.

"You know, as a teenager, what we heard at church was so legalistic: no rodeos, no dancing, no basketball games, no card playing or movies, no doing anything out of character that would ruin your image, like, not being on time.

"Beyond that even, there were some things that we knew were automatically out as far as being a Christian. Cultural things like ceremonies and squaw dances, even our Navajo weddings were automatically out because you just sort of knew what was "in" and what was "out," and so you no longer went to these things. This sweat lodge experience definitely fits into that "out" category. I remember being asked by my uncle to help cook and gather wood and things at a traditional social gathering but had to tell him no, that I was a Christian. I go to church and revival services now, so I can't help you in these things that you ask.

"You know at one point I actually believed what they told us, that we'd "go to hell" if we went to those things. I don't really remember any Scripture references, but just the thought of that entire time was that Creator had taken us out from that and you shouldn't go back to those things. Otherwise, if you went back to these things, you were immediately a backslider. And every night at the revival or Sunday morning service, there was a call for all the backsliders to go up front to get right with Creator. Lots of times it would be the same people that would go forward because they went somewhere to a rodeo again or back to a basketball game [laughing], so there they'd be, back up there asking Creator to forgive them and get prayed for.

"I had close friends and relatives who were really good basketball players and rodeo riders who just quit going to church revivals because they would be condemned. Some of my relatives owned cattle and horses and loved to compete in bronc and bull riding or calf roping, which was extremely popular on the reservation for young people. With the church people, though, all that too was gone—no more."

"That stuff is so crazy," said Larry. "It's so crazy it's funny sometimes. Reminds me of a story my good friend, Samson from the Spokane Reservation in Washington, told me one time about this famous Lakota medicine man who came to his reservation. He said that guy

was all famous and they wanted him to run a sweat for them. He said
they did everything just right. You know, they built it facing east, with
twelve support branches, grandfather rocks that were asked permission to move and blessed; a good buffalo skull was used and a good
pipe and lots of prayer. Everything was going just right. So then
Samson says that they strip down buck-naked and start crawling in
when his nephew, who is following him, says, 'Uncle Billy, how come
your butt is so hairy?' He said everyone wanted to bust up laughing
but they tried to keep all stoic about it 'cause the famous medicine
man was there. He said later they just laughed and laughed about it.
They're still laughing about it."

Robert said, "I had some troubling experiences with some white
pastors in my city and leaders in my denomination. Their legalism
created questions in people's minds that led them to say I was deceived.
At one point, many people left our church because they believed we were
bringing Indian religion or spirits into the church. After I began following Jesus in college, things were very difficult, and remain very difficult as far as my Christian faith being expressed through my Nativeness. I've encountered a lot of opposition from the very beginning when
I became a Christian, especially after eighteen years as a pastor, because
the church was basically telling me that everything that I was doing as a
Native was wrong and sinful. In my Grace Brethren denomination, our
Native church had a sister church with the Pueblo people, and they had
concluded that all our dancing and Native cultural expressions were basically of the devil. This was a very discouraging time because our Indian
people were just starting to come around."

Will added, "Well, I remember one time in our mostly white church,
I did one of our tribal dances and sang a song during our worship time.
It made some people in the church very uncomfortable because they
thought all of the holy men in the old days were evil shamans and they
thought all of the stuff like that was demon inspired. I explained to them
those things and they received it. I told them that Creator placed people
in the Native nations before Christ was known, and a lot of those people
were good people that operated with general revelation of the Father, and

their hearts were to serve the people and they would be the equivalent to Abraham in the polytheistic culture of Babylonia. There were also evil medicine people who used their power to control the people and put fear to their own ends, and that is true in every culture—white culture, black, and Native American. I told them not to just automatically trash everything that Creator was working among our people before the message of Christ came to us. So it was kind of an eye-opener for me to realize that some people still looked at it that way."

Dale said, "It wasn't just a family or two or town or area, but our whole reservation was impacted by the Pentecostal revival movement that came to our Navajo reservation from around '69 to '74. It was pretty popular. And I think it started even earlier but we weren't too aware of it. My mom went to those revival meetings. We were introduced to the revivals through a very close family of ours. They took Mom there and she liked it. I remember two of my older sisters going with this family and they came back and told me about it and said that these people, they stand up and clap and some of them even get the Holy Ghost who would overtake their body. I don't really know if that's the Holy Ghost or what, but they would shake violently and they would go out to the front and they would dance.

"But one thing that puzzled me was some of these people never even accepted Christ, even though they were overtaken by their experiences. And they would go up and dance. My sisters came and told me don't laugh at these people because I don't know exactly what they were saying. It was kind of like if you do, Creator will strike you with a lightning bolt. The message that I got was if you laugh at these people you better watch out, and so I still have questions about that [laughing]."

Will said, "You know, when I was a little boy in our village I learned our dances. I learned the songs and I knew they were good. They weren't bad; I just knew it. So I was just kind of like unaware and unconcerned about the people who had a problem with it. I just embraced these things in my Christian life and practiced it and did it in such a way that I didn't get much opposition. People just said, 'Oh, that's Will, you know; you may as well try and stop the wind because he is not going to change.'

Most of the people just said, 'Yeah,' because we would go to potlatches and there would be a mixture of different beliefs.'

"I encountered some Native believers who I guess must have been taught by somebody that their traditional dances and songs and the potlatch ceremony itself were demon inspired, and that it was including within it heathenistic forms of worship and belief systems that were opposing the Christian beliefs. They would try to say that, and I would say, 'No, you don't know what you are talking about. Tell me what your people believe if you are Eskimo or if you are Indian from some other place. Tell me what your people believe about Creator and about this and about that, about dances and what they mean.' They would say, 'Well, I was never taught it.' So I said, 'Who told you that this was not right?' They said, 'Well I went to Bible school or in my church or whatever.' I would say, 'Well, you're wrong and if you don't know what you are talking about, then you shouldn't be judging us or condemning our cultural ways.' So we would have those kinds of discussions, and there was really no big argument or it didn't ever blow up into something. I just did it and if they didn't like it they didn't say anything really. It would be just occasionally that we would have a discussion."

Bill said, "It took me about fifteen years, but I've come to the point, because of Christ in my life, where I think of myself as a Native man in this world from the perspective of victor, not victim; and because of this reality, I can be victorious in full regalia, with long hair, as well as leather vest and a white shirt on, and still retain my heritage. I think I'm finally close to fully believing that I can walk in the light of victory as a whole person in Jesus. It does require of me in some way something that I haven't fully grasped, a certain attention that just does something.

"It might be connected to something my daddy used to say to me, 'to stand up straight, to walk straight, and to walk tall.' When I started embracing the victory I have in Christ as being fully realized as a Native Christian, as I repented of things I'd done and really turned in a new direction like the ceremonies encourage us to do, I was empowered to become a whole person. For me, participating with you guys in this sweat lodge, or praying and fasting as I hold the pipe to the east lifting it up to

Creator or attending other ceremonies, these things are like a sacred altar of worship for me and have brought about drastic positive changes in me! I guess what I'm saying is that my intention is to live in a good way and to live out my heritage in a balanced and disciplined way as a follower of Jesus."

Will said, "I had the great experience of being mentored by a well-respected elder. In my tribal nation we had an elder by the name of Peter John. He was our traditional chief in our region for many years, and he died a few years ago and I think he was a hundred. He was a believer. He came out of a lot of pretty wild life and was a rough character, and later in his life he accepted Christ but he was very traditional and he knew a lot about our culture and about things we don't hear much about anymore. He really encouraged me with different things that he would see in the Bible and he would say, 'This is how we believed way before we knew about the Bible and the Bible would show us so many of the teachings that Christ taught, like the Sermon on the Mount—the whole thing is just filled with parallels in our Native culture.' He talked about the various principles of Christian living from the Sermon on the Mount that are so close and exact to what we already knew. Creator had given our people a general revelation of himself and of his holiness and of his divine attributes of love and of giving that were known and taught among our people.

"So this elder would speak to me and say, 'Yes, this is what we would do before we knew Christ: we would do the fasting and we would give. We are a very giving people.' He drew these parallels; it was things like 'do onto others,' 'the golden rule' and all these foundational principles. He pointed out that they were all a part of our culture before we even knew about Christ because Creator had revealed himself to us through general revelation, and there were people among our old leaders who were good people, and there were good stories about them and then there were evil people.

"So he kind of took me through a Native Bible study, and he said a lot of our old stories paralleled Bible stories like the flood and other things. I just also liked the picture in Revelation where all the nations and tribes and tongues were there, and I would always think, *Oh, the tribes—wow! So there is going to be our tribal people there.* We don't know who they are because we won't know until we get to heaven but we will have our tribal people there and they will be identifiable, it sounded like to me, and that tribes are not an evil thing otherwise they wouldn't be referred to.

"These things helped shape my thinking early on and were always affirmed during our potlatch ceremonies because the elders that were there loved Jesus and knew all their songs and dances and participated in those ceremonies with such love and strength. If I would just have to go and if I had any concerns that my culture was somehow evil or that the practices were somehow demonic, I would just have to watch the love and leadership of these elders. They participated in these community and family events and the giving that took place.

"All of this was done without fanfare, without expectation or recognition, just out of love. I came to realize more and more, because I would see this, that it was a beautiful way that Creator made us, and these were beautiful cultural expressions. And really the only time that I really ever encountered a kind of a—I am trying to find the right expression here—where somebody else would stand up and declare their identity and express their worship through their identity up there, that Creator gave them of their regalia and the stories—'pride of identity'—was when this guy came up to Alaska from the lower forty-eight, just up in his traditional gear and long braided hair and stories of his people and his journey and the pride of identity that Creator gave him, that just came out. It was very affirming and I realized what a treasure it was because of that very unique expression of Christianity with the cultural identity that Creator gave to our people."

Larry added his perspective, saying, "My family practiced all of our traditional Pueblo rituals, like our cornmeal offering, which starts right at the beginning of the day and is used for everything. Let me elaborate. In Scripture we are shown many times how critical the breath is as bringing forth life. And essentially how that works in my cultural tradition is to become aware of this breath of life and to constantly be reminded that that's how all life is brought forth is through the breath of the Creator. And therefore if I am going to be alive with this life, then that breath is still coming through me and I must be conscious of it. And so the offering of the cornmeal is to place my breath upon that to bring the life that is within me into being—just the very same way that the Creator has shown us that life comes forth. And in this it is also the spoken word that comes on that breath, and that word is alive and therefore I must be very watchful of thoughts that are forming and coming into being by speaking what they are.

"I grew up speaking Laguna Keres Pueblo on my mother's side as well as the Santo Domingo dialect. My journey and coming to know Jesus is extremely personal and also very much an Indigenous perception. All my growing-up years, of course, there was always the Catholic church and all the teaching in the Catholic church, and I knew Jesus more like associated with all of the Christmas, Easter, that kind of teaching. And that's how I knew Jesus. I always had these questions about this man but I wasn't getting any of them answered in any way. But really my intro-duction to Jesus as Christ came in a very personal way in my mid-to-late thirties, about 1979 or 1980. It was one of the first times I'd ever been in a non-Catholic church where I had this amazing experience. I was watching the person that was leading the singing all of a sudden have light come around him. This perked up my interest in what was going on in this congregation.

"Before I knew it this guy disappeared and there was the most amazing beautiful wonderful human being I'd ever seen in my life right there in front of me, and I recognized the spirit of this being as Christ. It was immediate. And it was like my whole life had just all of a sudden come to this point. It was powerful and it lasted throughout the whole hour- to hour-and-a-half service, and the details of all of this are just too in-credible to me as I still remember them. That's how I came to know this man Jesus.

"And then from that point it was a very Indian experience in that it was like very visionary and a vision into the heart and a sense of nothing to do with my intellect. This had to do with my spirit. It was really life changing and powerful, and one of the things as a result of it in the time that passed was I had a tremendous desire to talk to people in the church.

"I thought for sure they were going to just embrace this and understand this and make me welcomed. And it was totally the opposite. People in the church—I'm talking about church leadership—they had no way to relate to what I was describing or even relate to the experience. It was very, very disheartening and disappointing, and then I followed more on a personal learning quest. One of the things I gained out of this was I had this phenomenal companion whose name was Jesus, and he truly became my spiritual brother and he was constant in my life after this whole time.

"I remember one time essentially questioning why I was an Indian. Why are we here? What is our purpose? And along the way I've heard many elders describe this and talk about it, but it was never completely satisfying for me to hear it all until I had another perspective coming direct. And that's how my learning about Christ has been. It's been very Indian in that it's been very direct. I've been guided and led to find things in the natural world, and my study of the Bible has been a very Native study, not a super intellectual one. Not just my mind but my whole being. And I've since then gained knowledge that I always associated with Indian experiences. Now I was having spiritual experiences as an Indian person, but they were more related to this awakening sense of what Christ is in terms of Christianity.

"As I think about what ways the Bible theologically supports these things, I believe that it can be summed up very succinctly in freedom, the word *freedom*. That when something is truly of that divine quality, there's freedom and you're under no restraints, except that you're just expressing that divinity—very freely. And only human beings who are truly lacking in that sense of freedom begin to become restrictive. It brings a great joy to know that you are in the presence of overcoming. And you get to witness how incredibly exquisite and powerful that is in human lives. I believe that Jesus the man leads everyone to the cross. And Jesus then makes actual the experience of freedom which he had been describing and no one seemed to catch on to, was able to catch on to, now he's setting them the example that death has no hold."

Robert said, "As children growing up we were basically brought up with the teaching that there was only one Creator—one Creator—and with that we formulated a whole philosophy, a religion, I guess. We did have a fall ceremony kind of celebrating the end of harvest; we did have our string ceremony kind of bringing in the new life. Among our Apache tribe, traditionally, we had very few ceremonies like praying with sage or cedar or like praying in this sweat."

Dale said, "What you said, Robert, reminds me of the fact that my mom doesn't read or understand English very well or speak English that well either. So it is very tough for her to read the Word on a daily basis. But she told me when she looks around and looks at the creation, that she sees Creator and she knows what got us here and so that is what keeps her going. Her faith is strong. One of my favorite verses confirms what she told me. Psalm 19:1 says that creation shows Creator's handiwork."

Robert continued, "I later attended Grace Theological Seminary in Indiana from '85 to '88 and I kind of hid the fact I was Native for a while until one day when my son told my wife that he wanted 'the Indian to come back.' Of course, the Indian was me! I started attending powwows and ceremonies, and being who I was trying to be as complete as possible.

"After seminary I returned to McAllen, Texas, the place of my birth, and started a church in January of 1989. Things were going really good. One day two Indian ladies came into my office in our nice building and said they were very concerned. They kept inviting a lot of Indian people to come to church and the Indian people would just say, 'Well, that is just a white man's church,' and they would say, 'Our pastor is Native,' and the Indian people would say, 'It's still a white man's church.' So these ladies asked me if I would consider starting a ministry that was particularly for Indian people. I prayed and started calling around and asking questions and trying to get someone to give me some direction, because I had never heard of an Indian church, you know for Indian people. I even called Mormons to see what they were doing. I called the Baptists and the Methodists and the Presbyterians and the Assemblies of God, just to see what they were doing because it might be different and basically everyone would give me the same old, same old.

"Finally, the most helpful person was a Catholic priest whose church was on the Comanche Reservation in Oklahoma, and so when I talked to him he just started sharing some of the things that he was doing because I heard rumors that his church was full every Sunday and that he was using the Comanche culture to reach the Comanche people for Christ and so I called him. We talked for quite a while and he shared some of the things that they were doing in the Comanche church, and it sounded like something that I could possibly integrate into our service. Well, that was about fifteen years ago.

"One of the first things the Lord laid on my heart was that our music was going to have to change because the people wanted to worship the Lord in something that was more theirs than Caucasian. So my problem was that I called around and asked and there was no music to be found, and then I remembered an Indian from Oklahoma who sang at a wedding/powwow that I officiated and this Indian was part of a Native American Church. So I remember when I did this Indian wedding/powwow that they brought their singers, and for the wedding they were singing all these songs called Jesus songs. All of them were quotes of Jesus in the four Gospels, and I called them and asked if they had any songs recorded. They didn't but were willing to record something for me. I waited and waited and nothing happened. So finally I thought, Well, if the Native American church can do it, then I can do it too, and the Lord just started telling me to start singing songs and that was the first thing that changed in our Native service was that we changed the music. That was in 1994.

"So the first thing I told Creator was that I don't know anything about writing music, and I just saw Creator filling my heart. He said, 'You have been singing in powwows since before you were a Christian. You know how to write the songs; all you got to do is start singing.' So that is what I did, and little by little Creator started placing songs in my heart and we started our Native service with some music. And so when we started our Indian service the main source of music for worship was the drum."

Joseph said, "You know, music made a huge impact in my life too. In

2002, there was a gathering at Cottonwood where Richard Twiss, Mary Glazier, and Jonathan Maracle were the main speakers and leading worship. At that time my wife and I were helping a church on the Hopi Reservation that you would describe as basically an Anglo church. There was nothing contextual, nothing cultural, allowed in service. It was kind of like an old Methodist or old Wesleyan style service. It was just a one-hour service, nothing charismatic, just old hymns, and anywhere from two to twelve people came on a regular basis. Well it was at this gathering in Cottonwood that I first ever experienced this pan-Indian cultural style music using Native instruments and drums and people dressed in Native regalia. I met a Hopi lady that we had met out at the Rez, and it was the first time I ever saw her dressed out in her Native outfit. She was telling us how it was healing and had set her free. During this gathering there was an opportunity for me to sit at the powwow drum with a group of people. The first time I hit the drum, I actually felt like my sternum broke [touching his sternum]. There was a physical noise; it actually felt like something in my chest broke. And as I sang with the group of people there, I felt like Creator was actually pumping something new into me over that weekend! I got to sing a few times at the drum, and each time it was like Creator was dealing with and ministering something to me personally. I felt freedom in worship that I have never had being in Pentecostal, charismatic, pretty lively churches. I felt really close to Creator and that he was dealing with me but never really danced or got involved with the charismatic stuff. I loved it but I never did it until then, and I really felt a freedom that I had never had before."

Robert responded, "Wow! What a powerful story. So after my first experience I started the little church that was called the Native American New Life Center, which was just cultural worship. That went along really good. The service actually kind of grew and I had about thirty to thirty-five Indian people all meeting around in a circle, and that was another thing we did different with our service. We did it in a circle and everything was going great until the newspaper got ahold of our church and did a four-page article on us, and I thought that would be good to let everyone know what we were doing in an urban setting. Instead I got the opposite and learned that the church fears what it doesn't understand. The church saw it as demonic and satanic, and so rather than supporting what I was doing, all the churches in that area—well, the majority of the churches in the area, I can't say all of them, but at least fourteen churches in the area—came and started speaking against me and warning the people that I was a New Age pastor.

"I started hearing lots of rumors about me from the local church community. One brother would attend our church's Wednesday evening services and say to me, 'You know, I went to this church that was about twenty-five miles away and the pastor there gave a very interesting sermon.' I asked, 'What was it about?' He said, 'It was about the wolf in sheep's clothing.' I said, 'Oh, must have been a powerful message.' He goes, 'Yeah, he revealed who the wolf was.' I said, 'Really, who was it?' He said, 'It was you!'

"He was warning the people that there was this man, and he was telling them to stay away from me and that I was the devil in the flesh, I was a wolf in sheep's clothing, I was deceiving the church. So what ended up happening with that is some of my older church members that knew this pastor outside were maybe trying to leave the church, and so basically at the end I lost. Our Sunday service had been averaging about seventy-five to a hundred, and within two months it was down to twenty-five to thirty people because there was so much opposition to our new Indian ministry. I wasn't forcing Indian ministry on the rest of the church; we had a separate church. It wasn't like I was saying we are going to start playing the drum on Sunday morning, so you all should get ready for this. It was entirely a separate service, it was more of a home-church environment, and so basically we ended up losing everything. We lost our building, we lost our land and pretty much were very defeated, and yet I still felt in my heart that this was what Creator wanted me to do."

Tony said, "You know, it wasn't that many years ago that I was visiting different churches and was told I was not good enough for this or that church. I was abused by church members who would say I was being disrespectful to Creator by not sitting up straight enough, or my clothes were not what is expected in the house of Creator but that was all I had. After this I did not want to go to church ever again, so I stopped going and decided I would have nothing to do with those Christians. They were a mean group of people, not like us Indians. That is just a little background. Today my faith is restored and I have learned not to put my faith in man for he will always fail me. Today I understand Creator does not fail me."

Joseph said, "For me I learned pretty young—even though going to church was not a bad experience for me—that being Indian was hard. When I was about twelve my father said to me one day, 'You're a Native American and it is in your blood. You are one, you are part of me, but don't tell anybody because they will treat you different and they will treat you poorly so keep it to yourself.' Of course I didn't understand that at twelve, but then later I understood it and I did not talk much about it except with my very close friends. So I did that for a while; then I started embracing it more around my cousins who were very committed to the Indian way and it just grew from there. My journey toward learning about my culture started in 1964 when my father told me but I stayed pretty cool until 1973, when I first re-member starting to say, 'I got to do more about this.' I definitely wanted to be in nature and I felt connected to life, trees, and all of the things—they were part of me. That was just what I knew to be part of what was deep in my heart.

"Then in 1987 I was speaking with a tribal woman one day and I said, 'I am part Indian' and she said, 'Which part, your leg? You either are or you aren't.' So that was the day I embraced my culture.

"I am learning every day to embrace who I am, and that is critical. Jesus says he is going to meet you right where you are at and he will take care of the rest, so we have to embrace those things. I struggle with some things, but as far as dance and regalia, that is not of the devil and never was unless that was what the person wearing it was doing. Any of those things are positive as long as it is not hurting the people that Creator gave you."

They all agreed that their experience in the sweat, and especially their conversation as they sat together cooling off, had been extremely encouraging.

Joseph said, "Let me just tell you guys that in 1991, after discovering my tribal roots, I began to voraciously study American Indian history, including the church's role, and I became demoralized by undeniable facts. By the mid-1990s I no longer fit into church. Since that time I found no satisfaction in any church setting that seemed irrelevant to me as an Indian person. This left me both feeling alone and a little lost, though not weakened in my faith in Jesus. So, that being said, today was very meaningful and important to me. *Wado!*" (Cherokee for "thank you").

Dale then spoke up and invited everyone into the main house where his wife and some of the other wives had prepared a little food for them. Russell's wife, Mary, along with Denise, Charlotte and Susan, were sitting around the kitchen table.

"Boy, you guys really look like red men now," laughed Char. "I hope the rest of your brains didn't melt away too with all that lard you burned off—aaay," she quipped, as they all laughed.

Dale and Char had built this sweat lodge on their country property several years ago to support the local Native community with a good place to come and pray. Their lodge was used several times a week by both believers and nonbelievers. The only challenge was keeping a good supply of firewood on hand.

After Larry took a big swig of cold, fresh well water, he commented again on how encouraging this time together was. Char said, "I know this was the first time for some of you, so how was it?"

Joseph said, "I guess you can say we had church today in that sweat. Honestly, when I led the Assemblies of God church behind the pulpit, it was spirit filled, and Creator led, moved, touched and healed people. In the Native gathering that I have now, when I talk about Woodland culture and do a Bible study that relates to Native people and burn some sage once in a while and incorporate the pipe ceremony into our prayers and sing around the drum, I see that same desire and that same level, if not a little bit more. There is a fervency for Creator, and our Native people come and sit down—many of them for the first time—whereas before, in the AG church, you were assimilated—you were a city person. There was no Native identity, no decor, and there was no tie-in to our Native community."

Tony said, "Good stuff happened in there. You know I attended this reconciliation ceremony in Minnesota that was very life changing for me, like today. The spiritual leader of the gathering one evening had everyone bring all their regalia and lay it on the makeshift stage. Everything you can imagine was up there. There were pipes of all kinds, eagle feathers and claws, gourds, rattles, drums, sage bundles, tobacco ties, sweet grass braids—everything was there. It was just loaded, the whole stage, down the steps. Then everyone prayed and worshiped and dedicated it all to Creator and the purposes of his kingdom. That's how I feel about this sweat. It was dedicated to Creator and we felt his presence in there with us."

Russell said, "I used to pray with a pipe before I began following Jesus and going to church."

Char said, "I used to attend a Wesleyan church. The boys sat on one side and the girls sat on the other side. They just sang traditional white man's church hymns. They weren't allowed to sing happy spiritual songs, or sing in their language. They always had to sing out of a book. I later attended a Christian evangelical boarding school in Phoenix, Arizona, from 1972 to 1977 until I was eighteen. You know, us Navajos, traditionally, have certain ways of believing about creation, the world, spirits, powers, ceremonies and rituals. Everything from wedding ceremonies to 'coming of age ceremonies' for young women, to burying the umbilical cords of our newborn babies, to first-laugh celebrations; we have many beautiful traditional ways. None of these things however were part of our Christian experience. I remember we weren't even allowed to hang out with our grandma because she didn't go to church; it became wrong to hang out with grandma! We were told to no longer wear our beautiful turquoise jewelry—like squash blossoms, earrings, concho belts—or wear our traditional woven wool blankets. There are ladies who were buried without their blankets and all their personal belongings and cultural

items that they had before, because they were associated with 'traditional non-Christian people or Indian religion.' For a long time I used
to get very angry toward Christianity for those things."

Summary

The hegemony of colonialism, Westernism, manifest destiny, ethnocentrism, paternalism and all the other negative influences identified in
earlier chapters is clearly visible and evident in these, my friends', stories.
The oldest person in these stories is sixty-seven, but the median age is
fifty-four. Their experiences did not occur hundreds of years ago in a
less-informed, ideologically inflamed colonial era, but recently. These
stories are not exceptional or rare, but are typical. This has been the
common experience for many First Nations people and their introduction to contemporary American Christianity and its past and ongoing missionary enterprise in Native communities today.

Yet, despite the loathsome cruelty experienced by many of them and
their relatives in Christian-run boarding schools, and the dehumanizing,
shaming paternalism in the local churches, they have held on to their
deep faith in and love for Jesus Christ. Sadly, many others have rejected
their faith because of their experience in the "white church," in which
they found no room or acceptance to be who Creator made them to be
as human beings.

These are stories of hope. They are stories that are pointing to a better
way of being united in Jesus while maintaining the beauty of cultural
diversity. These stories reflect the work of the Holy Spirit who is inspiring
and empowering Indigenous followers of Jesus, here and worldwide, to
begin embracing the pain of our histories and to begin choosing a path
of healing and redemption. In the case of this study, this path is mani-
festing in a dynamic, new contextualized movement of the gospel led by
Native people.

Discussion Questions

1. Discuss the author's views on "organic" versus "academic" intellectuals. What are your views on this topic?

2. What is a "historical correctionist"? Give examples.

3. What do you see as a continuous theme running through the narrative—that is, what do all these people have in common in spite of their differing background stories?

4. The author said that the narrative in this chapter is the "heart and soul" of this book. Describe how these stories affected your views—how did they affect your heart and soul?

A VIEW FROM THE HILL

Emerging Native Expressions of the Jesus Way

Our traditional ceremonial ways are ancient. They have evolved, and will continue to adapt and change to new realities. While core meanings remain relatively intact, methodologies are fluid and personal. There are hundreds of tribes that share or appear to share certain ceremonial ways, yet they are genuinely different.

Although sweat lodge ceremonies are still led as "traditional sweats" in many sweat lodges today, instead of sage branches on the ground and buffalo hides covering the outside, you will find carpet on the floor and canvas, sleeping bags or U-Haul blankets on the outside. These new items might not be considered innovations but more as adaptations. If a group of Christian Native folks gathers in the sweat lodge to pray to Jesus and to help young people reflect on the Bible as a source of wisdom and knowledge in how to live a good life, this might be considered an innovation.

Rogers describes *innovation* as "an idea, practice, or object that is perceived as new by an individual or other unit of adoption."[1] In this chapter I will provide an accounting of specific examples of the introduction, implementation, and diffusion of significant new decolonization contextualization endeavors, "innovations," and the "innovators" who have emerged in the past twenty years. While some of the contextual practices I've identified may not be "objectively new," they are very new for many Native evangelical Christians today and can also be controversial. For example, the "sweat lodge" is an ancient ritual, but the way it is being used by these followers of Jesus within the Native evangelical community is considered a "new thing."

CREATION SPEAKS

The story of Creator's self-revelation to us in the person of Jesus is a two-thousand-year-old story. While the Jewish people anticipated the day when the long-promised Messiah would come, when Jesus came in fulfillment of those ancient "living prophecies," they, as a whole, did not recognize Jesus as the Messiah. In the metanarrative of human history, is the incarnation of Christ "divine innovation"? The essence of the gospel story centers on the incarnation of Jesus, the Creator coming to earth as a human being. This reality "serves as a key paradigm for a contextualized mission and theology."[2] In John 1:14, John declares, "The Word became flesh and blood, and moved into the neighborhood" (*The Message*). "[Jesus] embraced the human context in all of its 'scandalous particularity'—as a male Palestinian Jew, 'born of a woman, born under the law' (Gal 4:4)—in a specific time and place."[3]

As is certainly true of my findings, Rogers notes, "whether or not an idea is objectively new as measured by the lapse of time since its first use or discovery" is not so important as is the "perceived newness of the idea" because if, essentially, it appears new to someone or to a group, for them it is an innovation.[4] Critical contextualization as it applies to Indian Country continues down a two-thousand-year-old path of contextualization. Yet it seems, in the light of centuries of hegemonic colonial paternalism, to be a "new thing"!

These new ideas have spread rapidly in the past twenty years. In the late 1990s there were a handful of innovators, whereas today there are hundreds and the numbers are growing. Rogers describes this growth or diffusion process:

> Diffusion is the process by which an innovation is communicated through certain channels over time among the members of a social system. Diffusion is a special type of communication concerned with the spread of messages that are perceived as new ideas. Com-

munication is a process in which participants create and share information with one another in order to reach a mutual understanding. Diffusion has a special character because of the newness of the idea in the message content. Thus some degree of uncertainty and perceived risk is involved in the diffusion process.[5]

Many Native Christians imagined, hoped or longed for a greater openness to their cultural ways in their churches, denominations, networks and among their Christian friends. Some privately prayed with sage or sweetgrass or danced away from home. For many Native Christians it was their fear of denominational or organizational "discipline" or the risk of ostracism that kept them unwilling to openly accept these new ideas.

A Native Christian elder told me some years ago he had been waiting forty years for these things to come into being. Fifteen years ago a Native pastor told me he dreamed of the day when there would be a "Christian powwow," but said he doubted it would happen in his lifetime. There are now several Christ-honoring, traditional intertribal powwows held every year, though the majority would say they are *not* "Christian powwows."

Early innovators. I know Native ministry leaders who gathered to discuss these innovations before 1989 but never gained wider acceptance of their ideas as many do today. In fact, several were painfully marginalized by their respective denominations or Native ministry peers and even ostracized for their ideas, labeled "syncretists." Among these early innovators were Lloyd Commander, Adrian Jacobs, John Grosvenor, Jerry Yellowhawk, Andrew Begaye, Spencer Cody and Bill Baldridge. I knew some of these people personally. Some of them I had only heard of or had simply read some of their writings. They had been considering and talking about these things in the late 1980s. There were many more who labored in obscurity, trying to stay under the radar of their denominations.

In a paper published in the 2006 North American Institute for Indigenous Theological Studies (NAIITS) Journal, Randy Woodley comments on James Treat's very important book, *Around the Sacred Fire*, which tells the story of the Indian Ecumenical Movement (IEM) that convened annual conferences from 1969 to 1992.[6] This movement was a kind of precursor to the "contextualization movement" I am describing. I will only reference this unique interreligious dialogue phenomenon. It is worth reflecting on both its direct and indirect influence as a forerunner to the contextualization movement.

One thing worth noting is that some of the denominational churches involved in the IEM (Lutheran, Anglican/Episcopal, Methodist, American Baptist) were contextual in many ways. Four Directions Episcopal and later the Lutheran Church have been holding contextualized services in Portland, Oregon, for nearly thirty years. They pray using sage or sweetgrass, include drums songs, and have various Native designs in their sacramental objects. On several occasions they held a Christmas pageant where are all the biblical characters were dressed in full regalia, and drum songs were used along with language that reflected a Native story form. Around 1985 I attended my first service with them and was very touched by the Christmas program, but I remember feeling they were syncretistic because of the smudging. Still, I was intrigued—they fit into my then "liberal church" category.

Revolutionary paradigm. Rogers notes that "[a]ny given field of scientific research is launched with a major breakthrough or reconceptualization called a revolutionary paradigm that provides model programs and solutions to a community of scholars."[7] While I have not discovered a "singular breakthrough," I have discovered an organic "coming together" of key leaders through relational connections that coalesced at several key events in time, opening the door to wider reflection and acceptance. In light of the emergence of the contextualization movement, I believe they can be considered, collectively, a *revolutionary paradigm.* This launch set into motion national recognition of the new paradigm, inspiring a significant amount of intellectual dialogue and debate as "later" adopters, opinion leaders and change agents were attracted to the conversation. Many "followers" were already interested, and they were doing initial experimentation, but they had no theological or philosophical constructs, nor did they have a vocabulary to explain this growing interest. They only knew that "it felt right" and "it seemed like the right thing to do." This project is one of the first to "advance the new conceptualizations with research,"[8] the phenomenon of Native-led contextualization efforts.

These innovators have tremendous potential to reach "critical mass." For example, six Native students are completing doctoral studies from the E. Stanley Jones School of World Mission at Asbury Theological Seminary, Kentucky. Others have completed graduate-level theological studies in several other seminaries that are part of this community of scholars. These realities affirm the fact that "[g]radually, a scientific consensus about a field is developed and perhaps after some years the invisible college is formed to advance the new conceptualization with their research."[9] This has proven particularly true with the seventh Annual North American Institute of Indigenous Theological Studies (NAIITS) symposium held in June of 2010. There a memorandum of agreement with George Fox University and Seminary in Newberg, Oregon, was signed on June 12, 2010, resulting in the creation of a master of arts degree program in intercultural studies in 2011. All but one of the Asbury graduates sit on the board of NAIITS, as of this writing.

Different Kinds of Leaders Are Needed

Rogers provides sufficient overarching theories to explain a process of innovation and diffusion, but I have found his categories of "innovator," "change agent," and "opinion leader," though helpful, to be too static and definitive. These categories should be used as more flexible concepts with significant overlap, often functionally embodied in one person. The men and women who have emerged as leaders exhibit qualities of all three. Each in their personal development began innovating, then sharing their stories of discovery. They inspired and persuaded others. Over time they coalesced into a collective (movement) through meeting other leaders on parallel journeys. Because of the nature of cultural and crosscultural dynamics in the early days of the movement, the leaders fulfilled the functions of all three categories.

The majority of Rogers's research is based on the empirical framework of science and technology and less so on behavioral science disciplines,

OPINION LEADERS

Rogers identifies several generalized summaries of various empirical studies designed to differentiate leaders from followers. These
characterizations provide an analytical lens to help us understand
how these contextual practices have diffused and grown to their
current form. Because Rogers doesn't address religion or spirituality, his categories are limited in their capacity to interpret my findings. However, they do provide structures, categories, paradigmatic
constructs, and language helpful in explaining my data.

- *"Opinion leaders have greater exposure to mass media than their
followers."* The leaders/innovators I have identified in the early
stages of their processes worked with and frequently held significant positions in national denominations or parachurch ministry organizations. They had access to their group's various communication channels, but more importantly to national media.
They all had some formal biblical/theological education. They
were talented writers whose articles appeared in local, regional
and national publications. They were all skilled verbal communi-
cators and had access to and influence upon larger audiences.

- *"Opinion leaders gain their perceived competency by serving as an
avenue for the entrance of new ideas into their system. The exter-
nal linkage may be provided via mass media channels, by an opinion leader's cosmopoliteness* (access beyond geographic, cultural,
social and organizational boundaries) *or by the leader's greater
change agent contact."* Native innovators' organizational positions put them into contact with various ecumenical groups
where new ideas found greater acceptance. Since these were
Native men and women who often struggled with the paternalism of their respective evangelical organizations, they found
sympathy, encouragement and agreement with other leaders in
similar situations. Here ideas of resisting the control of paternalism and envisioning other ways of doing ministry in more culturally relevant ways were shared with one another. Thus, a fellowship grew. At other times, however, the innovator perceived as
more "radical" was excluded from the group because he or she
went "too far" with the cultural expressions.

- *"Opinion leaders are more cosmopolite than their followers."* They
can be described as "people on the edge." This cosmopoliteness
brings them into contact with new ideas from outside their social
group, which they then bring back to their members. They "carry
information across the boundaries" between groups. These Na-

tive leaders' exposure and involvement with other leaders outside their particular groups permitted them to work along the edges and serve as brokers between groups. It was always challenging for these leaders to balance organizational loyalty and "doctrinal adherence" with the refreshing liberty to consider new ideas. It was always a "multicultural" leader who could comfortably and confidently move back and forth across the cultural divides within their own First Nations community and—perhaps more importantly—between the dominant "Caucasian" culture of the evangelical church and their Native cultural world.

- *"Opinion leaders have greater change agent contact than their followers."* They work to gather other opinion leaders in order to leverage diffusion activities through training events, conferences and programs.

- *"Opinion leaders are more innovative than their followers."* The openness of opinion leaders to adaptation and implementation of new ideas early in the game helps invite a sense of competency and trustworthiness toward them by followers who see them as "experts." This confidence opens the way for followers to first consider the innovation as biblically legitimate and later acceptable.

- *"Opinion leaders have greater social participation than their followers."* While a new idea can begin in anyone's heart, even from the "lowest ranks of the people," for that innovation to gain widespread acceptance and expansion it requires some "loft of social elevation." Being an opinion leader requires having a "higher socioeconomic status" than their followers. This situates them into circles of more powerful, influential people who add their support, recommendation and approval. These influential people then help create a sense of credibility and legitimacy among evangelical circles. This is necessary in order for the innovations to find wider acceptance on a larger national scale.[10]

The leaders I have identified as key leaders all began with "precontemplation" of this innovation-decision process. One key event that served to fully affirm and legitimize their deepening embrace of contextualization was the World Christian Gathering of Indigenous People (WCGIP). The inaugural WCGIP was hosted by the Maori people in Rotorua, New Zealand, in November of 1996. More than two thousand Indigenous/tribal people from thirty-two countries attended that historic event, where people shared the gifts of their cultural music, dance, language, art and stories in honor and worship to Jesus Christ. It was truly a historic, catalytic event that served to help launch and fuel a global Indigenous-led contextualization movement.

although reference is made to "anthropological research tradition." Almost no reference is made to crosscultural innovation and none at all to cultural religious innovations. This missiologically framed study adds to Rogers's work. The study seeks to understand how Native followers of Jesus have integrated Eurocentric Christian practices with traditional "non-Christian" spiritual or religious practices, in light of current understandings of contextualization.

A Decolonizing Contextualization Movement Emerges

Fifty-two Native North Americans attended and participated in the 1996 WCGIP New Zealand gathering. Among those were some key leaders: Lynda Prince (former grand chief of the Carrier/Sekani); Garland Brunoe (Wasco/Chippewa), who has served on the board of Wiconi International and as chairman of the Confederated Tribes of Warm Springs in Oregon; Terry LeBlanc (Mi'kmaq/Acadian), who served as manager of Aboriginal Programs for World Vision Canada and as executive director of My People International and of NAIITS; John Sandford (Osage), a highly respected evangelical leader and elder; my wife, Katherine, and me (Sicangu Lakota), cofounders of Wiconi International; Fern Noble (Cree), national prayer leader; and others who were beginning to give leadership to/within ministry organizations that embraced and supported the new contextual innovations. The international leadership team agreed that the next host region would be North America.

World Christian Gathering of Indigenous People. In September of 1998, Terry LeBlanc and I served as cohosts of the second WCGIP in Rapid City, South Dakota. It was a remarkable catapulting and galvanizing event, both for those who attended and for those who heard about the Gathering. For the second time, hundreds of like-minded people were brought together to declare publicly that the gospel can and will be contextualized among Native North Americans. It was here that many early adopters met for the first time.

News of the Gathering spread across the land as *Charisma Magazine* published an eight-page feature story that went to their 220,000 subscribers worldwide. *Indian Life Magazine* also published a feature article covering the event. Since the inaugural event and the Rapid City Gathering, there have been six more: Australia (2000), Hawaii (2002), Sweden (2004), the Philippines (2006), Israel (2008) and New Zealand (2011). There has been a significant level of participation by First Nations delegates in every gathering. With the exception of the Sweden gathering in 2005, which I missed, Terry LeBlanc and I attended every one of the global events.

Many Nations One Voice Celebrations. Three months after the Rapid City Gathering, twenty of us First Nations national leaders met in Florida to discuss how to keep up the momentum created by the Gathering. Some of those in attendance were my wife, Katherine, and I (Sicangu Lakota); Terry and Bev LeBlanc (Mi'kmaq/Acadian); Lynda Prince (Carrier/Sekani); Suuqiina (Inuit); Doug and Gloria Yates (Haida/Tsimshian, Yupik); Kenny and Louise Blacksmith (James Bay Cree); Mary Glazier (Haida) and several others. We met for two and a half days. We decided to hold a series of North American conferences patterned after the WCGIP to promote this new contextual approach that was beginning to grow in acceptance and practice.

The first event was held four months later (April 1999) in Kansas City, Missouri, and it was called the Many Nations One Voice Celebration (MN1V). More than three hundred people attended from across Canada and the United States. Much of the excitement and enthusiasm from Rapid City carried over. Several dozen again wore their traditional powwow regalia and danced with great joy and freedom during the extended and free-flowing worship times. Lynda Prince had commissioned the making of 120 hand drums, each with a biblical image painted on its head, along with a large powwow drum she called the "Abba Drum." Jonathan Maracle (Mohawk) played this large drum during part of the two evenings as the 120 hand drums were randomly distributed to people in the crowd so they could play along in time with him. This created a dynamic sound that filled both the building and the hearts of all the people there. People who attended that gathering then went back to their local communities and churches across the land and convened similar gatherings—patterned after what they had experienced. Often, these early innovator leaders were invited to speak and/or lead the music worship times at these new gatherings.

After the Kansas City Celebration, Wiconi International took on the primary responsibility of planning and organizing the MNiV Celebrations. From 1999 to 2007 we convened twenty MNiV Celebrations in eighteen cities across North America. They were attended by more than ten thousand people.

The Celebrations typically began on a Thursday evening and ended on Saturday evening, mostly held in church facilities. One of the most important contributions to contextual thinking made by the MNiV Celebrations was that they provided a national speaking platform for Native leaders. Dozens of leaders representing over forty different tribes and twenty-eight organizations spoke at the events.

There were workshops that addressed a wide variety of issues related to faith, culture, leadership, theology, missiology and land—all with a focus on critical contextualization as a core value. In the evenings and especially on Saturday nights, all Native people were invited to wear their traditional regalia and dance in worship to Jesus. In eighteen of the twenty Celebrations, singer/songwriter Jonathan Maracle and his band Broken Walls led the music sessions. They always incorporated traditional powwow-style drum music, and were one of the early groups to begin fusing contemporary-style worship music with traditional Native sounds, rhythms, instruments and lyrics. They became leaders of a new innovative genre of contemporary Native worship music.

The purpose and vision of these MNiV gatherings was to convene national gatherings where Native theologians and spiritual leaders could present their unique perspectives to challenge colonial Christianity— and to equip Western/American Christians with a broader understanding of biblical notions of Christ's kingdom and its relationship to the life of a diverse church.

According to the brochures, the Celebrations were times for all people to join together and dance their prayers for the healing and unity of their communities. The historic and groundbreaking emphasis of the Celebrations was an invitation for participants to follow the lead of the

Host People of the land—Native North Americans—in a zealous pursuit
of biblical truth, justice, righteousness, cultural revitalization and spiritual renewal.

FRUITFUL RESULTS

Many people now involved in various contextual endeavors point
to the MN1V gatherings as "the" place where they felt affirmed, empowered and "called" to pursue the contextualization of the Gospel
in their unique local cultural contexts.

Emmett (Navajo) and dozens of others told me their deep and
very personal stories of how they experienced significant moments
of healing because of their attendance at a MN1V Celebration. Emmett says,

> I was rejected by Navajos and whites alike because I was
> not enough like either to be accepted as one of them. This
> led me to despise my Native heritage and to blame my Na-
> vajo mother for the pain she caused me. Through the years
> and many talks I found significant healing for the contempt
> I used to have toward my Native side. Though I have been a
> Christian since I was sixteen, I have recognized who I am as
> a Native person because of events like the Many Nations
> One Voice Celebrations [2005].

Kyle (Pawnee/Choctaw) describes his experience:

> It was at my first MN1V Celebration at Christ for the Nations
> in Dallas, Texas [2001] that Creator spoke to my heart about
> "Common Ground Evangelism." Had Richard not invited me
> it may have taken a little longer to be in a position that Cre-
> ator wants for my family and me. My wife Marcia is Euchee
> and I am Pawnee/Choctaw. Today, we and our entire family
> have embraced our cultural ways as followers of Jesus. That
> has resulted in a new passion for serving our Creator. We
> are so glad our children are growing with a healthy blend of
> faith and culture, and they are too! I can honestly say this is
> the result of Richard's influence in our lives. As Director of
> Native American Student Programs at Bacone College, I in-
> clude traditional expressions and forms of worship in every-
> thing I do with all my students.

Attendees found in these events a "safe" and affirming place to meet other like-minded Native followers of Jesus with whom they could share experiences and exchange ideas, what Rogers refers to as "Homophily—the degree to which people are alike."[11] Native people who heard of these innovations and questioned whether they were "correct" or not had the opportunity to watch, listen, observe and participate in the innovations presented in the formal gatherings. More important perhaps were the new insights gained in interpersonal conversations in small groups, over meals and during serendipitous encounters. As people shared their stories with one another, they learned of other similar and often identical stories of how people were processing this new information, which they say "spiritually confirmed" they were on the right track. All of these smaller conversations served the larger contextualization movement; Rogers refers to them as "interpersonal channels":

> A communication channel is the means by which messages get from one individual to another. Mass media channels are more effective in creating knowledge of innovations, whereas interpersonal channels are more effective in forming and changing attitudes toward a new idea, and thus in influencing the decision to adopt or reject a new idea. Most individuals evaluate an innovation not on the basis of scientific research by experts but through the subjective evaluations of near peers who have adopted the innovation.[12]

The process of the acceptance and adoption of these new ideas was confirmed by thousands of Native Christians through the course of the MNiV Celebrations. They were able to watch others do what they had previously rejected as wrong, but secretly dreamed of doing. They were then invited to participate, which, as in Emmett's case, brought healing and wholeness to their internal world.

"Hal's" (Apache) story exemplifies how both mass media and interpersonal communication occur and impact a person and diffusion:

> I heard a radio broadcast of Focus on the Family [1997] where two Indians spoke of their faith. I contacted Richard Twiss—one of the radio guests. That led to awareness of more Indian ministries all

across the country. I found many Indians like me with my concerns about if and how there is a correlation between Indian and Christian religions. Through the work of Richard Twiss and his Many Nations One Voice Celebrations [2000] and his and others' writings, I have learned the value of and need for contextualization.

These MN1V Celebrations were not simply educational conferences addressing innovations at an intellectual, theological level. People were deeply, spiritually impacted. My friend Ben Stoner has humbly and lovingly lived among the Navajo people, learning their language and walking among them in a good way for many years. For a long time he was perplexed as to why Navajo followers of Jesus would not incorporate their own music and ceremony into their prayer and worship experience. After decades of praying, hoping and planting seeds of possibility, a historic breakthrough occurred. He wrote to me of his profound experience:

At the Many Nations One Voice Celebration in Farmington, [New Mexico] I was blessed to see my many years of prayer beginning to be answered. I am still overwhelmed with what happened with my friend Johnny. He is a traditional seventy-one-year-old Navajo elder who sang Revelation 4:8–11 to Creator in his heart music style—his tribal chant style—at the invitation of Richard Twiss. Creator's Spirit blessed everyone there with a sense of birthing a new way of worship for the Navajo people, the Diné. A few other Diné were there and recognized the power of singing in their own heart style with a drum. The Diné are looking hard at what they can and cannot do from their culture as Christians. The work of the Many Nations One Voice Celebration was a boost to move forward with power. Johnny recognized that what he did opened something, too. That same evening he and his wife Nellie went to a revival and he got up to share the song. He prefaced singing it with telling the folks he was going to sing a song that is not in any of their song books. He sang it and one man clapped, a man I know, but I never knew the man to go to church! He asked Johnny where he got the song and Johnny pointed to his Bible and said there are many more in there!

Stories of Creator's work in their lives through the MN1V Celebrations, like these, were told hundreds of times by Native people to their friends and families across North America. The MN1V Celebrations served as a vitally important launching point nationally for contextual thinking and innovation, but many people who attended the Celebrations wanted more time to just be together in a relational environment. The informal conversations between sessions of a rather heavily scheduled conference setting did not allow participants to delve deeper into the multidimensional ramifications and implications of this emerging "contextualization community."

Mni Wiconi Wacipi *("Living Waters Powwow" and Family Camp).* In August of 2004, as a first step in response to this expressed need for more community, Katherine and I and Wiconi International hosted our first annual Living Waters Family Camp. The following year it became the *Mni Wiconi Wacipi*—"Living Waters Powwow" and Family Camp. Initially we thought in terms of it being a Christian powwow. It is now considered a community-centered, intertribal traditional powwow where Jesus is honored, but not a Christian powwow. By that I mean it is not organized specifically as a Christian gathering or event. It is a community event with local Native "powwow people" on the steering committee. It is currently held the last weekend of July at the Aldersgate Conference Center in Turner, Oregon. The family camp runs Thursday through Sunday, and the powwow takes place all day Saturday. See attendance figures in table 4.1.

Our vision for the gathering is to strengthen families, enjoy friendships, support communities, teach cultural ways and encourage people in their spiritual journeys. As First Nations communities are faced with significant socioeconomic, cultural and spiritual challenges, people are challenged and equipped to make wise and courageous commitments to strengthen their families and communities. Wiconi International, through its Living Waters Family Camp and Powwow, has created a fully

Table 4.1. Living Waters Family Camp and Powwow

Year	Camp Attendance	Powwow Attendance
2004	125	---
2005	225	425
2006	222	450
2007	226	475
2008	259	540
2009	232	600
2010	265	1200
2011	258	1050
2012	262	1150

contextualized family/social gathering that provides hope and support for participants. It is making a life-changing, positive impact in the lives of Native people for a better tomorrow. And these are the results:

- Children learn cultural ways: beading, painting, drum and drumstick-making, copper plate–making, traditional games and competitions. They learn traditional Northwest tribal stories and enjoy fun activities under trained and trusted leaders.

- Mothers and fathers take parenting classes led by mature leaders married for many years—with healthy families—that address topics such as principles of raising/parenting children, developing healthy relationships, dealing with financial issues, establishing spiritual values in the home, and learning the importance of cultural values from the elders' perspectives.

- Participants learn about biblical values, love, honor, respect, forgiveness, generosity, prayer, wisdom, courage, humility and worship.

Sweat lodges. Two temporary sweat lodges are built before people arrive. The land and the construction process are prayed over and blessed by spiritual leaders using sage, cedar and water. Elders, who often happen to be pastors, conduct prayer times inside the lodges in the early morning, every day. There are separate times set aside for men, women, and couples, and at times for youth. The sweat lodges are considered sacred places of worship and intercession in the Spirit of Jesus, conducted in exactly, or in much the same way, as you would find on any reservation. They are led by a traditional spiritual ceremonial leader, but contextualized to reflect faith in Jesus as the Creator, attended by the Spirit of the Almighty Creator. People always experience the ceremonies as times of great personal spiritual reflection, accountability, liberation, encouragement and healing.

We have four leaders for the sweats: Randy and Edith Woodley (Keetoowah Cherokee, Shoshoni), Casey and Lora Church (Potawatomi, Navajo), Bryan Brightcloud (Chiricahua Apache) and John Grosvenor (Tsagali Cherokee). All have pastored in different denominations and learned how to conduct a sweat in different tribal traditions, and all guide people to focus on the Spirit of Creator in their ceremony. Each conducts the ceremony in similar ways, reflecting their own personal journey of contextualization in light of "how they were taught." Each sees it as a very spiritual time of personal reflection, healing, cleansing, restoration, repentance, commitment and worship.

The sweat lodge ceremony is today widely practiced all across North America. Each region and tribe has its own unique traditions, practices and history with it, yet certain aspects are common to all.

"Each sweat is unique," writes Raymond Bucko in *The Lakota Ritual of the Sweat Lodge: History and Contemporary Practice.* The Lakota word is *Inipi.* Bucko, as do most people today, simply says "sweat" when referring to the sweat lodge or *Inipi* ceremony.

It is the unique nature of the sweat, from both its experiential and its structural aspects, that makes the ceremony so compelling. But, despite the uniqueness of each sweat, there is a significant continuity among sweats historically and on the reservation today. Sweats proliferate on the reservation, both in multiplicity of lodge structures themselves and in the frequency of use of each lodge. The sweat represents a transformation of the past as understood by participants in the present, which they designate as *tradition*. The participants in the sweat bring the past into the present, not as a whole, but according to current understandings, needs, and circumstances.[13]

The sweat lodge was used for a variety of reasons but always for the purpose of prayer. It was done "before performing other ceremonies such as the . . . 'vision quest' and the . . . 'Sun Dance'" and most other sacred ceremonies.[14] It was and is still used today to pray for healing from sickness; to petition Creator for favor and blessings, "for success in endeavors"; "to communicate with spirits through the leader in order to learn the outcome of future events"; "to achieve ritual purity"; for personal health and well-being; to counsel, console and purify mourners; and traditionally to ready yourself for war and sanctify your weapons.[15] The lodge is built by inserting eight tree saplings in the ground in a circle, ten feet or more in diameter, then bending them over to the middle and tying them together to create a rounded hut. Supporting saplings are then tied around the other saplings for structural strength. Today, it is then covered with canvas, blankets, sleeping bags, or as in the old days, if available, buffalo hides. A hole is dug in the ground in the center of the structure. An altar is constructed in front of the door using the dirt from the central hole. The altar, which has a buffalo skull placed on it, usually faces west. The buffalo skull faces into the lodge and sweet grass, eagle feathers or other items are placed on or next to it. Special rocks that can withstand the heat are selected, typically volcanic rocks. They are considered sacred and are often called "grandfather rocks." A special fire pit is dug. Wood is brought to the site, and a fire is made in the pit with the rocks stacked in the woodpile and then heated until glowing. A special person is designated as the fire keeper. It is his or her job to keep the stones heated and—at the appropriate time—usually with a pitchfork or shovel, to carry the rocks from the fire into the lodge where they are removed with deer antlers by the one conducting the ceremony. Typically then there will be four rounds of prayer, singing and talking. A round consists of closing the flap, making the lodge airtight and pitch black, then pouring water from the buckets onto the stones, which have been prayed over often with tobacco or cedar sprinkled on them, creating clouds of intensely hot steam. Once everyone has prayed around the circle, the flap is opened, drawing in fresh air and allowing an opportunity for those who wish to have a cup of cold water. This is considered a "round."[16]

The sweat lodge ritual is a sacred place of divine encounter where a Holy Creator helps us face the frailty of our humanity, and pours grace, forgiveness, healing and love on a willing recipient in the name of Jesus.

Powwow. Saturday is set aside as a full-on traditional, noncompetitive intertribal powwow called the *Mni Wiconi Wacipi*, "Living Waters Powwow." It is a community-wide event where everyone is welcome to attend and enjoy a great day of music, drumming, dancing, food, fellowship and fun. Many traditional Native people and families from the local powwow community attend each year. Singing/drum groups are invited from the region every year, regardless of whether they are "Christian" or not. Over the years, traditional people who were skeptical about participating in what they heard was a "Christian powwow" have left saying, "We really liked the spirit we felt in this place, and we'd like to come back."

Participation in traditional powwows has for many Native Christians been discouraged or forbidden. Long considered a seditious threat to government control and an obstacle to the evangelization of tribal people, there was a long-concerted effort on the part of the United States government and missionary organizations and workers to put an end to these practices. These traditional social/spiritual gatherings have, however, been an irresistible force in maintaining a sense of cultural integrity, endurance and pride among Native people. Two of the key features of the powwow, along with the socializing, are the drumming/singing and the dancing, with the beautiful dance regalia, as well as the prayers and cultural protocol.

The drumbeat is considered the "heartbeat of the people." The dances are thought of in terms of "dancing our prayers." Zahniser, in his discussion about the importance of ritual ceremony in assisting followers of Jesus in their unique cultural contexts to grow into spiritual maturity, comments on the importance of music in its capacity to convey truth:

> Music is one of Christianity's most consistent symbolic connections between the sensory world of human life and the meaning of Christian faith. Songs can be powerful symbols. Some songs greatly appeal to believers because they condense and unify more reality for them than do others.[17]

The crucially important expressions of traditional cultural music and dance have been denied Native followers of Jesus, yet are integral in the development of an "Indigenous hymnody." K. A. Dickson's time in Ghana, Africa, led him to closely examine areas of Christian worship. In his article "Christian and African Traditional Ceremonies," he focuses on areas of Christian worship such as liturgy, order of service, music and the resulting "personal inward feeling of being in the presence of God." He notes that much has been written about African music and dance, including innovations already in use by African nationals. His comments about the critical cultural importance of music forms in Africa are very relevant to the situation among the tribes here in North America: "Where traditional life cannot be described as the Plotinian flight of the alone to the alone, it is important that the church's corporate acts should be such as to help its members achieve that corporateness which underlies society's very integrity."[18]

It is interesting that he would view the importance of music and dance as fundamental to a society's integrity. It is no less true for the Native American context as it is for the African context. Sadly, however, were it solely in the hands of Native evangelicals to determine what Native ceremonies, rituals or other cultural practices would be allowed, there would be no intertribal powwow, sweat lodge ceremony, Sundance, Kiva dance, green corn dance, or longhouse potlatch held in North America today, let alone still in existence. All would disappear forever, considered by the historic evangelical mission position to be "of the devil," thus requiring total elimination.

As I have previously written,

> During the past 15 years several inter-tribal powwows have been or-
> ganized by First Nations Christ-followers, with the expressed aim to
> bring together biblical faith and Native tradition. Randy and Edith
> Woodley in Anadarko, Oklahoma; Rosalyn Alemany (Dakota); and
> Ric Ross and Bryan Brightcloud (Chiricahua Apache) started the
> annual Pasadena Powwow in Pasadena, California, in 1999. Peter
> and Marcia Mason, "missionaries" from Australia, organized and
> hosted the Sacred Gathering Powwow in Colorado Springs, Col-
> orado, in 2002 and held three more in the ensuing years. Marshall
> "Tall Eagle" Serna (Apache) and his Native church gathering hosted
> a "Christ-centered powwow" in 2007 in Salem, Oregon. Pastor
> Robert Soto (Lipan Apache) has hosted the Annual South Texas In-
> tertribal Powwow in McAllen, Texas, since 1980. Bill Gowey hosts
> The Peoples Powwow in Flagstaff, Arizona annually, and Doug
> (Haida/Tsimshian) and Gloria (Yupik) Yates hosted a mid-winter
> traditional potlatch gathering in the Tsimshian village of Metlakatla,
> Alaska, in 2008.[19]

A beautiful example of how contextualization is being done in partnership within a local community is The Peoples Powwow in Flagstaff,
Arizona. In 2004, Bill and Jan Gowey (Yaqui), directors of Reztoration
Ministries, put on a small social powwow at a local Flagstaff city park as
a ministry "outreach." For their first-ever powwow, thirty dancers and
two drum groups showed up. Most of the dancers were from contextual
Native American ministries, and one of the drum groups came as part
of a ministry team. Many people from the community attended, and two
hundred hamburgers and three hundred hot dogs were served! They
held this powwow two years in a row, with many local traditional people
supporting and attending the second year. After each of these two
powwows they held a contextual Native Christian church meeting. Not
everyone who attended the powwows came to church, but many did, and
a few said that they really liked what they did and that they had been
touched by Creator in powerful ways.

In 2005 they changed the emphasis of their powwow from a more formalized ministry to a community-building focus in partnership with the local Native community, and named it "The Peoples Powwow." Their goal was to put on a fully traditional social powwow to serve and bless the local community.

To raise local awareness and create a sense of ownership and participation, as well as to raise funds, Bill presented their vision to some Christian churches, families and businesses around Flagstaff and across Arizona. Their vision was to seek financial support from Christians to pay for this powwow as a point of reconciliation for the church's involvement in the Indian Boarding School abuses of the past. There are many Native people in northern Arizona whose lives were deeply, negatively impacted by their boarding school experiences. After sharing the vision for healing and reconciliation with both traditional Native people and churches, both communities embraced the vision and stepped up to help make this event happen by donating six thousand dollars. While the churches gave most of the money, traditional people offered to serve in the powwow as head staff, host drums, and headman and lady dancers at little or no cost. All wanted to be a blessing and desired to see healing among peoples.

At their first annual The Peoples Powwow in 2005, more than seven hundred people took part, with more than 125 dancers and eight drum groups participating. The powwow has grown in size and influence every year, and 2008 was the best ever by all accounts. Bill states that, "In 2009, despite a torrential downpour with over two inches of rain and some cold, unpleasant weather, many people stayed all day and told us that it was still a major blessing for them." Bill's assessment: "We are seeing many people touched by the Holy Spirit, and we have had many letters from traditional people and Christians alike telling us how much they love our event. It really has become a community event, and many people have been blessed by the support of Christians and churches for a Native event that has no strings attached." Bill received a letter of support from a highly-respected traditional Navajo woman:

YOU DID A WONDERFUL JOB! I heard many positive compliments from different individuals. The event was wonderful! I really enjoyed myself. This was the first time some of our family members came to see a powwow. They enjoyed watching the dances. The event was very SPIRITUAL for me! Thank you for all your hard work to make this event a SUCCESS! I'm here to help, if you need my assistance. *Hágoónee'* ["farewell" in Navajo].

The intertribal powwow is one way First Nations followers of Jesus are "doing theology in the context of engaging their cultures and offering their audiences a fresh and fitting articulation of the good news."[20]

HISTORIC ATTITUDES

In 1902, Commissioner William Jones identified "a few customs among the Indians which . . . should be modified." . . . The festivals and dances, which could spread over weeks, were anathema to BIA leaders. The Court of Indian Offenses placed growing restrictions on Indian dances, and they met remarkably little resistance. A few activists did protest. Sioux writer Zitkala-Sa complained that "I would not like to say any graceful movement of the human figure in rhythm to music was ever barbaric," and that banning Indian dances made sense only if all dancing were banned throughout the world. But the idea of suppressing the relics of paganism was echoed by some "civilized" Indians themselves, the Christian and Americanized leaders who represented a growing faction on most reservations. In 1921, *Christian Lakota prohibited* [emphasis mine] traditional dances at the Powwow.[21]

At the WCGIP in 1996, our North American Native delegation was unable to find any "Christian" Native powwow music that we could use to dance to as part of our entrance into the auditorium. This was important at the time, as we didn't feel the liberty to use "non-Christian" powwow music for a distinctly Christian event. A contemporary Christian song by a Caucasian worship leader using some Native words and a good beat was selected. Pastor Robert Soto and others unknown to us at the time (1996) had been writing and singing contextualized powwow songs for several years by then. This fact was indicative of the effectiveness of the church to keep Indian music out of the church.

Except in a handful of cases (believers among the Kiowa, Seminole, Comanche, Dakota, Creek, and Crow tribes, to name some)—and those always in a local tribal context—Native believers were not allowed or encouraged to write new praise or worship music in their own languages utilizing their own tribal instruments, style and arrangements. What they were encouraged to do was translate Western-style music, hymns and songs (for example, "How Great Thou Art," "Amazing Grace," "The Old Rugged Cross," "A Mighty Fortress is Our God") into their own languages, which fully retained their Western cultural musical constructs. As I've mentioned before, much of the opposition to using traditional Native musical instruments, music and dance comes from Native church leaders.

Cultural heart music. In recent years there have been several papers written and circulated by First Nations evangelical Christian leaders who are critical of contextual efforts. Native pastor and Bible teacher Jim Chosa and coauthor Faith Chosa have demonized the Native drum in their book *Thy Kingdom Come*. To demonize the drum is to demonize the songs and the stories that go with them—and the entire genre of traditional Native music. The Chosas write, "We also are aware of many cultural elements which are distinctly in contradiction to the Word [Bible] and unredeemable such as the use of drums as the sole musical instrument for worship of God." They continue,

> In many regions of America, ancient people established drum cults, which worshipped the drum and established religious ceremonies centered on the use and sound of the drum. Modern musicians know the power of the drum to rouse the carnal elements of the soul with its repeated rhythmic sounds. When used with fasting, dancing and/or mind-enhancing drugs, the drum can quickly cause the participant to enter a trance-like state where the soul is open to spiritual influences. This is what happens in the sun dance

ceremonies. Rhythm must be balanced by harmony and melody to produce a sound pleasing to God. Remember, it is God, not man, who is to be worshipped.[22]

The Chosas's demonization and dismissal of the Native drum and elevation of Western music (that is, harmony, melody, arrangement, and churchly dependence on the pentatonic scale as reflective of "a heavenly sound") is a prime example of neocolonialism. I am saddened by such views, but recognize they emanate from the worldview assumptions of modernity, colonialism and paternalism that were accepted by earlier missionaries. While these attitudes are diminishing in popularity and "authority" under the weight of the favor contextual efforts are finding, they still prevail in many conservative circles.

What these attitudes reflect is a dualism that neatly divides the human experience into isolated compartments that can be individually analyzed, categorized and assigned meaning apart from the whole of the experience. Within that worldview framework, Indigenous music as a "cultural category" has suffered under the weight of the hegemonic bias of a "Western-tuned ear" that cannot hear the beauty of Creator-Jesus in it. This mindset is absolutely predisposed to reject Native music, dance and art as uncivilized, pagan, unsophisticated, primitive, base, evil, satanic, and so on. Tara Browner (Choctaw/Mohawk), in *Heartbeat of the People: Music and Dance of the Northern Pow-wow*, presents a juxtaposition of a compartmentalized and holistic view of music:

> In their [Native] worldview, religion and spirituality are not separate from the business of daily life, and activities cannot necessarily be conceptualized with the Western binary categories of sacred and secular. Therefore, traditional dance and music, even when performed at large, competitive pow-wows and for a non-Indian audience, can still exist within the realm of the spiritual or sacred. It often seems as if Indian participants move in a reality set off from non-Indian observers, who tend to perceive a pow-wow as a combination carnival and sporting event. These differing sensibilities enable Indians to perform dances that, al-

though in a commercial setting, have profound spiritual meaning for them.[23]

Many Native believers engaged in contextualization efforts are finding a very similar, if not identical, experience of meaningfulness as they put on their powwow regalia and dance in a church or Christian gathering or traditional powwow. It helps bring wholeness to their world as both Native *and* Christian.

Over the past twenty years I have found myself debating—personally and in print—with our critics, defending the new contextual efforts. It's been dumbfounding at times in that contextualization seemed so logical and obviously a better way that I couldn't understand why the critics were so vehemently opposed. Rogers addresses this phenomenon:

> Simply to regard the adoption of the innovation as rational (defined as use of the most effective means to reach a given end) and to classify rejection as stupid is to fail to understand that individual innovation-decisions are idiosyncratic. They are based on an individual's perceptions of the innovation. Whether considered right or wrong by the scientific expert who seeks to evaluate an innovation objectively, adoption or rejection is always "right" in the eyes of the individual who made the innovation-decision (at least at the time the decision is made). Diffusion scholars would do well to remember that an individual's perceptions count in determining their innovation behavior.[24]

To follow Jesus is to allow the spirit of Jesus to address our own internal issues of offense, anger and forgiveness—and lead us to new places of love and acceptance. For many years I felt attacked, misunderstood and unjustly criticized for embracing notions of worshiping Jesus in the midst of our cultural ways. Undoubtedly, some of it was deserved for the immature and arrogant attitudes I had as an innovator, thinking my new ideas were better than the old ideas held by long-standing church leaders. I was perceived as threatening their status, and many of them became defensive and opposed me and many of the rest of us in the contextualization movement. I hope I am much more gracious than I was ten years ago!

In 1995 Mohawk musician Jonathan Maracle wrote a song that was selected to be part of the national *March for Jesus* soundtrack used all across Canada. The song utilized some Mohawk words, drumming and style. Jonathan had written dozens of songs as a contemporary Christian artist and church worship leader up to that time, but all had been Western-style music. The popularity and success of the song opened his eyes to the possibility that Creator could use and bless traditional Native-style music, contrary to what he had been taught by church and ministry leaders in his early Christian experience.

In 1998 he was asked to participate in the World Christian Gathering of Indigenous People (WCGIP) in Rapid City, South Dakota, by leading a session of music for younger participants. It was then that he fully realized the power of Indigenous-style music to convey biblical faith to Indigenous audiences in a way they would enjoy and appreciate—and that would uniquely speak to their "Native heart and soul." Beyond that, he found this style of music very moving for listeners of every ethnic background. He and his band Broken Walls (as of this writing) have written, recorded and distributed more than 130,000 CDs and performed concerts or led music for Christian events in more than three hundred venues. His songs are sung in Native and non-Native churches all across North America.

R. D. Theisz, in his extremely helpful booklet *Sharing the Gift of Lakota Song*, provides insights into the worldview assumptions of Lakota (and most First Nations people) regarding singing and drumming. He also offers a solid critique of Western assumptions regarding musical perceptions and pedagogical expectations: "The contact with Native American music and dance by European colonial powers and later European immigrants has produced a history of opposition and negativism toward tribal music." Theisz says that Native Americans were sometimes viewed as howling savages, and missionaries and those who favored assimilation believed that *all forms* of Native music and dance amounted to devil worship. "The Western musical tradition has, with very few exceptions, found little use for American Indian music, and although some Native Americans have participated in Euro-American music, the latter had little influence on composition or performance of traditional tribal music as well."[25]

Ben Black Bear, Sr. (Lakota) and R. D. Theisz offer historical traditional views of Lakota music and dance in their very enlightening book *Songs and Dances of the Lakota: Cokatakiya Waci Uwo! Come Out to the Center and Dance!* Black Bear writes:

> I want to speak about what is already known. The Lakota don't sing for just one certain thing. The first thing they sing about is the sacred ways. Some songs were given to the holy man, the medicine man and the holy men. And then, through the songs, men and women and boys and girls ask things for themselves and they also sing sacred songs. In addition, they sing to merely enjoy themselves. This is for recreation and they will be happy.[26]

Music has always been a very special part of everyday Lakota life. While traditional Lakota people may still today enjoy traditional-style music and dance as part of their worship and connection with Creator, this has not been true for Lakota Christians. Our Lakota churches are filled only with the sounds of Euro-American music.

In 2002 Clyde Ellis recorded a conversation with a woman at a Sac and Fox powwow in Stroud, Oklahoma. Her words show how traditional Native music can touch the heart of a Native person. All music has the power to "move" listeners familiar with their own style of music at a deeply emotional, psychological and spiritual level. Listening to the powwow drum music, she said,

> "You know, this is just the *best* place for me to be this evening. That music—it soothes me. Makes me forget my aches and pains. In my mind I see my dad out there again, hitting that drum." Pay attention to the children who come out for the first time in the arena, and listen to the family members who speak for them. "It's your *right* to have this way," said one man on behalf of his grandson at a small dance in Oklahoma that I attended a decade ago. "But you have to be careful with it. Take care of it. Respect it. Your people are here, in this arena. Be proud of it." Do that, and you'll know . . . "that

anyone who is not well and feeling bad and anyone that is mourning, the sound of the drum will revive them and make them happy."[27]

This Indigenous-style music has been missing in the Native church. It is music that moves the Native soul—unlike a piano, guitar, or synthesizer. Some tribes do not use big powwow drums, only hand drums. Many tribes do not use drums at all. Historically, few tribes actually had a powwow that resembles today's intertribal powwow.

Gabriel Ward is a member of the Desert Cahuilla tribe of Southern California. Over the years Gabriel, a local pastor, slowly embraced the traditional singing of his tribe as an expression of worship in the church. The musical style of the Cahuilla people is traditional "a cappella bird singing and bird dancing." They do not use drums, but hollowed-out gourd rattles with dried seeds inside for rhythm accompaniment. Seeing the beauty, history and grace of bird singing, Gabriel is a strong supporter of his people's music today.

Speaking of this kind of "heart language," using different terminology, Kraft notes that the longer a people or group utilizes a majority of foreign forms, the longer Christianity will remain a foreign religion, which I think is particularly true of music:

> When the [Native] Christians think of the Lord as their own, not a foreign Christ; when they do things as unto the Lord meeting the cultural needs around them, worshiping in patterns they understand; when their congregations function in participation in a body, which is structurally Indigenous, then you have an Indigenous Church. Note that it is extremely important what forms are used and where they come from, since they have to convey the proper meanings if the result is to be properly Christian. Any society can, of course, borrow cultural forms from another society. If, however, the proportion of borrowed forms is very high and the proportion of Indigenous forms very low, the character of their Christianity is strongly affected.[28]

In large part, the growing contextual movement for a generation of younger Native ministry leaders sprang from the increasing disappointment they felt with the "white character of the Christianity" they had been brought up in. They loved the music, dance, ceremony and notions of ritual they were beginning to discover in a different reading of the Bible. Moving away from their modernist and culturally Eurocentric-informed view of their own faith journey, they began to long for, dream about and experiment with new models and forms of expressing their faith as Native men and women.

Jonathan Maracle and many other Native Christian musicians compose and perform today in order to serve contemporary purposes and needs, though their music is drawn from and inspired by historical tradition. They come from a background of never or only recently sharing their tribal music as Christians in a Christian setting. These musicians would be considered "adopters." They were inspired by the early innovators who encouraged Native believers to break away from the paternalistic and rejectionist views church leaders held toward Native music, dance, ritual and ceremony. The "adopters" have become "innovators," creating a new genre of music to support the contextual movement and "carry the sound of the people" along with the message of the gospel of Jesus.

More conservative Native evangelicals have vigorously opposed the acceptance of these musical innovations and ceremonial adaptations as being profoundly syncretistic. Every tribe in North America has its own unique language, music and rituals. Music is both social and religious, though not so cleanly compartmentalized as "one or the other." Ceremony and ritual serve to connect people with the spiritual world, regardless of nationality, culture or religious affiliation—whether inspired by the Bible, Torah, Koran, Bhagavad Gita or oral tradition. Tinker, in *American Indian Liberation: A Theology of Sovereignty*, comments on the ceremonial or ritualistic history and experience of First Nations people:

> Virtually every tribal nation in north America has had a variety of ceremonies whereby the individual might take on a discipline of ceremonial vicarious suffering for the sake of the people as a whole.

In every case, the first european and amer-european invaders of their lands, including especially the missionaries, mistook these ceremonies for something they never were intended to be. Because they misunderstood, sometimes very intentionally, these ceremonies, the missionaries and the amer-european government proceeded to condemn our ancient rites as devil worship or idolatry. Yet, these ceremonies have much in common with the sufferings of Jesus in the christian gospels because the individual undertaking the ceremony willingly undergoes a discipline of suffering on behalf of the people.[29]

Contextualization efforts have been viewed with suspicion by more mainline liberals as being "not authentic enough" or disingenuous, being manipulated for "evangelizing the sinner" versus being embraced as deeply sacramental in a worship context. They have been resisted by the traditionalists because these efforts were viewed as compromising Native religion, or being co-opted by Christian Indians who didn't really know what they were doing. The traditionalists saw the contextualization efforts as "invading" Indian ways to take them away, or at least to inappropriately borrow them. These tensions still exist.

As a boy growing up on my reservation, I loved attending all the small local community intertribal powwows. These were the gathering places where friends and relatives would go to enjoy the drumming, singing, music and dancing that took place. There were other music and dance ceremonial styles that were private and for specific spiritual purposes. Currently, powwows are held year-round all over the United States and Canada, usually on weekends. Many attract dancers and drummers from far away to compete for monetary prizes. People also come to watch the dancing and purchase a variety of foods and crafts from the vendors. Where I live (Vancouver, Washington), there are several annual powwows. These powwows provide fellowship and fun for urban Native community members. In this way they are able to stay connected to traditions, songs and family "from back home."

It is informative for my observation of the innovation and diffusion of contextual music and worship to consider Browner's assessment as she traces the evolution of today's modern "intertribal powwow":

> Yet in the late twentieth and early twenty-first centuries, when so many things Indian have been commodified, powwows remain contradictory, challenging both observers and participants to find meaning within a pastiche of tradition and commercialism. Continually changing musical repertories, dance styles, and regalia combine with new traditions to create an ongoing state of transformation that often coexists in dress, behavior, and music. Yet, underneath the layers of representation is a living event, central to the lives of participants who may travel hundreds of miles each week for the chance to "dress to dance" or sing for the money collected during a Blanket Dance.[30]

For the First Nations community of Jesus-followers, there is the huge challenge of how to interpret and incorporate music, dance and ceremony in light of history, contemporary needs, adaption and acculturation. This emerging new hymnody is similarly a "pastiche of tradition" where people are seeking new meanings in old traditions as they attempt to transform a blend of historical/cultural musical constructs, styles and meanings into a new genre. It is inevitable that something will get lost in the process. Yet this new music has been one of the most attractive and meaningful components of the contextual movement as people experience great personal spiritual enrichment within the context of Native cultural ways. In addition it has served as a dynamic tool of diffusion as thousands of recordings of this style of music have been distributed across the land.

Besides those mentioned earlier, other Native Christian musicians who are writing, recording and distributing music and have emerged in the past ten years include Robert Soto (Lipan Apache), JoAnn Storm (Blackfeet), Michael Jacobs (Cherokee), Bill Miller (Mohican), Tom Bee (Lakota), Jan Michael Looking Wolf (Grand Ronde), Terry (Yaqui) and Darlene Wildman, Jim Miller, Stephen Tindle (Cherokee) and Cheryl Bear (Nadleh Whut'en). This is only a small representation of those who

are engaged in contextual music. Because of their relative national commercial success and the wide distribution of their recordings, their songs
are played in the more musically progressive churches (Native and non-
Native) throughout North America.

Bill Miller is a three-time Grammy Award winner and in 2009 received
a Lifetime Achievement Award (NAMMY) from the Native American
Music Award Association for his contribution to the Native music industry.
Terry and Darlene Wildman won a NAMMY in 2009, and Jonathan Maracle and Cheryl Bear won major awards for their music at the 2009 Aboriginal Music Awards in Canada. Jan Michael Looking Wolf was named
2009 Artist of the Year at the eleventh NAMMY awards ceremony.

REPRESSION OF NATIVE DANCE

In the early 1920s, Charles H. Burke, Commissioner of Indian Affairs,
drafted BIA Circular 1665 outlining specifics of what he called "Indian Offences," including the repression of Indian dance:

> The native dance still has enough evil tendencies to furnish a
> retarding influence and at times a troublesome situation
> which calls for careful consideration and right-minded ef-
> forts. It is not the policy of the Indian office to denounce all
> forms of dancing. . . . The dance *per se* is not condemned. . . .
> The dance, however, under most primitive and pagan condi-
> tions, is apt to be harmful, and when found so among the
> Indians we should control it by educational measures as far
> as possible, but if necessary, by punitive measures when its
> degrading tendencies persist. The sun-dance and all other
> similar dances and so-called religious ceremonies are con-
> sidered "Indian Offences" under existing regulations, and
> corrective penalties are provided.[31]

Today, seventeen years after the inaugural World Christian Gathering
of Indigenous People, when no "Christian" Native powwow dance music
could be found, there is a new and steadily growing "ethnomusical library" of Native-style worship music being written, recorded and dis-

tributed by Native artists. All societies have their own unique music, and now an "Indigenous hymnody" has begun to emerge out of the contextualization movement in North America!

Native drums and music are experiencing a spiritual renaissance. By comparison, Native dance—which was militantly opposed and identified with demonic activity and as a seditious threat to national security—is more slowly being considered as a legitimate expression of church worship.

My friend Mark McDonald, who served as the first national Indigenous bishop of the Anglican Church of Canada, and also ten years as a bishop of the United States Episcopal Diocese of Alaska, offered an intriguing perspective on music and dance: "I heard a young Cree clergyman say, 'You know all this stuff about the drum? In a lot of ways it's just about lipstick and rouge. What we are really after are the values that produce those things.'" While I think this Cree clergyman's analogy of music and ceremony as purely cosmetic "window dressing" is absolutely mistaken, I do, however, completely agree with his juxtaposition of a Western assessment of these things and a Native view of the same realities as being both biblical and essential for an authentic biblical faith to thrive among Native people. The MN1V Celebrations and other contextualization gatherings successfully introduced early innovative ways and practices of incorporating powwow music, dance and protocol into a worship context. They helped widely communicate and promote these innovations across North America, and it is only just the beginning!

For contextualization to be effective, heart issues must be addressed. The Christ-honoring *Mni Wiconi Wacipi*—Living Waters Powwow is much more than an evangelistic outreach. It promotes the "restoration of souls" in a holistic way and encourages involvement in tribal identity. The powwow brings the tension between faith and culture into balance and allows participants the biblical freedom to dance their prayers in worship to Jesus.

I want to now selectively highlight several key happenings that served as communication channels for the diffusion of these new ideas. I will arrange them in the two general categories of "events" and "media." There are far too many to list here, so I have selected examples that I believe best capture the primary focus of these contextualization efforts.

IMPORTANT EVENTS, GATHERINGS AND
THEOLOGICAL EDUCATION

Christ and Culture: Missionary Influence on the Plains Tribes. In 1991 Randy and Edith Woodley hosted a conference called "Christ and Culture: Missionary Influence on the Plains Tribes" at the Anadarko Christian Center, Anadarko, Oklahoma. It was one of the first Native-led gatherings that demonstrated Native contextualization practices in a conference setting. Like many innovators in that time period who were launching new ministries, they experienced strong opposition from Native brothers and sisters in Christ who vehemently disagreed with their methods and theology.

The recognized leaders of the opposition movement were all invited to participate, including those representing Christian Hope Indian Eskimo Fellowship (CHIEF) Ministries. There were about two hundred people in attendance, and the format was one of presentations from a five-person panel. The panel format allowed for each side to make a case, and then they broke into smaller groups for discussion. After the small groups met, they reconvened and people brought their questions and concerns from the floor to the whole group. Randy Woodley was the emcee and host for the event. According to his recollection, about halfway through the gathering things began to heat up as the topics "powwows" and the "sweat lodge" were included. By the end of the conference, battle lines were drawn deeper. Those who seemed to want to move toward a more open position were sought out and individually proselytized by those who were against cultural contextualization.

Regardless of the stiff opposition, there *were* new "converts." There were also others who had been waiting for the time to arrive when they could once again express their love for Christ through their Southern Plains Indian culture. This was especially true of younger Native Americans in attendance who were searching for their own identity in Christ, but only finding a Euro-American option. News of the gathering slowly and quietly traveled throughout Oklahoma and beyond. This encouraged others to pursue their interest in incorporating more Native-style musical, dance and ceremonial forms into their Christian faith.

Because of the controversy over the direct confrontation during the first conference, the Woodleys decided not to use the same format in the future. The irony was not missed the following year when they hosted the conference again with a new emphasis, and called it "Christ and Culture: Native American Peace Traditions." The attendance was much lower than at the first conference, but many of the people who were growing toward a contextualization approach attended—which showed there was increasing support for this emerging movement. The Woodleys would continue to push the issue, but it would be done more indirectly than they had first imagined. They decided simply to move forward with cultural contextualization without allowing a format for the opposition to gain a foothold through direct confrontation. Yet people did find ways to interrupt Bible studies and other meetings to publicly criticize the Woodleys' methods.

In 1991 and 1992, the Woodleys hosted winter powwows and summer Native American youth culture camps at the Anadarko Christian Center to encourage the movement. Randy was the executive director. The Woodleys exposed the youth to their Indian cultures by having Native American elders teach drumming, dancing, the use of the sweat lodge, beading, bow and arrow construction, storytelling and basket making. Randy and John White Eagle, his assistant at the Anadarko Christian Center, continued to run sweat lodges with Bible studies at the Woodleys' home, drawing young men from the Riverside Indian Boarding School, some in substance abuse recovery.

Gathering of the Five Streams. After the Woodleys' conference, I convened the second major contextual ministry conference (Gathering of the Five Streams) in November of 1994. This was in the early days of the movement. People gathered together on the Warm Springs Indian Reservation in central Oregon. Seventy-five key leaders from across the

Western states attended, as well as three leaders from New Zealand and a couple from Hawaii.

The delegates looked at five areas: worship and music; prayer and intercession; economic development; cultural contextualization and leadership development. The highlight came as the two Maori men from New Zealand prayed over the North American tribal leaders in a traditional Maori war dance, the *Haka*, challenging them to embrace their cultural identity as followers of Jesus. That night, for the very first time, many of us First Nations men and women danced (Native style), drummed and sang Native-style songs in worship to Jesus in a group setting. It was a pivotal time for people as they left affirmed and deeply encouraged to pursue critical contextualization as a fundamental approach to living their faith in Jesus among Native people. Furthermore, it helped formally recognize an emerging relational network of Native leaders who were all on the same page.

Soon other leaders, inspired by these earlier gatherings, began to organize and host a number of other important national events: Sacred Fire Gathering in March of 2000, in Leeds, Alabama; Many Tribes Sacred Council Fire—A Gathering of Nations in April of 2001 in Cottonwood, Arizona; and another Gathering of Nations, led by Kenny and Louise Blacksmith in 2001, 2002 and 2005 in Ottawa, Canada. Besides these, dozens of small local and regional contextual gatherings were convened.

Youth With A Mission (YWAM). In October of 1989, Youth With A Mission hosted a Native American Leadership Summit in Denver where approximately sixty participants began to earnestly dialogue about the appropriateness of using Native cultural forms as part of their worship experience. To attend an event with more than the two or three people we were already having discussions with was a new encounter for most of us. Syncretism was a significant concern and most of us were just beginning to consider new ways of thinking about faith and Native culture. Those who attended were mostly Native people who were new to each other and had been pondering these things independently, thinking they were the only ones.

Christ, Culture and Kingdom Seminar. In 1996 I wrote and self-published a spiral-bound eighty-six-page study guide, *Christ, Culture and Kingdom Seminar Study Guide—Presenting Biblical Principles for Native Ministry that Honor Creator, His People, and His Creation* (CC & K). I used this study guide to teach a seminar on developing contextual Native ministry models. I taught this CC & K Seminar to Native audiences around the country from 1996 to 2002, including in Rapid City, South Dakota, with Wesleyan Native American District national leadership; Pasadena, California, at the US Center for World Mission; Ignacio, Colorado, on the Southern Ute Reservation; Tucson, Arizona, at Faith Christian Center for their First Nations University Ministry; Spokane, Washington, at a gathering of regional Native ministry leaders; Portage le Prairie, Manitoba, Canada; Fairbanks, Alaska; Vancouver Island, British Columbia, Canada, with Saanich First Nations members; Portland, Oregon, at Multnomah Biblical Seminary; and Albuquerque, New Mexico.

Northwest Native Women's Conference. Wiconi International, in partnership with several organizations, hosted two Northwest Native Women's Conferences in the Seattle area. One was held in 2003 (some 200 attended) and another in 2005 (about 250 attended). The conferences were remarkable gatherings where women experienced healing and spiritual wholeness. They were freed from the pain of abuse and brokenness in their lives, which in many cases had been caused by their boarding school experiences. Many of the women wore their traditional dresses/regalia, and numerous hand drums were played. For many of the women it was the first time they wore their regalia or drummed as an expression of their worship to Jesus. Speakers included Grand Chief Lynda Prince (Carrier-Sakani), Mary Glazier (Haida), Rita Bear-Gray (Cree) and my wife, Katherine, and me (Sicangu Lakota). Music was performed by Michelle Clark (Cherokee) and her team. The ministry team included Fern Noble (Cree) and Cheryl Barnetson (Yinke Dine). "Native Grandmothers" included Della Hill (Tulalip), Cecile Hanson (Duwamish), Doris Allen (Muckleshoot), Martha Franklin (Yakima) and Norma Blacksmith (Lakota), who welcomed all the guests who came, and then they in turn were honored.

Theological Education and Leadership Training

Looking at the state of the Native church in light of the absence of First Nations theologians and theologies, Kraft's words—gloomily and prophetically—describe the consequence of that absence saying, "where there is no surge toward independence, and theological experimentation has not occurred, only apathy toward Christianity remains."[32]

Since the early 1990s, many of us early innovators dreamed about and discussed the need for advanced theological and leadership training. The "self-theologizing" by Indigenous theologians discussed by Hiebert has been slow in developing in North America.[33] Over the centuries there has been but a handful of First Nations theologians who have contributed to the body of theological literature here in North America. While Native leaders have become adept at borrowing, then modifying, the theologies of others—be they ancient or modern— these efforts have not helped them interpret Scripture, the kingdom, and the work of the church from their own worldview constructs. Among seminaries today, there is a dearth of theological textbooks written by Native scholars.

Ministerial inequality for Native scholars. The struggle for equality by Native Christian leaders serving in the dominant culture church today is part of a long-standing historical stream of resistance, one with very little success to show for it, particularly in theology. In many ways this has been true for the cross-cultural innovators in this study. There has been a ceiling prohibiting them from becoming professors, theologians or deans. The leaders in this study are working to mediate and then inhabit a permanent place between the demands of neocolonial educational presuppositions and the ways of Native peoples in decolonizing Christianity. In this way they will fashion new learning centers or opportunities for theological education and leadership development. But things are changing; they are beginning to find their voice as welcome coequal participants in the North American church.

Examining the progressive growth of theologizing and church maturity in places like Africa, India, Latin America, Oceania and others, where there has been significant Western mission presence, Kraft writes:

Christianity has been like a pot-plant transplanted into a garden. In the early days the imported soil in the foreign pot sufficed to sustain its growth. But, as time passed, the roots grew large and shattered the pot from within, often to the dismay of the foreign "gardeners." If we could both understand the pressing need for the development of homegrown, culturally relevant theologies which freely borrow from, but are not dominated by, foreign theological models and encourage Christians everywhere in dependence upon the Holy Spirit to theologize freely, the Christian church would be much richer. And we of the West, as well as those of other cultures, are being denied theological insight because of this lack of positive regard and respect for the perspectives of those other cultures. By cutting ourselves off from the insights of people immersed in other cultures, we of the West are in danger of developing and perpetuating certain culturally-conditioned kinds of heresies.[34]

Native self-theologizing. A closer look at the current "self-theologizing" coming from these early innovators reveals the fact that the "theological roots are growing and the Western pot is cracking"! In the North American context, there are a growing number of excellent Native theologians who have offered a profound and excellent critique of the American colonial missionary enterprise. A significant number of those in this study have contributed to this conversation. Over time, however, they came to believe that a thoughtful critique—regardless of its helpfulness in the early stages of deconstructing the hegemonic modernist assumptions that informed their early Christian experience—did not take the conversation far enough. As years passed, spiritual maturity grew and new understandings emerged. A time came when they collectively began to take self-theologizing and contextualization to a deeper level.

While acknowledging their connection to the stream of theological thought as a new generation of scholars and theologians, they gradually "felt free of the obligation to conform to the theological maxims of another culture or subculture."[35] While several of them did pursue a course of formal theological education, they're guided, rather, by their own Spirit-led understanding of Scripture and its applicability to their own cultural world. If a theology is to be a culturally relevant expression of supracultural truth, theologians must not keep looking over their shoulders to see if they are in step with Aquinas or Calvin or Barth; rather they must "look unto Jesus," the hope of glory who is present in his church.[36]

Philip Jenkins notes that among the Protestant and evangelical traditions that have so totally dominated American culture, the thought that Indian religion might have something to teach them would seem ridiculous.[37] (It is the inherent distrust of all things Indigenous that First Nations theologians are challenging, and correcting biblically, theologically, and missiologically around the world.) Western-evangelical propositionalism that assumes that one's own statements are the essence of eternal truth precludes any ability to accept new information or context.

Ray Aldred (Cree) is one of founding board members of the North American Institute for Indigenous Theological Studies (NAIITS). He is a brilliant thinker and provides an example of the kind of contribution Native innovators are positing when he reflects on the gospel as narrative, versus proposition. His view offers both a critique and an alternative to the inflexibility of modernity to willingly change, which is inherent to Western theology and effectively prevents Aboriginal people from developing an Aboriginal Christian spirituality. An excellent source for these emerging Indigenous theological reflections can be found in the NAIITS journals. There are currently nine volumes in print.

Several early attempts were made to establish a viable teaching center or program that embraced a contextual approach. Today these leaders are hopeful that, though most of those early attempts failed, much was learned and they are now encouraged by new developments and initiatives.

National Native Bible College. Ross Maracle (Mohawk) started the National Native Bible College in Deseronto on the Tyendinaga Mohawk Territory in Ontario, Canada, in 1977. The student body, though small, was largely First Nations. Its curriculum was "non-Native" and was the same used for all such schools within the Pentecostal Assemblies of Canada denomination. Adrian Jacobs, who had served on the board from 1985 to 1993 and as a guest lecturer, developed a two-year contextualized theological curriculum during his tenure as academic dean from 1993 to 1996. Jacobs noted that of the five thousand volumes in their library, perhaps only twenty-five were about Native people. After years of struggling with lack of funding and administrative management issues, the school closed in 2000.

First Nations Institute. One of the schools that held enormous potential to become a national learning center, sadly, figuratively, "went up in flames." In September of 1999 the Wesleyan Native American Ministry launched the First Nations Institute. It was started on the location of Brainerd Indian School in Hot Springs, South Dakota. Adrian Jacobs (Cayuga) and Phil Duran (Tewa), in partnership with Jerry Yellowhawk (Lakota), gave leadership to the institute and developed an excellent fully contextualized curriculum. Jacobs had moved from Ontario, Canada, and along with Duran, who relocated from Washington State, further developed the two-year curriculum he had begun at the First Nations Bible College. Students began attending and momentum was building. They built a traditional brush arbor for a dance arena and remodeled a room in a circle for their chapel.

Due to financial mismanagement in the denominational office, however, the school was forced to close its doors after only three months. Adrian had raised enough money and materials to restore the property, which had remained dormant for six years after major flood damage. While the financial issues were difficult, according to Jacobs, they were not irreversibly so. The closure had more to do with members of the various denominational governing boards having growing concerns over syncretism and contextualization. These concerns, fueled by complaints from Wesleyan Native leaders, led to the decision to "pull the plug." Once that decision was announced, Jacobs contacted several Native leaders in the contextual movement (including myself) to raise funds for a down payment to purchase the property. This was accomplished. When the offer was made to the governing board, however, the spokesperson quickly backpedaled and said the amount was not what they meant and raised the price out of reach, which effectively aborted the First Nations Institute. The property was then sold with the proceeds going to the "Anglo" denominational district headquarters, not the Native ministry that raised the money to restore the facilities that had housed Native ministry for sixty years. Sadly, that property is now part of a pheasant reserve. This is but one in a long string of aborted visions conceived in the hearts of Native leaders, but not wanted by dominant-culture Christian ministry leadership.

North American Institute for Indigenous Theological Studies (NAIITS). The closing of the First Nations Institute did not diminish the commitment to create new learning opportunities for Native leadership. In 1999, following the World Christian Gathering of Indigenous People in New Zealand and Rapid City, South Dakota, and then three Many Nations One Voice (MN1V) celebrations, Terry LeBlanc and I took leadership in the ongoing dialogue with other Native leaders and began discussing a theological gathering. We then formed many years of conversation into an idea. We began raising money, making plans, finding partners, and inviting leaders to become part of a leadership team, which in 2000 became the North American Institute for Indigenous Theological Studies.

NAIITS, an Indigenous learning community, is a nonsectarian Christian organization dedicated to encouraging the Native North American evangelical community to develop and articulate Native North American perspectives on Christian theology and mission practice. Terry LeBlanc serves as CEO and executive director, and I serve as the board chair, along with a board of ten others who provide oversight.[38] The NAIITS board encourages implementation of Native North American learning styles and worldviews by supporting the development of a body of written work that addresses scriptural, theological, ethical, and missiological issues from Native North American perspectives. One of the primary objectives of NAIITS is to facilitate a written theological foundation for the visioning of new culturally informed paradigms of gospel telling among Indigenous peoples.

In December of 2001, NAIITS hosted its first Missiological Symposium in Winnipeg, Manitoba. The conference was convened as a means of responding to three documents in circulation at the time. The documents were written by conservative Native evangelicals decrying the use of culture in the exercise of Christian faith. The purpose of the symposium was to facilitate open dialogue about various aspects of contextualization in Native North American history and experience. Initially it was our goal to bring together academic and practical ministry leaders to engage in honest dialogue around the contextualization controversy and other issues being raised across Indian Country. Today the symposiums address a wide range of concerns impacting ministry in our First Nations communities.

Since the initial symposium, there have been eight more, held in various locations: Canadian Mennonite University in Winnipeg, Manitoba, 2003; Crestmont College, Crestmont, California, 2004; Asbury Theological Seminary, Wilmore, Kentucky, 2006; Sioux Falls Seminary, Sioux Falls, South Dakota, 2007; Trinity Western University, Langley, British Columbia, 2009; George Fox Seminary and University, Newberg, Oregon, 2010; Ambrose University College and Seminary, Calgary, Alberta, 2011; and Wheaton College Graduate School, Wheaton, Illinois, 2012.[39] Journals have been produced from each. NAIITS uniquely reflects the collective journey of discovery of the twelve founding board members (and many others) who had wrestled with these questions for years.

Stephen Neill comments on how the "West looks eagerly to the East for new insights into Christian theology."[40] The evidence of this study suggests that in the North American church context, an entire generation of young believers is not only looking to the East for insights to make sense of following Jesus in this new world, but also finding great hope and inspiration in the understandings of these First Nations leaders. A great challenge lies before these First Nations leaders, many of them completing postgraduate studies at American seminaries. They work to take what they've learned of theology in the Western academy and to reinterpret this knowledge into a cultural framework that helps produce true Indigenous theologies. Neill articulates this challenge from church history: "The West has done its work too well; the trained theologians of the younger Churches have been so conditioned by the effort of mastering Western theology that they have little to offer in the way of Native and original understanding."[41]

A monumental historic outcome of NAIITS, signaling the emergence of these new insights referenced by Neill, was the signing of a memorandum of agreement with George Fox University and Seminary in Newberg, Oregon, on June 12, 2010. This MOA resulted in the creation of a master of arts in intercultural studies degree in 2011. George Fox hired NAIITS board member Dr. Randy Woodley as associate professor of faith and culture and as director of Intercultural and Indigenous Studies in 2010. The majority of the courses are written or edited, that is, contextualized, by First Nations scholars. NAIITS board members and other Native scholars (six PhDs, one DMiss, one DMin and two MAs), along with Dr. Woodley, serve as faculty. The program is creatively delivered through a variety of methods considerate of Native students' concerns of wanting to remain "living in community." It is the only degree program like it in North America! Beginning in June of 2013, a master of arts degree in ministry leadership is being launched in partnership with Tyndale Seminary in Toronto, Canada. Additionally, plans are moving forward to create a PhD program in community development with William Carey University in Pasadena, California.[42]

Nazarene Indian Bible College. Lloyd Commander (Cayuse) graduated from Nazarene Theological Seminary in Kansas City with a master of arts in missiology in 1990. In 1992 he was appointed academic dean at Nazarene Indian Bible College in Albuquerque. We first met and became friends in 1987, and during these years Lloyd became an inspiration to me. He encouraged me to begin educating myself missiologically, focusing on how faith and culture need to be understood in balance within Native ministry. Lloyd was becoming increasingly frustrated and disappointed by the ongoing resistance and opposition—by both Native and non-Native faculty and administration—to his attempts to introduce ideas of contextualization at the school. In 1994 he reluctantly resigned from his position because of his regard for the students. He was no longer able to endure the intense opposition of institutional leaders. Sadly, his Native students were just beginning to feel increasingly empowered to embrace their cultural ways and their faith in Jesus.

Lloyd and Adrian Jacobs participated in the 1994 "Gathering of the Five Streams" conference and helped lead the discussion around one of the "five streams" or topics that dealt with leadership training and theological education. Numbers of others participated in these conversations, several of whom became active in the contextual movement. Through a series of events a year later, the International Bible Society hired me as their director of Native Ministries. I worked to get Lloyd hired as well. One of my first decisions was to create a Native Board of Reference, and one of my first members was Adrian Jacobs. Adrian, Lloyd and I had many conversations about the need to develop contextualized Native ways of doing theological education and leadership training. NAIITS was the eventual outcome of many untold conversations like these, challenging the status quo of Native ministry, mission theology and ecclesiology that had been circulating for many years.

InterVarsity Christian Fellowship (IVCF) Urbana Missions Conference. At the Urbana 03 student missions conference held at the University of Illinois, some seventeen thousand people from around the world observed and participated in a remarkable event. The evening main-stage program of worship was led by First Nations leaders in full regalia dancing to powwow drum music. Reports of this innovation spread across North America and beyond.

That night actually began in 1999 when two national IVCF staff members attended the MN1V Celebration in Winnipeg and met with me. It was the beginning of an enduring friendship between IVCF/ Urbana and Native leaders from the new and growing contextualization movement. From that meeting I was invited by Paula Harris, then senior associate director of the Urbana program, to attend the Urbana 2000 conference to teach two seminars. I recommended that Terry LeBlanc, CEO and executive director of NAIITS, also be invited to attend. This resulted in the Urbana 2000 conference having signif-

icant Native participation. Five leaders taught seminars, and a team of
dancers shared traditional Native dance, stories and music in the
student lounges.

One evening at the Urbana 03 conference, Mohawk musician Jonathan Maracle and his band led everyone in worship using a solo
powwow drum in his unique blend of Native and contemporary music
styles. There were ten Native powwow dancers (including me) on stage,
dancing in full regalia. Then Ray Aldred (Cree) gave a keynote address
that many later said was one of the most "cutting edge" messages ever
heard there.

Our team was highlighted on the main stage. Because of the respect,
favor and solid evangelical reputation Urbana enjoys, this served as a
significant national act of approval and affirmation of our collective contextualization efforts! This impact was felt far beyond that one evening.
It served to diffuse these new ideas to a new, younger international audience. These young emerging leaders found this especially meaningful
in their multicultural realities and search for identity.

Despite the overwhelmingly positive response of Urbana attendees
and staff to our message of contextualization, the relationship with IVCF/
Urbana has been tenuous at times. Over the years, several meetings were
required to settle misunderstandings and offenses that seemed to be the
result of "institutional memory loss." Native contextual leaders have participated in each Urbana since 2000, both as seminar presenters and
platform participants, including Terry LeBlanc serving on the board of
directors for IVCF of Canada and delivering the keynote closing message
at Urbana 12.

Promise Keepers. During the 1990s there was a growing recognition
of "neglect" on the part of national evangelical Christian ministries concerning the contribution of Native American leaders/voices in their respective movements. Promise Keepers (PK) was another organization
having "racial reconciliation" as one of its "guiding values." Promise
Keepers invited a national Native American evangelical leader, Huron
Claus (Mohawk/Kiowa), executive director of Christian Hope Indian
Eskimo Fellowship (CHIEF) Ministries, to sit on their national board.

He was not, however, supportive of contextualization and was actually strongly opposed. Thus he intentionally excluded the influence of contextual ideas and innovations in shaping how PK developed their Native men's ministries as they were emerging in North America.

I was considered as a national platform speaker, and in 2000 I was formally invited to speak at the Albuquerque event. Shortly before the event, however, I received a call from a PK senior staff member informing me that some Native ministry leaders from the Assemblies of God Native American Fellowship in Albuquerque were threatening to boycott the event, and would work to get all the Assemblies of God pastors in New Mexico to boycott as well if I were allowed to be a platform speaker. In the "spirit of unity" they asked me to voluntarily withdraw from participating as a result of the hostile threat. There was no mention of dialogue or a meeting to resolve any differences in the "spirit of reconciliation." They paid me my agreed-to honorarium and I "voluntarily" withdrew.

In 2002 I actually did speak at the Grand Rapids, Michigan, Promise Keepers event through the sanctified subversive effort of a Native staff member and close friend of mine. It was the last time I, or any other Native leader from the contextual "camp," was allowed to speak, though conservative "noncontextual" evangelical leaders were frequent speakers. So, while PK did make room for a segment of the Native community at the table, they did not serve to promote reconciliation among individuals with varying views of contextualization—thus fostering even greater division.

IMPORTANT BOOKS, PERIODICALS AND LITERATURE

Getting published is no easy task for anyone, but harder still for Native Christian authors. Books and literature have served as key diffusion and communication channels for the widespread introduction of contextualization.

In 1994 I wrote and self-published a study booklet titled *The Story of the Turtle and the Snail*. Over the next two years I added new chapters and more stories. In 1996 I renamed it *Five Hundred Years of Bad Haircuts—Understanding God's Heart for First Nations People: A First*

Nations Christian Perspective on Culture, Reconciliation and Unity in the Church. I printed and distributed several thousand copies of it as a 136-page spiral-bound book. In 1999 Regal Books decided to publish the book under a new title, *One Church, Many Tribes: Following Jesus the Way God Made You,* and it was released in 2000.[43] There are more than forty thousand copies in print.

In 1996 I wrote and self-published a spiral-bound, eighty-six-page study guide, *Christ, Culture, and Kingdom Seminar Study Guide: Presenting Biblical Principles for Native Ministry that Honor God, His People and His Creation.*[44] To date, I have published and distributed more than one thousand copies. I use it to teach a seminar by the same name and parts of it at other Native gatherings around North America. In 1998 I wrote and self-published a forty-five-page booklet addressing the highly controversial issue of syncretism in Native ministry titled *Dancing Our Prayers: Perspectives on Syncretism, Critical Contextualization and Cultural Practices in First Nations Ministry.*[45] To date, 1,200 copies have been published.

As a columnist for *Charisma Magazine,* I wrote seven editorial articles under the heading *Smoke Signals* from September 2000 to September 2001.

Randy Woodley wrote *Living in Color: Embracing God's Passion for Ethnic Diversity.* There are more than ten thousand copies in print. He also wrote *Mixed Blood, Not Mixed Up: Finding God-given Identity in a Multi-cultural World* in 2000 (revised in 2004), and there are 3,500 copies in print. In 2007 his book *When Going to Church is Sin and Other Essays on Native American Christian Missions* was published. His book *Shalom and the Community of Creation: An Indigenous Vision* was published in 2012.[46]

Adrian Jacobs has written and self-published several books and study guides. His first, *Aboriginal Christianity: The Way It Was Meant to Be,* is a spiral-bound eighty-three-page book that was released in 1998. His second is *Pagan Prophets and Heathen Believers: Native American Believers in the Creator of the Bible,* a spiral-bound forty-four-page book, released in 1999. *Sacred Clowns* is a spiral-bound book of thirty-five pages. He estimates more than 1,200 copies are in print.[47]

My People International (a Native North American ministry), under the leadership and editorial direction of Terry LeBlanc, wrote, designed, illustrated and produced a five-volume, five-year Vacation Bible School curriculum. The titles include *Creator Creates the World, Our Relationship with the Creator, Creator's Promises, Our Creator Saves Us* and *Building Together.*[48] It was the first-ever effort to produce a study guide that fully incorporated traditional Native stories, artwork and worldview values, composed entirely under Native leadership. There are now 1,200 copies in print. This kind of contextualization allows the gospel "to be expressed and applied using languages, images and ideas that make sense to the audience,"[49] in this case to young Native children. The curriculum presents the gospel story to them in a way that affirms their cultural identity, not denying or demonizing it. Good News! Jesus is not pictured as a blond-haired, blue-eyed Caucasian sitting under a tree. Jesus is portrayed as a Middle Eastern man with long black hair, black eyes and dark skin from the tribe of Judah who was an amazing storyteller. He looks a lot like these young Native boys and girls who may be reading about him for the first time.

Qaumaniq Suuqiina (Cherokee) and Dr. Iglahliq Suuqiina (Inuit) coauthored *Warfare by Honor: The Restoration of Honor: A Protocol Handbook* in 2007. There are more than five thousand copies in print. From 1999 to 2006 they used the contents of the book as a training manual to conduct fifteen "Healing the Land Seminars" and presented the material hundreds of times. In 2004 Dr. Suuqiina wrote and released *Can You Feel the Mountains Tremble? A Healing the Land Handbook,* and there are more than ten thousand in print.[50] All across North America, people have begun applying the principles of "protocol" when creating new relationships with the Native people in their communities and regions. Their seminars and books are classic examples of Rogers's view of how leaders influence change:

> Opinion leadership is the degree to which an individual is able to informally influence other individuals' attitudes or overt behavior in a desired way with relative frequency. A change agent is an individual who attempts to influence clients' innovation-decisions in a direction that is deemed desirable by a change agency.[51]

Every MN1V Celebration began with protocol, which in Native culture means seeking the blessings of the "host people of the land" (local tribal leaders). Guests who wish to be welcomed to traditional territories show proper honor and respect by following this custom. The tribal leaders were all given various gifts, often beautiful Pendleton blankets.

In the past several years various books have been produced by Native authors with a contextual bent. Included in these are works by dozens of good authors such as Robert Francis (Cherokee), Anita Keith (Ojibwa), Phil Duran (Tewa) and Casey Church (Potawatomi). The writings, like the movement, continue to expand.

Indian Life newspaper (indianlife.org). *Indian Life* is the only North American Native Christian periodical. This distinction makes it very important as a major communication channel. For most of its history it was opposed to contextualization, then later more tolerant of it. *Indian Life* was founded in 1968 as a free evangelistic publication of a ministry in South Dakota run by Raymond Gowan. It was supported through Mr. Gowan's vision and generosity and grew until one hundred thousand copies were being distributed across the United States. After eleven years he could not continue publishing the newspaper, so in October 1979, it merged with another publication, *The Indian Christian*, but kept its name, *Indian Life*. From 1979 through 2012, it produced six issues per year, thus 198 issues printed and distributed over thirty-three years.

When Jim Uttley came on board in 1988, they were printing around sixty-eight thousand copies per issue. Half of them were distributed to prisons at no cost. In 1995 they had to drop the free prison circulation due to a decrease in funds. They came up with a program in which sponsors can send ten copies of each issue to a prison at a cost of fifty-two dollars per year. Prisons only receive one copy per issue unless they have a sponsor. Because of this change, circulation dropped to thirty-two thousand.

Despite early attempts to be culturally relevant when it came to choosing photos for the magazine, those that included Native people holding eagle feathers or dressed in regalia were rejected. References to powwows, drumming and other contextual practices were omitted.

In the fall of 1998, Terry LeBlanc and I cohosted the second World

Christian Gathering of Indigenous Peoples in Rapid City, South Dakota. *Indian Life* sent a delegation of two. It was at this major contextual event that *Indian Life* met the man they had been cautioned to avoid some two years prior, namely, me! At this same event they also came in contact with many other individuals with whom they'd had a long-standing relationship, including Adrian Jacobs, Jonathan Maracle, *Indian Life's* founder, Ray Gowan, and his son David.

At this conference, *Indian Life's* editor, Jim Uttley, realized that Indigenous leaders from across the world were working to escape the colonial paternalism of Eurocentric missions to make the gospel knowable in their unique cultural ways. He began to believe that *Indian Life* ought to be covering these various events and reporting on what Creator was doing in many different circles, churches and denominations.

When the newspaper published a report on the WCGIP in Rapid City, a small number of those opposed to contextual ministry withdrew their subscriptions and support of Indian Life Ministries (ILM). Throughout this time, *Indian Life* received only a handful of complaints about this issue. Most were from very conservative Christian individuals and organizations.

As a result, the leadership of ILM initiated a "neutral policy" where the contextual movement was concerned. Under this policy, *Indian Life* could not publish any articles about or authored by those in the contextual movement. This particularly included me, Wiconi International, and a host of other leaders and organizations I worked with.

In 2000 Wiconi International sponsored a MNiV conference in Winnipeg, Manitoba, Canada. Jim Uttley and several *Indian Life* staff had the opportunity to attend. Jim met with me during the conference to discuss various issues. Following this conference there was a growing sense among some of the staff that *Indian Life* needed to become as contextual as possible for the sake of the gospel. However, it was becoming more and more difficult to hold this position, considering that the leadership wasn't entirely open and was determined to continue the "neutral policy" when it came to contextualization.

In 2004 Jim no longer felt that he could continue as editor without the support of ILM's leadership, considering their approach to contextual ministry. He resigned and joined Wiconi International as communications director.

In 2005 *Indian Life* had a philosophical policy shift in support of a more contextualized approach to Native ministry. Bob Neufeld, the new director, saw the importance and necessity of being in touch with the contextual movement. In 2005 he suspended the "neutral policy," giving *Indian Life* the liberty to publish news reports of Creator working throughout Native North America, whether through contextual or noncontextual ministries.

In September 2005, ILM's director asked Jim to see if Wiconi would agree to allow him to return as editor. Realizing the importance of *Indian Life*, Wiconi agreed. Jim is currently "on loan" from Wiconi to ILM as *Indian Life's* full-time editor, spending most of his time managing the publication in Winnipeg.

Since the time of their policy shift, about 450 subscriptions were dropped. However, about one thousand subscriptions were gained. Currently there are fourteen thousand *Indian Life* newspapers printed for each issue. So in the past four years, twenty-four issues representing some four hundred thousand copies have been distributed across North America in support of contextualized Native ministry. During this time, several articles featured Wiconi events or staff ministries and numerous other leaders and organizations representing good contextual ministry.

Mission Frontiers magazine. For many years, *Mission Frontiers* was a premier publication in the global missions community under the guidance of the late Dr. Ralph Winter. It is a publication of the US Center for World Mission. In September of 2000, the editor of the magazine asked me to write the lead article and also to be interviewed for an issue devoted entirely to covering the emerging Native contextualization movement. The cover headline read *A New Day: In Ministry to Native Americans*. I invited Adrian Jacobs, Randy Woodley and Terry LeBlanc to write articles for the issue as well. Each of them presented compelling theological and missiological positions supporting and promoting contextualization. It was sent to sixty thousand people in the global missions community. This issue of *Mission Frontiers* introduced the movement and its leaders to the national and international mission community. The articles reached out to like-minded thinkers, and by default, or at least tacitly, "approved" the work of the early innovators.

Some ten years later in September 2010, *Mission Frontiers* again dedicated an issue to covering the Native contextualization movement titled *Making Jesus Known, Native Americans Lead the Way in Reaching Their Own People.*[52] Rick Wood, the editor, invited me to serve as editorial advisor for the issue. I wrote the lead article and invited Native ministry leaders Bill Gowey, Fern Cloud, Casey Church, Cheryl Bear-Barnetson and Terry LeBlanc to write articles. The publication has a worldwide circulation of ninety-two thousand. In addition, Rick Wood generously agreed to print and send me an additional ten thousand copies at no cost. These were distributed across Indian Country in North America.

Trinity Broadcast Network (TBN) and the 700 Club. TBN is the largest Christian television network in the world, watched by millions of people. The 700 Club, though considerably smaller, is watched by hundreds of thousands. It is surprising how many charismatic/Pentecostal Native believers regularly watch TBN, especially those in more rural areas. It becomes "their church." Since 2005 I have appeared as a guest eight times on the *Praise the Lord Program*, highlighting the new contextualization efforts taking place among First Nations people. I have shown video footage and still photos of the Living Waters Powwow and the World Christian Gathering of Indigenous People on several occasions, always with great approval and response. Several other Native leaders have appeared as guests on the 700 Club program to explain and promote contextual ministry. It is difficult to measure how these programs have influenced attitudes toward Native American people, ministry and contextualization. That being said, Wiconi International has received hundreds of emails and letters from viewers expressing their appreciation for our humble efforts and the words I shared.

First Nations Monday. First Nations Monday (FNM) is a Native American/First Nations Internet prayer mobilization endeavor formally launched by Jenny Covill (Cherokee) in May of 2000. It was a catalytic diffusion mechanism for the early adapters of contextual ministry. The original purpose was to network various Native American ministries with one another, as well as to connect these ministries with intercessors from around the US. The networking would be accomplished via the Internet on a monthly basis for the purpose of prayer. Hence, the name comes from combining the two key elements of the project: "First Nations" and the "first Monday" of each month.

In part, FNM grew in response to the fact that most people involved in Native ministry, to one degree or another, were relatively isolated from one another. Many expressed, "It seems like I am the only one on this path," or "I feel so alone and discouraged," or "If only there were others who could relate to my calling."

This isolation was most likely due to two main factors: (1) lack of awareness regarding Native ministry on a national level, and (2) those serving in Native ministry were so given to their own work that they had little time or opportunity to meet colleagues, much less build relationships with them.

The prayer network started in 2000 with about forty subscribers, including fifteen different Native American ministries. The website launched in July 2000 with the purpose of providing a directory to all of the ministries involved in the prayer network. Shortly after FirstNations Monday.com was available on the Internet, Jenny Covill partnered with Dee Toney (founder of Polished Arrow) and Tim Stime (My People International) from Canada in creating an exhaustive web-based directory of Native ministries. This gave birth to FirstNationsMonday.com as a directory. It became better known than the prayer network, almost overnight. It was obvious that a long-time need in the Native ministry community was being recognized and met through the labors of all involved.

By 2003 the data for the directory had grown immeasurably. Managing the information became overwhelming. It was decided that Dee Toney would take over sole supervision of the directory, and it was officially moved to PolishedArrow.com.

By 2005 this aspect of the ministry had grown so big that it was almost too much to handle. There were hundreds of ministries listed by region and then by state. There were over four hundred subscribers to the prayer letter, including about two hundred US-based Native ministries, plus about fifty others in Canada, Mexico and other countries. The letter included prayer requests, contact information, progress reports and schedules of meetings and events.

The need for administrative help, combined with the phenomenon that most of the ministries had grown by leaps and bounds, left FNM in a unique position. It was too short-handed, and the various leaders in Native ministry had become too busy to compile and submit their monthly prayer needs. After much personal prayer, Jenny Covill felt that FNM's overall purpose had been accomplished. People were networking and ministries were developing their own individual prayer teams. So in March of 2005, after posting one last exhaustive list of ministries with their contact information, FNM discontinued the monthly prayer letter.

In December of 2000 Jenny started an online e-group for posting prayer requests and other communications that needed attention immediately throughout the month. There are about two hundred subscribers still utilizing this resource. Other e-groups were developing at this time as well. One called Native Believers was created by Gene Brooks. It was the first online discussion group specific to Native ministry. In 2001 Gene passed the Native Believers discussion group to FNM for the next two years. Native Believers was discontinued in March of 2003.

From 2001 to 2003 many ministries were creating their own e-groups for the purpose of communication with their supporters. It was common for people interested in Native ministry to subscribe to several of these different ministry e-groups, trying to glean information and be connected. Yet, there still was a need for online discussions.

International Bible Society (IBS). In 1995 IBS established a national Native American Ministry office in Plummer, Idaho, on the Coeur d'Alene Indian Reservation. In 1994 I was contracted to write a set of introductory notes for a New Testament the society was producing for use in Native ministry. These notes (in the foreword) were intended to put the gospel story in the vernacular of the nonbelieving Native person and to teach new Native followers of Jesus.

At the time I was serving/volunteering as executive director of the North American Native Christian Council (NANCC), a group of Native men who were leaders of various ministries. Some of those leaders were Russell Begay (Navajo), director of the Southern Baptist Indian Churches; Julian Gunn (Acoma), director of the Nazarene Native American District; Craig Smith (Chippewa), director of the Christian and Missionary Alliance Native American District; Jonathan Maracle (Mohawk), chief of the NANCC; Bill Lee (Navajo), president of the Assemblies of God Native American Fellowship; Torrey Antoine (Kiowa), American Indian Crusades and several others. At my request, International Bible Society agreed to allow NANCC members to contribute to the notes. I wrote the majority of the notes in tandem with an IBS staff writer, and a few of the other leaders added comments or edits. With the deadline for final changes due in less than forty-eight hours, I made additions and edits in conjunction with IBS staff. Not all NANCC members "wrote off" on the final draft. The publication was called *The Jesus Way New Testament* and had a beautifully designed Native motif cover. Fifteen thousand New Testaments were printed. Two short paragraphs read,

> The Creator also loves Native culture. Jesus came to make our cultures better, not take them away from us. The Creator is pleased when people from different tribes and nations worship him. He delights when he hears many languages and sees many customs and ways of being used to praise him. With our songs, dances, and languages we can be fully Christian and fully Native! We must be careful not to mix the true worship of the Creator with the old religions that do not honor him. But at the same time, we must not be afraid to worship the Creator with all the unique beauty and gifts of our Native cultures.[53]

When copies were distributed to members of NANCC, a furor erupted over the inclusion of the word "dances"! Letters of vehement disapproval stating this was blatant syncretism were written to the president and senior vice-presidents of IBS. Several NANCC members refused to allow IBS to distribute the books with their names included in the list of contributors. A compromise was found in response to their ultimatum and IBS agreed to tear out the page with the "offending" section in it from all fifteen thousand New Testaments before they released them.

Later, at a meeting of the NANCC council, I was accused of deliberately including the word "dances," knowing they were against dancing. With the members assembled together in a room, a secret vote was called for (members wrote on pieces of paper, which were taken outside and counted, and the number reported) and I was summarily voted off the council.

In spite of this controversy, in 1996 I was hired as the director for IBS's Native ministry. In this capacity I participated in many evangelical ministry organizational leadership events. *The Jesus Way New Testament*, which was warmly embraced in many circles, also increased the number of invitations I received, although another consequence of the publication was that I became known as a controversial figure in Native ministry. At its final printing in 2004 there were thirty-five thousand copies of *The Jesus Way New Testament* floating around Indian Country.

EMERGING THEMES

My research has provided intriguing and compelling evidence that contextualization is and has been occurring in Native ministry. The following are some of the prominent events, practices, themes and trends that my research has identified as being at some stage of emergence in the contextualization conversation:

- There are now several "Christ-honoring" traditional powwows and social gatherings occurring across the country—organized and hosted by Native followers of Jesus. Some are "blatantly Christ-honoring," as stated in literature, symbolism (a cross) or promotions. Other powwows are organized and hosted by Native believers, but have no outward indicators that they have a distinctly Christ-honoring focus. Yet they are operated in a very respectful and traditional way.

- Hundreds of believers have contextualized traditional rituals as expressions of discipleship, worship, gospel-telling and cultural revitalization—for example, marriage, sweat lodge and naming ceremonies.

- Native artists are carving traditional Northwest Coastal totems and masks with symbols and designs that purposefully communicate biblical themes, expressing their personal faith in Jesus. In addition, various other art forms are being used in a similar fashion.

- Indigenous forms of prayer (formerly condemned) are now being utilized by many, including praying with burning cedar, sweetgrass or sage, using a traditional tobacco pipe, and certain dances and songs.

- A variety of dance styles from across the country are being used and in some cases reinterpreted for biblical worship, personal edification and discipleship.

- An entirely new "Indigenous hymnody" supporting these contextualization efforts has emerged since 1998. These musical innovations include drumming, singing styles, music composition, instrumentation, language and protocol that follow both modern and traditional forms. They also include music that combines traditional elements with contemporary style and instrumentation. This music is serving as a vehicle to explore theology, corporate worship and its use in private devotional situations.

- New models of church planting, ecclesiology and missions are emerging that might be considered more reflective of a North American "Indigenous Christianity or church." Several networks of new Native churches now exist.

- Over the past several years, the International Church of the Foursquare denomination has emerged to "officially" embrace, fully support and participate in contextualizing the gospel in their ministry efforts among First Nations people.

- Several churches are using traditional names for Creator in their worship services, along with contextualizing traditional linguistic concepts, ceremonies and story as part of developing Indigenous theologies.

- New First Nations biblical scholars are emerging and are formally introducing innovative paradigms for the theological training and education of Native leadership. They are working together in various networks, forming new organizations, producing literature and becoming a recognized voice in the North American theological and missiological community.

SUMMARY

In this chapter I have selected just a few examples of the many I had to choose from in my research to show how these contextualization innovations are growing in acceptance, practice and awareness. Through the various diffusion channels of media, literacy, relational and organizational networks—communication channels—awareness of these innovations and their innovators has thoroughly spread across Indian Country in North American and even the wider international Christian community. In comparison to the Indian Ecumenical Movement, they may not qualify historically as "new," but in Rogers's view, "new" can be any "idea or message perceived as new."[54] The contextualization innovations are not considered new because they have never been heard of before—they are new because they are now considered an appropriate cultural expression of biblical faith by many Native and other evangelical Christians, whose prior experiences had involved complete rejection and resistance.

DISCUSSION QUESTIONS

1. What are the innovations that these contextualization initiatives are adopting, and what is the theology that supports them?

2. What are the responses of current Christian leaders and organizations—both Native and non-Native—to this contextualization movement, especially those whose experience of Christian faith has occurred within distinctly Anglicized models?

3. Describe how you see a "truly Indigenous church."

4. Do you see contextualization as manipulative or "deeply sacramental," that is, sincere? Describe the tension the author mentions.

5. Describe how the innovators mentioned in this chapter are working
   out "Native self-theologizing."

6. How does a person trained in a Western theological institution develop a truly Indigenous theology?

5

FROM COLONIZATION
TO CONTEXTUALIZATION

S tories are people, people are their stories, and stories are alive. Traditionally, Native American stories are never fully explained. The power and influence of the story does not lie in the exact correctness of its telling, but in the life of the "teller" and in the "telling" (difficult to nuance with ink on a page). While doing the analytical work for this book, I have felt the strain and tension between trying to interpret and explain stories with empirical methodological devices and allowing the inherent mystery of Creator working among us to remain unexplained. Evan Pritchard writes about the ancient practice of storytelling among Native peoples in *Native American Stories of the Sacred: Annotated and Explained*. He comments that Native stories were not to be explained for several reasons, including,

> out of respect for both the intelligence of the listener and the Great Mystery. However, stories are as three-dimensional as the objects and creatures that inhabit them, and so no matter how much you explain them, there is always a great deal left over to wonder at and ponder over, becoming clear to us later, when we are ready, each according to his or her own capacity. Everyone gets what they can from them, and the rest is left to dawn on you later.[1]

So also it is with the stories I have been given. Natives and non-Natives across North America have entrusted me with their stories, included me in their journeys of faith, and let me into the larger stories of their lives.

I had the great honor and privilege to prayerfully search in order to discover how these unique stories fit together in the context of a bigger story being written by Creator in the Native community of North America. As I have carefully read, listened to and sorted through the living stories of friends, strangers and acquaintances, I have come to some conclusions— all while seeking to address the core questions regarding the emerging Native-led contextualization efforts in North America.

Multicultural Leaders/Interpreters

Based on the stories and data I have gathered over three years, a pivotal commonality among these contextual innovators—and consequently this movement—has become evident. In light of hundreds of years of colonization and missions history, the Native leaders best suited as innovators to introduce and negotiate new contextualization efforts are multicultural people who can navigate the Anglo, Native, urban and reservation cultural worlds as interpreters. It is important to understand this because of the historical tension typically confronting these types of people in a colonial context. They are often misunderstood by both sides, while playing a critical role, for better or worse, as cultural brokers or interpreters within a governing dominant culture. Bernd Peyer, in *The Tutor'd Mind: Indian Missionary-Writers in Antebellum America,* comments on this centuries-old problem:

> The literary bequest of Indian missionaries in antebellum America should be regarded as a historical testimony to a conquered people's creative accommodation to social change. Their lives and works can only be appreciated in association with the extreme nature of the relationship between Indians and whites at the time, or what might be called their contact environment, which is understood here as the physical and philosophical space in which social encounters take place. Since the character of that relationship was determined by a colonial situation, that contact environment imposed unusually harsh conditions for their advancement as individuals, as writers, and as cultural brokers.[2]

This is exactly the precarious position faced by many of the early innovators in this study. We can be blind to this situation because of their perceived "normalness"—the result of their ability to "successfully" operate as participants within the dominant culture.

It is important to understand the historical context in order to see the degree of enduring difficulty facing Native Christian leaders. They must overcome the hegemony of American colonial Christianity so they can develop Indigenous contextual theologies. Peyer narrates this lasting historical dilemma:

> Yet another common manifestation of literary chauvinism in a colonial situation is the fabrication of racial stereotypes to set the proper mood for conquest. . . . Of particular relevance to the topic at hand, however, are the more elusive negative images that surround many of those who try to find ways in which to adapt to the colonial contact environment. Labeled contemptuously as sellouts, apples, Uncle Tomahawks, or, in its kindest form, progressives, transcultural Indians often find themselves stigmatized as the bastard offspring of two incompatible societies.[3]

To survive in a colonial situation, an ethnic minority needs to establish some form of internal balance mechanism in order to cope with social change.

In a helpful study, anthropologist Malcolm McFee makes an attempt to measure "levels of acculturation" among the members of the Blackfeet Indian tribe of northern Montana. As a result of his study he coins the phrase "the 150% man" to describe a person who is of mixed blood ancestry. The "150% man" is able to easily and freely move between his Native and white cultures to effectively serve as an interpreter between the two and on behalf of both.[4]

While I am always highly uncomfortable with anthropology as "science," which is infused with epistemological notions of "certainty," (though anthropologists would say this is not true) McFee's study is helpful in understanding the Native leaders I have identified as "multicultural people."

Throughout my study I have put myself in the position of "participant observer" in order to tell the stories from the perspectives of the storytellers. I did this to capture the essence of their day-to-day experiences. My hope is that by doing so I will have gained "a holistic perspective of the lifestyles, worldviews, and social relationships" of my friends, associates and respondents.[5]

While I find his definition of the term inadequate, certain features of Rogers's reference to the "emphasis on intercultural diffusion" and the manner in which "concepts of context and culture"[6] are taken into account have been helpful—especially when considering the ways an innovation is adopted over time, and which factors (such as the perceived attributes of the innovation) explain its speed of adoption.[7] He does not specifically address the point that I think is critical to the diffusion of the contextual innovations I have identified. I am saying that for Native-led contextual innovations and early diffusion to occur, a unique crosscultural interpreter is required—a "cultural insider." Without this person there will not be genuine contextualization, only modifications or surface-level adaptations of the cultural, theological and ecclesiological status quo, or outdated paradigms of ministry and mission.

REDEFINING/CONTEXTUALIZING CONTEXTUALIZATION

There will come a time when enough of the general Native population will adopt contextualization efforts that a "tipping point" will occur. Then those efforts will be carried along to the majority of the community. But, there is also a "tipping point" that seems to make a difference in spreading the innovation. This has to do with how the innovations first spread among individual innovators and then become "shared" or "commonly held" innovations through personal relationships, friendships and, to a lesser degree, collaborative partnerships. The innovations are then widely and quickly spread as a synergistic movement. This process of diffusion or "tipping point" is what Malcolm Gladwell refers to in *The Tipping Point* as "the biography of an idea."[8] He uses the dynamic metaphor of a contagious virus that can produce an epidemic as a way to describe how a simple idea can infect others and then spread. Borrowing the mathematical formula of geometric progression, he infuses this into his contagion metaphor, stating, "Epidemics are another example of geometric progression: when a virus spreads through a population, it doubles and doubles again. At some point a new idea, social trend or phenomenon spreads and multiplies until it reaches the 'tipping point,' the moment of critical mass, the threshold, the boiling point."[9] I have identified enough indicators to say the shift toward critical contextualization as the accepted norm in Native ministry is close to reaching that point in time.

That being said, however, while reflecting on the writings of Flemming, Nida,[10] Hiebert, Smalley, Kraft, Whiteman, Hesselgrave and many others, I find making sense of contextualization a difficult and disturbing task because it is commonly defined by these authors in an "over there" geographic context. An example of this would be a "foreigner-missionary" looking across an ocean or distant land at an exotic or "foreign" people, culture, history, tribe or nation, strategizing about how they are going to evangelize *those* foreigners.

The authors of the books I have referenced explain the evolution of the connection between anthropology and mission. They note how within various traditions and at certain times the words *localization, context-indigenization, ethnotheology, enculturation, indigenization, critical-contextualization, structural-contextualization, incarnation* and *dynamic-equivalence* have been used to describe gospel telling or our participation with Creator in making Creator known.

Here in the United States and Canada, contextualization seems to be more of a subtext within the bigger text of an Indigenous church movement among colonized people. How are we negotiating our own colonial theological oppression and contextualizing the gospel amongst ourselves as we resist assimilation and struggle for survival within a neo-colonial reality? With more than four centuries of colonization, social and political subjugation and religious oppression, it is problematical to imagine what a truly Indigenous church would look like today. Massively compounding this problem is a half-century of the forced removal of Native children from their homes and their forced attendance in typically Christian-run boarding schools. In light of the deterioration, and at times complete loss, of original languages, traditional and sustainable economies, governmental structures, kinship systems, religious ceremonies and social-ordering mechanisms, perhaps a better questions is: What could an Indigenous church look like in this modern world?

It is true that the gospel always engages human cultures, and that we cannot know the gospel apart from culture. Culture is never static but

WRESTLING WITH DEFINITIONS

According to Kraft, the term *contextualization* has helped us acculturate Christianity and the Scriptures to a particular audience. Kraft is urging caution when using the terms *contextualization, localization, enculturation* and especially the earlier term *indigenization*, because he fears the focus is placed on culture rather than on people. Kraft makes a distinction, noting that "people and culture are quite different." For example, he says, "People do things, culture doesn't do anything. Culture itself does not behave, people behave. So our adaptations of Scripture need to be thought of as people-centered, not culture-centered."[11]

Kraft, along with others, has suggested the word *appropriate* as a way of saying that gospel telling is best done when it is both appropriate to a given social or cultural context and to Christianity or the Scriptures. He writes, "The term appropriate . . . raises the question 'appropriate to what?' And our answer will be twofold since the subject is twofold: gospel on one side and culture on the other."[12] Still wrestling with defining words and concepts and now suggesting that "appropriate" more accurately nuances the ways in which we should communicate the message of Jesus among us as Creator and Waymaker, he fundamentally says:

> We believe that God wants His church incarnated in the cultural way of life of every society (people group). Just as Jesus totally participated in first century Palestinian life, not as a foreigner but as a native son, so contemporary Christian communities should not be living like foreigners in their own lands, speaking their language with a foreign (usually Western) accent, performing foreign-looking rituals at strange times and in strange-looking places.[13]

always changing and evolving. The question still remains, after five hundred years of colonial assimilation, how will the gospel of Jesus be best understood in this emerging "modern Indian culture?"

To reinforce my point that Native leaders need to lead efforts to move away from neocolonial models of mission and church toward an Indigenous one, I want to introduce the work of David Scates, a missionary among the Navajo people in Red Mesa, Arizona, from 1966 to 1979. Based on his fourteen years of ministry experience and three years of research, he wrote a doctoral dissertation for Fuller Theological Seminary that became the book *Why Navajo Churches Are Growing: The Cultural Dynamics of Navajo Religious Change*.[14] It told of his participation in and observations of the unique spread of Christian faith among the Navajo.

Scates graciously acknowledges that the cultural assumptions and worldviews of the early missionaries (who were ill-equipped for the task) made them unknowing participants in the ongoing colonization of the Navajo people by teaching them to reject their cultural identities. In fact, he spends considerable time developing the idea of what a worldview is, and shows specifically how the clashing worldview assumptions of the Navajo and the missionary resulted in the miscommunication of the gospel. This was especially true during the period of widespread anti-white sentiment in the 1940s. His perceptive recognition of the need to assign equal value to both the worldview assumptions of the Navajo people and those of the missionary is critical. With this summary background he tells the intriguing story of how the providence of Creator had already provided a dynamic cultural pathway for the gospel.

The key principle he identifies for the growth of Navajo churches is their traditional clan system. It was an already-existing cultural core value that connected the people. The shift away from considering them as "cliquish" or exclusive and divisive, to being recognized as a natural pathway for the gospel, opened the door to a true grassroots revival and church-planting phenomenon. As noted in Scates's thoroughly documented survey, this shift was measured by the fact that there were 38 Navajo churches in 1950, increasing to 255 by 1978.

Scates notes that a variety of ways and means are needed to communicate the gospel to a tribe that is comprised of subcultural groups, that is, clans. In addition, he fairly and genuinely recognizes that to reach every segment of Navajo society, which is at varying stages on an "assimilation continuum," a variety of methods and strategies are required. He describes an assimilation continuum ranging from those who reject all the ways of the white man to those who reject all their own traditional ways in favor of assimilation. Rather than seeing one end or the other as the preferable one, he sees the need for the gospel to be communicated to both the conservative and contextual communities in terms that make sense and are meaningful to them. As Scates points out, for some, one way may seem radical, even syncretistic, to reach those who reject an Anglicized Christianity as the "white man's religion." For those who are moving toward full participation in the dominant culture, a more "westernized" style of music, worship, preaching and liturgy is what is most effective, but may be viewed by the other end as "apple Indians"—red on the outside and white on the inside.

While Scates addresses the "communication" dynamic of missions, he does not develop the idea of the Indigenous church, specifically, self-theologizing relative to contextualization. Because churches are being planted and are growing in the context of the traditional clan system, Navajo believers are leading these churches and the Navajo language is being used. This is sufficient for him to define this as an Indigenous movement. He seems to view the three-legged stool—self-supporting, self-governing and self-propagating—as an adequate model. One would question how a grassroots movement revival could prosper and endure without the development of adequate Indigenous theologies that would emerge from within the culture itself. Scates's book is excellent in that it shows how the gospel can most effectively impact a people when it follows natural and cultural societal structures and values, but still leaves the question of "what next?" unanswered.[15]

Based on my interviews with Navajo believers who were raised on the Navajo Reservation and who had friends and family who were part of the movement Scates describes, my observation (with limited specific research) indicates that those once-thriving churches have slowly, gradually, faded in vibrancy, numbers and reproduction. Without more re-search, and based only on these believers' comments, I can tentatively say that this movement was a bright light, a flash, but has already quickly faded. It was not a multigenerational movement and did not adapt to the growing changes or needs of the people because it did not adequately contextualize the gospel to the cultural, spiritual, religious and spatial worldview of the people. Despite the fact that these new churches were located in, and spread through, the traditional network of Navajo "chapter houses," they remained the "white man's religion."

Contextualization done well is part of the process of decolonization in pursuit of freedom and justice. These stories illustrate that without an intentional breaking away from colonial Christianity, decolonization—true realized freedom for Indigenous people and the Indigenous church—will not happen.

Cultural liminality. North American Native culture has been in a prolonged liminal state for several centuries. In order to survive geno-cidal colonization, Native people have been forced to adapt, adopt and assimilate the values and forms of a Euro-American culture in creating their own new reality. Lesslie Newbigin in *Foolishness to the Greeks: The Gospel and Western Culture*, enlarges the culture category, reminding us that "Every statement of the gospel in words is conditioned by the culture of which those words are a part, and every style of life that claims to embody the truth of the gospel is a culturally conditioned style of life. There can never be a culture-free gospel."[16] While it is understood that there is no monolithic cultural representation of North American Native culture, we do possess a relatively common history as inhabitants of this land and in our collective, subsequent encounter with European culture and Christianity. According to the 2010 United States Census, "Seventy-eight percent of the total Native population of five million two hundred thousand [Native Americans, Alaska Natives and those of mixed Native/other blood] live off their tribal homelands or reservations," with the majority living in urban centers.[17] This sixty-year-old phenomenon has given rise to a new "pan-Indian" reality. In this new, often inner-city reality, Native people have struggled valiantly to maintain their cultural ways and identities in a world dominated by foreign ways. It is in this world that these contextualization innovations are occurring.

In his study of the biblical record of the spread of the gospel throughout the first-century world, Dean Flemming in *Contextualization in the New Testament, Patterns for Theology and Mission*, understands that, "The gospel and culture is complex and multidimensional. The gospel is both at home in every culture and alien to every culture."[18] In what ways does the current dissonance in traditional Native culture today both inform and shape how we do contextualization? How can the gospel be contextualized in a fragmented, hybrid, sometimes tension-filled culture? That contextualization is difficult is especially true in light of five hundred years of colonization, intermarriage between Native and non-Native, the influence of formal Western education and the hegemony of evangelical Christianity/theology. In examining the tensions experienced by the Hebrew church as it expanded into the Greco-Roman world, Flemming acknowledges that the church has always existed in a multicultural world, which helps make sense of our current condition in Indian Country:

> The mission of the church to which the New Testament bears witness, then, is not simply a monocultural or even a classic "cross-cultural" mission, in the sense of moving directly from one culture into another target culture. It is an intercultural mission, which requires enormous creativity, flexibility, and Spirit-inspired wisdom.[19]

Those who have been the innovators and early adopters in contextual thinking have all been multicultural persons who were able to serve as interpreters among various communities, both Christian and non-Christian. Rarely has the "first-generation mother-tongue speaking traditional believer" been the one who has done the contextualization work. Rather, it has almost exclusively been the second- or third-generation believer. The innovators identified in my research—though they may be the first in their families to embrace faith in Jesus—are all multicultural persons. William A. Smalley, in *Readings in Missionary Anthropology II*, comments on the apostle Paul's cultural background. He notes that as a

MULTICULTURAL CHARACTERISTICS

Rather than posit a succinct definition of the term, here are the characteristics of those I am calling multicultural. Most were raised in a mixed home (Native/non-Native parent) and were nearly all of mixed-blood ancestry. With some exceptions, few were raised on the reservation or traditional homeland of their people, or were raised with their tribal language and religious practices, ceremonies or rituals. Most received some education and all had relative freedom of choice to do the necessary biblical study and experimentation with their contextual ideas. Nearly all learned and later carried out their early ministry in a mostly urban Caucasian context. Some learned of their tribal traditions through the stories of a parent, family member, tribal leader or elder. Many learned through books and individual study. Some chose, at a point in time, usually in their twenties, to strongly self-identify as a person of their tribe or nation.

Jewish man he was no stranger or foreigner to the Greek world. Like the men and women in my research, Paul "was a bicultural individual, one who was as much at home in the Greek world as he was in the Hebrew world and whose preaching carried to the Greek world the message which came to him from the Christians of the Hebrew world."[20] In fact, his claim to "become all things to all people so that by all possible means I might save some" (1 Cor 9:22 NIV) is rooted in his own ability to move back and forth between different cultural settings.

The contextualization efforts relative to this study have come out of these innovators' Christian experiences in a mostly urban setting. There are exceptions like Randy and Edith Woodley in their work among the Kiowa, Comanche, Apache, Cheyenne and Arapaho tribes around Anadarko, Oklahoma, and then later among the Western Shoshone, Paiute and Washoe peoples near Carson City, Nevada. These were or have now become traditional homelands for those respective tribes. The theology and contextualization occurred with traditional Christian and non-Christian leaders who helped the Woodleys "figure it out." Other innovators would include Adrian Jacobs, who grew up in the Handsome

Lake Longhouse tradition of the Cayuga Six Nations, where he worked to make sense of his faith in Jesus as a Cayuga man. Jerry and Johanna Yellowhawk lived most of their lives in and around Lakota communities in South Dakota where Jerry has served as a Lakota translator.

Most of them started off in a denominational context where they received either informal or formal theological training, introduction to biblical studies or biblical leadership, and local church government. If they came to faith in a Southern Baptist church, they became a good Southern Baptist. If they came to faith in the Assemblies of God, they became a good AG Christian. If they came to faith in the Dutch Reformed church, they became a good Reformed Christian. In the early years of their faith, wanting genuinely to follow Jesus, they lived out their faith unquestioningly within the Euro-American contextualized Christian culture in which they found themselves.

Stephen Neill, in *A History of Christian Missions,* speaks of the natural tendency of a new believer to follow the pattern in which his Christianity was learned. Neill has observed that a "convert is imitative; he wants to do things exactly in what he conceives to be the proper Christian pattern and in no other way." Neill observed in the church in Bali (Republic of Indonesia) how extreme this reality can be: "In all its inner and outward life the Balinese Church is more like the Dutch Reformed Church than the Dutch Reformed Church is like itself. It manifests hardly a trace of the wonderful art and culture of that most beautiful island."[21]

This was also true to varying degrees and over various periods of time for many of the leaders in the contextualization movement. Within a few years, however, their views of and their comfort level with their early experience of Christianity began to change—and soon radically changed.

Reflecting on his own experience as a missionary, scholar and theologian, Kraft shares his conviction that every follower of Jesus is obliged to "risk whatever theological frame of reference we have been trained into in order to assist and support new believers in their journey of growing spiritually." The Native innovators in this study exemplify Kraft's assessment of what it takes to fully live out the gospel. He identifies a necessary quality of those engaged in challenging old paradigms, saying that, "Only by risking prior, less mature understandings can we gain more mature understandings."[22] I see this as a prerequisite quality of faith in order to successfully engage in contextualization efforts in preexisting, well-established church realities.

Most of these innovators were multicultural persons who were not raised in the traditional religious environment of their particular tribe. They often were equally at ease in both the Native and Anglo worlds. This level of comfort—along with their growing Native self-awareness, increasing confidence and sense of tribal identity—allowed them to become cultural translators. Their relative ease of movement among cultures and ensuing crosscultural competency placed them in the unique position of beginning to translate and reinterpret traditional Native forms, rituals, ceremonies and music from one culture to the next. This process began very personally—internally at first. Today many of them are equally or more at home in a sweat lodge ceremony as they are in a church building on Sunday morning.

This process of change is always clearly the work of the Holy Spirit. All of these men and women were actively engaged in various aspects of Christian ministry practicing contextualization before they gradually became aware of one another from a distance. From 1990 to 2000 most of the early innovators had met each other in a variety of settings in North America, most often at conferences.

Generational dynamics. As has often been noted in missiological studies, the first-generation Native Christian who comes to faith out of a deep-seated worldview often sees religion as foundational to the real world and not easily separable or redefinable as an expression of a new faith in Jesus. For them to take their traditional forms, sounds, structures and ceremonies and use them for a completely different purpose—worshiping this new Creator, Jesus—was too difficult, perhaps impossible.

Neill asks the question, "What, if anything, hinders the development of this spontaneous adaptation of the old to the new?" In attempting to explain believers' objections to contextualization, he identifies the source of that opposition:

Resistance comes primarily from the converts themselves and from their reluctance to have anything to do with the world from which they have emerged. Only in rare cases does the convert regard his former religion as a preparation for the new. The old world was a world of evil in which he was imprisoned, and from which he was delivered by the power of Christ. The last thing that he wishes is to turn back in any way to be associated with that which to him is evil through and through. . . . This attitude meets us so constantly, and in so many parts of the world, that there can be no doubt that it is spontaneous and not simply due to prejudices inculcated by the missionaries.[23]

While Neill may be identifying the reason that first-generation believers resist contextualization, this does not explain how, in our case, it is almost exclusively second- and third-generation Native evangelical Christians who are so resistant.

Craig Stephen Smith (Chippewa), a third-generation Native Christian, addresses a process of contextualization in his book *Whiteman's Gospel*: "I believe the best person to decide how a traditional person conforms his life to biblical principles is the traditionalist himself under the guidance of the Holy Spirit!" He issues a caution to church leaders not to attempt to persuade this traditional (perhaps first-generation) person one way or the other in how he "will evaluate his cultural ways in light of Scripture" and contextualize or reconcile his faith with his culture. Furthermore, Smith emphasizes disallowing people from outside this person's tribe, region or background to influence or assist the process, saying, "This process, however, must not be brought on him by someone not familiar with his particular situation."[24]

In 2000 Smith served as the district superintendent for the Native American District of the Christian and Missionary Alliance Church. While in this capacity he oversaw the writing and production of a booklet titled *Boundary Lines: The Issue of Christ, Indigenous Worship, and Native American Culture: The Official Guidelines of the Official Workers and Member Congregations of the Native American District of the Christian and Missionary Alliance (US)*. In this writing he reinforces his point: "It is our strong belief that the key people best poised to lead the Native church in the process of critical contextualization are the spiritually mature Native Christian elders and leaders who have had personal experience *in their respective cultures*."[25] This statement has been used to discredit and nullify the contextualization efforts of many of the innovators I've identified. He and other Native evangelicals label these contextualization efforts as "non-authentic," disingenuous and syncretistic.

Smith grew up traveling with his family ministry, singing, preaching and doing evangelistic work on several hundred reservations and in Native communities. He is widely known and respected in the Native evangelical community. He became one of several dozen outspoken critics of the contextualization efforts of the people in this study, along with Tom and Huron Claus and those associated with the CHIEF network of Native ministers.[26] Soon after the *Boundary Lines* paper was first published, it was regarded as a kind of Native evangelical "position paper" and was used by a number of Native Christian leaders and organizations to refute these contextualization efforts. Becoming more than a theological debate, it digressed to be more about control and power than anything else. It attempted to define and control the vocabulary of missiology and theology in the Native context, for example:

> Recently there has been introduced in the native evangelical church community the concept that drums, rattles, and other sacred paraphernalia formerly used in animistic worship can be "redeemed" for use in Christian worship. This position does not enjoy consensus among native evangelical church leaders. *Legitimate definitions* [italics mine for emphasis] of the terms "culture," "worldview," "syncretism," "cultural form and meaning," "sacred objects," and "critical contextualization" as they relate to this study have been provided.[27]

As I discussed earlier in the syncretism section, the obvious implication is that if one holds a view of contextualization differing or in disagreement with their definitions, an "illegitimate" view, it is easily dismissed. It is *not* open to dialogue. It appears then that the real issue is one of control and power and the maintenance of territory, not honest dialogue. It is like the contentious arguments surrounding syncretism which are "often taken to imply 'inauthenticity' or 'contamination,' the infiltration of a supposedly 'pure' tradition by symbols and meanings seen as belonging to other incompatible traditions."[28] This is fundamentally an issue of control.

In each generation Native leaders must answer new questions for which they must find biblical answers. "Exegesis and hermeneutics are not the rights of individuals but of the church, as an exegetical and hermeneutical community."[29] To overcome the fear that produces the need to maintain control and religious political power bases, we need to work toward a new kind of Spirit-filled interdependence and cooperation—a hermeneutical community. Leaders can then collectively—in a spirit of love, honor and respect—respond to the challenges facing our Native people today. In our generation, critical contextualization and our understanding of syncretism must be reshaped, reformed and adjusted by the biblical insights from the wider community of Native believers. It is only within this "community" that those "spiritually mature elders and leaders"—those Smith says are best qualified to do "legitimate" critical contextualization—will be found.

A "tipping point" among contextualization innovators? The gospel must always find a welcome place to land within the culture, the context and the history of a particular person or people—a permanent home. For more than four hundred years, from the Atlantic seaboard to northern Alaska, we have been waiting for the gospel to be absorbed into the soil and soul of our Indigenous communities. It has been a long wait. Neill writes that "time must be allowed" for this process of contextualization to occur:

> The old non-Christian past must sink below the horizon. That which has come from the West must be so absorbed and assimilated that it can be transformed and re-expressed in categories different from those of the world of its origin. But this is the work of generations, not of years.[30]

Based on the data from my research, I would contend that the time is now. We are far beyond years and well past generations of waiting for this to become the new reality. In the context of the New Testament alone, the time that it took for the apostles to accomplish the contextualization process was from A.D. 30 to A.D. 90. That is, in sixty years the gospel was contextualized in Hebrew, Greek and Roman cultures, and even in variations such as Greco-Roman religion, Eastern religions (Persia, Egypt) and incipient Gnosticism. If that could be done in *sixty* years, then *four hundred* years is far too long for Native Americans to wait.

I am stating unequivocally that we as Native leaders find ourselves in a new role in which to serve. In the words of David J. Hesselgrave and Edward Rommen in *Contextualization: Meanings, Methods, and Models,* the primary emphasis of contextualization lies with the

> "prophetic" insight of the contextualizer and the cultural, political, and other circumstances in which he [and she] finds him [her] self. Contextualization entails entering a cultural context, discerning what God is doing and saying in that context, and speaking and working for needed change. In short, it is prophetic contextualization.[31]

In spite of the significant opposition, criticism, and rejection, the men and women identified as innovators in my research have endured; they continue to "live prophetically," calling others to join together in making Jesus known and living out that faith in partnership with what Creator is doing.

Apostles Paul and John took innovative risks and used Greek terminology when sharing the gospel with members of the Hellenistic society. "Terms like 'mystery' (mystērion), 'transformation' (metamorphōsis), or 'word' (logos) had long-standing associations with Greek religion and philosophy; they carried the potential of being confused with their pagan meanings." Paul redefines mystery to refer not only to Creator's eschatological plan of salvation, but even to Christ himself. In describing Paul's boldness and courage to contextualize the Gospel to all he met, Flemming notes how he "co-opt[ed] the language of Hellenistic religious philosophy (especially from Stoicism) that would resonate with gentile readers." Paul

TO REFORM OR DO A CHURCH PLANT?

One of the biggest challenges is whether or not these contextualization practices will be accepted by pastors and leaders living and
working on reservations—thus far there has been great reluctance.
In many cases they are not only opposed, but actively engaged in
preventing any contextualization efforts from being accepted.
They have presented critical messages from their pulpits, dissemi-
nated erroneous representations and withdrawn fellowship. This
being the case, then, a major consideration is whether or not these
contextualization efforts will serve to help reform existing churches
(if possible), or whether an entirely new church planting movement
is necessary.

declares that Creator's "eternal power" and "divine nature" are visible to
all people through Creator's creation, giving them a genuine knowledge
of the Creator (Romans 1:19-20).[32]

As I reflect on the experiences of the people involved, it becomes
clear this contextualization of the gospel began largely as an evangelistic enterprise. Questions were asked about how the gospel could be
more effectively communicated to a nonbelieving Native person, community or audience. Thus, contextualization was seen as a means to an
end—salvation.

In the past twenty years this evangelistic focus has become more holistic. The gospel is seen as speaking to a way of life in the present world,
rather than merely being a destination/outcome-based philosophy or
evangelistic methodology, strategy or technique:

Contextualization is also comprehensive. It must take place at
many levels: evangelism, preaching, Bible translation, hermeneutics, theologizing, discipleship, Christian ethics and social involvement, worship, church structures and leadership, and theological education among them. In short, it has to do with the
mission of the church in the broadest sense.[33]

So, while contextualization does assist in translating the unchanging truths of the gospel message—the words and teachings of Jesus—and in translating them into the cultural context of a given people, it equally demands our attention to its social and ecclesiological dimensions as well. Does contextualization address economic, political, legal, health, agricultural and other issues as well? If not, it is not contextualization!

If contextualization is going to run its course within the wider Native community, then consideration must be given to how this will influence the way local churches are started, organized and led. Should there be a recognized Indigenous church-planting community, resource center or even movement? Certainly this means reframing the conversation of church planting into more of an Indigenous context of cultural revitalization, community development, relationship building and working for issues of justice.

Indigenous communities of faith. Smalley offers a definition of an Indigenous church as "a group of believers who live out their life, including their socialized Christian activity, in the patterns of the local society, and for whom any transformation of that society comes out of their felt needs under the guidance of the Holy Spirit and the scriptures."[34] It is worth considering Smalley's point that as we discuss Indigenous church-planting movements, "it is impossible to 'found' an Indigenous church."[35] He then suggests that our American conceptions of establishing churches are heavily weighted with assumptions of church growth, values and structures:

> No, Indigenous churches cannot be founded. They can only be planted, and the mission is usually surprised at which seeds grow. Often they have the tendency to consider the seeds which do grow in any proliferation to be weeds, a nuisance, a hindrance in their carefully cultivated foreign mission garden, and all the time the carefully cultivated hothouse plants of the mission "founded" church are unable to spread roots and to derive their nurture either from the soil of their own life or from the word of God in the root confining pots of the mission organization and culture.[36]

After listening to the people I interviewed, reviewing my surveys and recollecting the dozens of Native churches I have visited and spoken in on reservations across the United States and in Canada, I would concur with Smalley. Our Native churches reflect Euro-American/Canadian cultural church values and forms almost exclusively—far more than the cultural values of the people in the communities where they were "planted." Kraft suggests that instead of this copycat model

> what is desired, then, is the kind of church that will take the Indigenous forms, adapt and employ them to serve Christian ends by fulfilling Indigenous functions, and convey them through Christian meanings to the surrounding society. When the term "Indigenous church" means this kind of church, well and good. Christians should feel that their church is an original work within their own culture . . . not as a badly-fitted import from somewhere else."[37]

That being said, however, care must be taken that traditional ways are not simply co-opted and redefined by church folks apart from input of local community members. I can recall only one reservation church, "The Carpenter's Shop," pastored by Robert and Theresa Stead on the Rosebud Sioux Reservation in South Dakota[38] that is genuinely attempting to transform their church from a traditional Pentecostal-dominant culture background to a local contextualized one. On their church property they built a small circular dance arbor as a sacred place to conduct their worship and evangelistic services during the summer months. They have held small community powwows, and they have built a sweat lodge for discipleship gatherings for new believers. These "physical" structures and ceremonies, while surface-level adaptations, do reflect a return to deeper worldview values about being, place, identity, Lakota spirituality and a local theology that is rooted in the story of "this" people. While I am sure there are probably other contextualized reservation churches, this is the only one I am aware of and have personally observed. The Steads' attempt to contextualize their church is an example of what Kraft would define as a "Dynamic Equivalence Church," that is, "As with theologizing, translation, revelation and all other products of Christianity . . . it is crucial that each new generation and culture experience the process of producing in its own cultural forms an appropriate church vehicle for the transmission of God's meanings."[39]

Bob and Theresa have endured considerable persecution for their position from other church and ministry leaders. Smalley notes that Indigenous churches are not always appreciated by ministry leaders, saying, "Missionaries often do not like the product," and "A truly Indigenous church is a source of concern and embarrassment to the mission bodies in the area."[40]

HAVE WE REACHED CRITICAL MASS?

I doubt whether critical mass has been reached for the whole of the Native Christian community. It seems at this point in time to primarily be an urban Indian phenomenon. If critical mass is to be achieved, there need to be several critical masses—perhaps as many as there are communities. There need to be critical masses for reservation tribes such as the Apache, Navajo, Lakota and Hopi. There should also be a critical mass for traditional homelands and for urban centers. All these communities interact and are in relationship with one another. Because the Native Christian community is so small, there is always interaction between people living on the reservation and those in the cities. This happens through school attendance, job availability, weddings, prolonged visits, conferences, the media, and various relational and familial ties and connections. Neither location exists in isolation from the other.

Susan Lobo and Kurt Peters, American editors of *Indians and the Urban Experience,* point to the need to dispel the notions of what real Indians are, at least concerning the places where they come from and where they live. Since at least the 1950s, real Indians live in the cities in no less a genuine way than those living on traditional homelands on the reservation. Lobo and Peters note, "The reality and vitality of continuing Indian Life is urban, rural, and everything in between. For Indian people these varied settings are interrelated in multiple ways. . . . The rigid rural/urban dichotomy is not a true expression of Indian reality, yet it has been one of the molds and barriers that has continued to shape research, writing and, to a lesser extent, creative expression."[41] This migration of Native people back and forth between their reservation communities and their urban world is a major pathway to new ideas for the Christian Native community as well.

All these things speak of the difficulties Christian Native people encounter while attempting to live out their faith in Jesus in a matrix of issues related to identity, belonging, sovereignty and cultural vitality.

SUMMARY

It is true that the early innovators in this study are mostly from an evangelical tradition. They come from nontraditional families, were not raised in reservation communities, nor do they speak their tribes' languages. However, I do not believe these contextualization innovations could have occurred any other way in light of several centuries of oppressive colonial Christian mission—and the state of the Indian church being nearly completely Eurocentric. That is, the majority of Native Americans live off the reservation, and most of the Native American Christians in this study come from urban families. Why have contextualization efforts not occurred previously? Or, if contextualization efforts were attempted, why did they not find critical mass, become the norm, or give rise to what many would consider a truly authentic Indigenous church movement?

Earlier we discussed James Treat's examination of Native interreligious dialogue and the Indian ecumenical movement in the '70s and '80s. Why did those efforts not achieve critical mass beyond their traditional borders?

One would have thought that those efforts would have caught on. They were taking place in the mainline "liberal" church denominations that people would consider culturally friendly. However, they remained bound within that community and never crossed over into the evangelical community. I remember talking to an older, well-respected Native evangelical leader about some of our early contextualization ideas and efforts and his concerns about syncretism and biblical compromise. He said to me that it had all been tried before in the mainline liberal churches, and it did not work. He said it did not work then and it will not work now, because it is syncretistic.

So, fair or not, contextualization efforts in an Indigenous context have been dismissed with charges of being syncretistic or liberal. However, the gospel is either making sense in local contexts, producing a better quality of life for the people in every sphere of their human experience, or it is not. This has nothing to do with being evangelical, conservative or liberal. Yet, this conversation has been co-opted by conservative views of syncretism held by Native Christian leaders who are compelled to resist and oppose these efforts because they think that they are not truly biblical.

DISCUSSION QUESTIONS

1. Discuss the need for multicultural leaders/interpreters.

2. The author asks, "After five hundred years of colonial assimilation, how will the gospel of Jesus be best understood in this emerging 'modern Indian culture?'" What do you think the answer is?

3. Discuss your thoughts on Twiss's view that "these stories illustrate that without an intentional breaking away from colonial Christianity, decolonization—true, realized freedom for Indigenous people and the Indigenous church—will not happen."

4. Who do you think should have the authority to define contextualization as legitimate?

5. Discuss the author's view of "prophetic contextualization."

6. Do you think there should be "a recognized Indigenous church-planting community, resource center or even movement"? How would that look?

LOOKING DOWN THE ROAD

The Future of the Native Church

This book has identified dynamic movements that reflect the tension, process of change and transition between historical missions and the emerging awareness for and diffusion of new revitalization innovations among the First Nations people of North America. Lamin Sanneh, in *Translating the Message: The Missionary Impact on Culture*, notes how the apostle Paul "came to be in radical tension with his own cultural roots, not because the roots were unsound but because the Gentile breakthrough had cast a shadow over any claims for cultural absolutism, Jewish or other."[1]

Throughout this study I have envisioned that my findings will empower future generations of Native followers of Jesus to see, like the apostle Paul:

> Through the eyes of the Gentile [Indigenous] church, Paul encountered an unsettling reality about the seriousness of Creator's irrevocable design to draw all people to the divine. The death and resurrection of Jesus had inaugurated the new age in which Paul, like Peter, discovered on a Gentile frontier that "God is no respecter of persons but that in every nation anyone who fears Him and does what is right is acceptable to Him" (Acts 10:34-35).[2]

This has certainly been my experience and that of most of those I interviewed. I sought, as suggested by Lieblich, Tuval-Mashiach and Zilber in *Narrative Research: Reading, Analysis, and Interpretation*, to explore this world of contextualization "by listening to the voices of people telling their life stories, knowing that people create stories out of the building blocks of their life histories and culture. At the same time these stories construct their lives, provide them with meanings and goals, and tie them to their culture."[3]

More than four hundred years of missions cannot be undone. The effects will linger for decades to come. We cannot go back to a point in time before the avalanche of American assimilation buried our people under the social, political, economic and spiritual fallout of the cultural bomb of colonialism.

While I have not written of how tens of thousands of Native people today gather on Sunday mornings with hearts full of love and adoration for Jesus Christ, this is surely what is happening. There are still Native congregations that will continue to love singing their old Southern gospel, country-western hymnbook songs, or more contemporary music at Sunday services. As Christians they will see no problem with disassociating themselves from their "un-Christian" traditional cultural ways in order to be considered faithful "Bible-based" church people. This is not an unfamiliar pattern around the world—in fact in many ways it is predictable.

Yet, this has to be okay for me at some level, if I am going to love my neighbor and not be perpetually disappointed or judgmental of their experience. There are untold numbers of Native people in those churches who would testify to how Jesus genuinely saved them from enslavement to alcohol, violence, or drug abuse, and set them free to be better human beings. That being said, it is a kind of Christianity that is waning, but will nonetheless still outlive me. The hope for *this* project is that it will encourage and empower the next generations of Native followers of Jesus who are growing disillusioned with that old wineskin.

The social context in which this contextualization is taking place is a continuum of assimilation. It ranges from the full-blooded traditionalist living on a reservation and speaking his or her mother tongue to the comfortable, fully assimilated urban or rural Indian. It is an *ever-changing* continuum. There must be a place of inclusion for all believers to live out their faith in a way that brings them meaning. Some urban Christian gatherings formed by pan-Indian groups of believers disillusioned with the dominant-culture church are very much a hybridized blend of music, traditions and ceremony.

One such group is from the Florida Conference on Native American Ministry of the United Methodist Church. They have fully embraced a contextualized approach to worship, outreach, and community building as their normative style of worship. Leaders and members represent several different tribes, and they each bring their unique ways into their worship circle. In addition, they participate in traditional ceremonial gatherings from each tribe represented in the group. As they move forward in relationship, they are literally inventing their own church expressions as informed by their respective tribal traditions. Their need for a contextualized approach to worship has led to the adoption of earlier innovations for worshiping inspired by the innovators. Rogers says, "Reinvention occurs at the implementation stage of the innovation-decision process."[4]

In Portland, Oregon, there are some thirty-eight thousand urban Native people. There are three Native churches with a combined-average Sunday attendance of perhaps twenty-five to seventy-five. There are considerably more people who feel more comfortable attending non-Native churches. This would be especially true of urban Native professionals or those who embraced Christ in a particular Christian context. That context then became their affirmation of "authentic or biblical" Christianity. After reviewing and reflecting on the many hours of interviews and written data, I have made the following observations.

CURRENT CONDITION OF THE NATIVE CHURCH

Based on the findings of my research, these are my conclusions about the current condition of the Native church:

1. Christian mission as introduced and practiced by non-Natives among Native people and communities has found very limited success (depending on the definition).

2. Contextualization is the method of the Bible and the model of mission for today, according to missiologists globally—yet not in Indian Country.

3. New contextualization innovations have emerged, mostly in urban Indian contexts, and are spreading across North America at a steady rate.

4. Contextualization is also finding acceptance on reservations and in rural Native communities among individual believers, though at a slower rate. Contextualization is not yet finding that acceptance in already-established denominational churches.

5. Innovative thinkers are emerging, and they have specific characteristics:

   • They are competent in both worlds ("150%" men and women).[5]

   • They are reaching a critical mass that creates a tipping point among the group of innovators where they inspire, encourage and support one another.

   • They are working in a colonial context, not within cultures untouched by Western culture, thus accordingly are "re-presenting" the gospel within a complex matrix of diverse tribes and cultures where people have been "burned by" and perhaps "inoculated against" the gospel.

   • Most are not directly involved or employed in a denominational system. Thus they are free to innovate without having to be concerned with ecclesiological reprimand or censure, or loss of employment, funding or positional status.

   • They would all say their contextualization efforts were inspired by a handful of courageous Native leaders who worked for many years to see these innovations accepted in their denominations or networks, but never saw them gain the acceptance they enjoy today.

Challenges facing the Native church. Additionally, there are pressing and disturbing issues facing the Native church:

1. Current evangelical leaders are still resistant to contextualization because of the fear of syncretism, liberalism, relativism or biblical compromise.

2. The existing Native denominational churches in North America are still struggling with contextualization of the gospel among their churches.

3. Several evangelical Native denominational churches have been shrinking in numbers for the past twenty years. The Church of the Nazarene, Christian and Missionary Alliance Church and the Foursquare International Church have all dissolved their Native districts.

4. Mutual dialogue is desperately needed among Native leaders in these "opposing camps."

5. Both barriers and opportunities exist for establishing worshiping Indigenous churches within the local contexts of Native urban, rural and reservation communities.

6. Denominational non-Native missionaries and pastors who oppose contextualization still lead large numbers of Native churches.

7. Missions to Native people are still bound by a benefactor/beneficiary paradigm where Native people are typified as desperately in need of rescuing.

8. Because of their irrelevance to Native culture and because of the attraction to contemporary urban hip-hop "youth culture," Native churches are losing their youth.

9. One of my serious concerns with contextualization endeavors lies in the fact that there are now late adopters who, later in life, "discovered" their Native heritage and have primarily learned about their culture via literature or apart from tribal community. As a result of the manner in which they have "come into" their cultural experience, I have seen it negatively affect the "cultural integrity" or "cultural authenticity" of their contextualization efforts.

10. This raises an even more serious question about who is qualified to contextualize a particular tribal ceremony or cultural expression if

- A person is not from that tribe.

- They have not been raised in that particular tradition with "proper" instruction by a qualified teacher.

- A person is not connected with their community or with a person from the tribe from which this particular expression originates.

- They are not being mentored to perform this particular expression in a way that people in the traditional community would "mostly" approve.

Beyond these concerns for our North American Native community, I think a legitimate reflection of what contextualization means suggests we stop using the term *contextualization movement* to describe what we are attempting to do. It is our desire to simply tell Jesus' story in a way that fits into the simple narrative framework of a sacred story. At some level, notions of "doing contextualization" seem to only reinforce the constructs of a paradigmatic process that underlies the old paternalism. While "contextualization" might be a handy adjective or descriptor, I do not want the people on my reservation reading somewhere that I am working contextually among them (a real concern I have with the future publication of this manuscript) when I am back home. Over the past twenty years—as I have read about, observed, taught, practiced and now researched "contextualization" as a missiological innovation—I am compelled to use the term less and less to describe what we are doing. For me, it does not adequately capture a cultural sense of gospel telling that must occur for the story of Jesus to take root in the *soil and soul* of our Indigenous people.

Advancing Decolonizing Contextualization Efforts in the Native Church

As the issue of "way of doing story" has gained wider national interest in the church, non-Native scholars have been writing about it. Dr. J. L. Corky Alexander Jr. finished his doctor of missiology degree at Fuller

LEADERS ADVANCING DECOLONIZING
CONTEXTUALIZATION EFFORTS

Though I am growing discontented with the word *contextualization*, the purpose of completing my exploration of this new "way of doing story" among North American First Nations people is to contribute to the body of available literature that tells its story from the standpoint of an insider—and especially from a position of affirmation and advocacy. This book will contribute significantly to the dialogue surrounding decolonizing contextualization efforts between Native and non-Native leaders concerned about the legitimacy of the innovations identified. I am deeply grateful to report that several dissertations and theses written by my Native friends and colleagues at Asbury Theological Seminary and other theological institutions are completed or nearly finished as of this writing:

- Dr. Randy Woodley (Keetoowah descendant), Asbury Theological Seminary, PhD dissertation titled *The Harmony Way: Integrating Indigenous Values Within Native North American Theology and Mission* (2010).

- Dr. Terry LeBlanc (Mi'kmaq/Acadian), Asbury Theological Seminary, PhD dissertation titled *Mi'kmaq and French/Jesuit Understandings of the Spiritual and Spirituality: Implications for Faith* (2012).

- Dr. Cheryl Bear (Nadleh Whut'en First Nation), The King's University, DMin dissertation titled *Introduction to First Nations Ministry* (2009).

- Rev. Casey Church (Pokagon Band Potawatomi), Fuller Theological Seminary, MA thesis titled *Paradigm Shift: Understanding Transition and Change in the Native American Contextual Ministry Movement* (2006).

- Dr. Ray Aldred (Cree), Brunel University, supervised by the London School of Theology, working on his ThD dissertation titled *An Alternative Starting Place for an Aboriginal Theology* (2012).

- Dr. Wendy Peterson (Red River Métis), Asbury Theological Seminary, PhD dissertation titled *A Gifting of Braided Sweetgrass: An Analysis of Reindigenization, Retraditionalization, and the Reclamation Movement Amongst Indigenous Jesus-Followers* (2012).

Theological Seminary. His dissertation is titled *Inter-Tribal Pentecost: Praxis Transformation in Native American Worship* (2010). Thomas Eric Bates is finishing a PhD dissertation, *An Ethno History of Pentecostalism on the Blackfeet Reservation in Montana*, that incorporates theoretical aspects of Native American identity and critical contextualization. Dr. Cori Wiseman completed her doctor of missiology dissertation at Asbury Theological Seminary titled *Crossing the Great Divide: The Use of Sacred Traditional Native Symbols, Ceremony, and Ritual in Worship*.

In addition, this study will add to the broader church's awareness of innovative missiological paradigms emerging from the Native Christian community as viable biblical alternatives to existing models within the dominant-culture church. While admitting my bias and thus implicating my personal narrative in the beginning of this research, I sought to be both critical and appreciative and to combine historical analysis and contemporary field research as a participant/observer of these efforts. I obviously have a point of view and a fifteen-year-old network of relationships that influence the way I hear, read and interpret the stories.

Reshaping missions attitudes and practices. This study, as a careful analysis of these "ways of doing story" initiatives, represents the possibility of reshaping missionary attitudes and introducing effective, new Indigenous paradigms of following the ways of Jesus. My hope is that these findings will encourage other Indigenous contextual movements and communities in other parts of the world, something that would be of great significance.

As this new wave of Native scholars begins teaching and writing and contributing to the North American church's understanding of Scripture and the kingdom of Creator, we move from the margins of Christendom into the heart of our Creator's redemptive work among the nations. This new location for Indigenous self-theologizing will have an empowering effect for "ways of doing story" in the future, particularly for younger leaders.

Long-term implications. These new possibilities are especially encouraging in light of the devastating problems rampant in our Native communities today. After reflecting on the data, I am suggesting several possible long-term implications or outcomes these efforts will have in the future. They will reshape gospel telling and community transformation among First Nations people in North America:

1. Locating an ad hoc, working definition for contextualization will be helpful—something like "ways of doing story" that helps explain what a North American Indigenous church/gathering is at this point in mission and colonial history.

2. A formalized network, coalition or association will be created for recognizing ministry leaders, training ministry leaders, leveraging resources, and creating its own place in the body of Christ as a valued coequal member.

3. For the gospel to make sense in "real life" practical terms, Native leaders must be actively engaged in social justice issues in their respective communities.

4. A crucial, historical body of theological literature produced by Native scholars will contribute to American theological educational efforts.

5. This North American Native network will coalesce with other Indigenous efforts (networks) globally for significant theological reflection and development of Indigenous models of ministry.

6. Native leaders will find a greater voice, recognition and regard nationally and internationally.

7. A generation of young Indigenous leaders will be inspired, equipped and mentored by these innovators to creatively implement these innovations at a deeper, more localized level.

A critically important area for further research—which will help evaluate the effectiveness of various First Nations movements—is the criteria for how Native people are counted as Christians across Indian Country. Over the years I have heard people frequently state that only 3 to 5 percent of Native people are saved, born-again or "truly converted" and considered Christians. After my research, I seriously doubt the accuracy of these figures.

That being said, in 2011 my friend Vincent Yellow Old Woman (Siksika)

wrote to tell me that his reserve, Siksika in Alberta, Canada, has a population of 6,500, with about 300 Christians, which works out to 4.6 percent
of the population. Again, in Portland, Oregon there are some 38,000
Native people with two Native churches in the metro area as of this
writing. Their combined average Sunday attendance of approximately 75
worshipers equates to less than 1 percent.

My conclusion is that these percentages are based almost entirely on
church attendance on Sunday morning. In a typical Native community
of say, 1,000 people, if there are 50 believers sitting in the pews of the
eight churches on a particular reservation on Sunday morning, then
the conclusion is drawn that 5 percent of the people on the reservations
are Christians.

My strong hunch is that there is a considerably larger percentage of
Native people who would identify themselves as followers of Jesus. They
might regularly participate in powwows and other ceremonial gatherings,
but never attend a local Christian church for a variety of reasons. Problem-
atically, if they participate in cultural gatherings, as has often been the case,
they do not feel welcomed by the evangelical Christians in church on
Sundays. In the near future I hope to find funding to do research for a book
to answer the question, How many Native people would consider themselves followers of Jesus, but not necessarily "Christians" or "church
people"? Whether we like it or not, the fact remains that the Christian faith
is inextricably woven into the fabric of our Indigenous story.

As I stated earlier, stories are the heart of this book. They are the foundation and cultural lens that help make sense of my theological and
missiological reflections. Atkinson claims that "telling a story can be an
act of transcending the personal and entering the realm of the sacred.
Life stories portray religion and spirituality as a lived experience." He
then describes what I consider my role as researcher to be: "To respond
empathically to another's experience by understanding it in the teller's
own terms and then asking of the story specific questions, such as what
beliefs or worldviews are expressed in the story?" He identifies a critically important question that is also central to my research: "In what
ways does community play a role in the life lived deeply?"[6]

Stories that bear witness. The following stories will serve to summarize the heart and intent of this undertaking. They will help us to understand how the Holy Spirit is introducing new ideas of being both Native and "Christian" while walking with Jesus. I will conclude this study by returning to the *power of story* to reflect on the past—while pointing to future changes and trajectories in Native ministry.

Glen's story is typical of many Native believers. Glen is enrolled in his tribe, grew up attending his tribe's annual Sun Dance ceremony every year, and was raised in a traditional Native American Church (NAC), which he attended every weekend until he left home. His wife, Lea, is Caucasian and was raised in a Baptist church, baptized at age eleven, embraced Jesus and was brought up with a sense of right from wrong.

When asked how they got involved with Wiconi International's Living Waters Powwow and Family Camp, Glen responded that he had heard of Wiconi and started researching it on the Internet. He then decided to attend the one-day powwow. He liked what he experienced in 2008 and the next year attended all three days later saying, "It looks like the beginning of a good friendship." Lea reported that she did not come from a Native American background and was not raised around any traditional Native ways like her husband. She said that she'd had a lot of misunderstandings about Native ways, and the fact that she was brought up in a traditional Baptist church made their "intercultural marriage" at times difficult. She said that what was so profound about their experience at the Living Waters Family Camp is that they could both "worship in a traditional style and in a way that honors our cultures and that brings together both of our backgrounds . . . the merging of our two cultures."

In contextual gatherings such as these—though specifically organized for the Native person—non-Native believers find themselves equally encouraged and strengthened spiritually. Old fears are dispelled and new understandings open their hearts to the life of Jesus in ways previously rejected. These gatherings result in all people experiencing a revitalized sense of faith and worship because of the crosscultural influences of those involved.

Casey Church (Pokagon Band Potawatomi) told me how in 1995 he and his wife, Lora (Diné/Navajo), started a "house church" in Grand Rapids, Michigan, to incorporate some new ideas they had about Native American Christian worship. In this house church they began a service by cleansing their home and each other by burning sage and fanning it over themselves. He said, "We sang drum songs in our worship and prayed in our Native languages." In the summer of 1996, they joined with a group in Grand Rapids to start a new style of Native American worship service called All Tribes Gathering. Casey said, "We designed the service to reflect our Indigenous cultural religious expression into our new Christian worship service." Attendance in their new congregation was about fifty, with three quarters of the group being Native American. All of those attending felt comfortable in this new service. At All Tribes they also incorporated the use of burning sage (called smudging), fanning the smoke with an eagle-feather fan. They continued to explore using other aspects of Native American culture in their Christian worship service. Casey continued, "Over the years I was taught the use of the pipe and the sweat lodge ceremonies by Rev. Jim McKinney, a Prairie Band Potawatomi." Jim was the leader of a Gourd Society, a Northern Traditional dancer, and an ordained elder in the United Methodist Church serving in Kansas. Casey described his relationship with Rev. McKinney:

> With his spiritual guidance we began to bring the pipe and sweat lodge ceremonies into "All Tribes" Christian worship in various ways. We used the pipe in wedding ceremonies to make a covenant between the couple and Creator. We used the pipe and the sprinkling of tobacco during prayer times and also during funerals where many prayers were needed. During all of these years my family and I were powwow dancers. We were asked by powwow committee members to take part in the powwow by offering opening prayers and blessings of the grounds in sunrise ceremonies and other rituals as required.

In the summer of 2000 Casey and his family relocated to Albuquerque, New Mexico. While in Albuquerque they duplicated the methods from All Tribes Gathering in a new ministry called "Soaring Eagle." In this initiative they started a drum group to sing praises to Jesus Christ in their worship services and at many other Christian events in the area, such as the day-long Praise Gathering in Santa Fe, New Mexico, held in the fall. They continued to use all of the above-mentioned cultural expressions and also began to teach these methods to other Native ministries in the Southwest.

After an extended break from Soaring Eagle due to several deaths in his family, Casey said, "We once again are in active ministry in Albuquerque. We renamed our ministry 'Thunderbird' and have continued to develop a new faith community for the Native American people by the incorporation of Native American 'contextual' theology being developed by members of the North American Institute for Indigenous Theological Studies" (NAIITS). At Thunderbird they have also incorporated Native traditional and contemporary music expressions. They continue to use their drum group when called upon for various events, both Christian and traditional. One of the major additions to their ministry is the use of the sweat lodge as one of the components of a resident alcohol treatment program, where Casey conducts a "Christian sweat lodge" during each month of the program.

Casey described to me their experience of attempting to incorporate traditional cultural beliefs and practices as part of their faith in Jesus as Native people:

> During all of these years my wife and I have also used our culturally-appropriate Christian expressions in the life of our family with our five children. We celebrated our faith in Jesus during initiation and coming-of-age ceremonies, such as the first dance, vision quest, the naming ceremony, first laugh and the puberty rites in the Navajo tradition for our daughters. All of the mentioned culturally-appropriate Native American Christian expressions of our tradition have been performed in humility and the honoring of our traditional ways, so that we do not explain in detail how we conduct these ceremonial methods. It is not appropriate in our

ways to share these sacred rituals in writing or in a classroom setting. They are meant to be taught to individuals searching for understanding in these areas.

Casey and Lora are now highly regarded as spiritual leaders throughout the Albuquerque area. Both Christian and traditional people seek them out to mentor those wanting to learn their tribal ways and ceremonies.

These geographically isolated stories represent hundreds of other similar and steadily growing numbers of stories. These stories point to a tipping point, "a contextual shift" on the horizon of Native ministry, which will radically alter how ministry is carried out in Native communities. Gladwell, again using the contagion metaphor, describes this tipping process that I have followed in the lives of innovators, their innovations and the diffusion of those innovations:

> Epidemics are a function of the people who transmit infectious agents, the infectious agent itself, and the environment in which the infectious agent is operating. And when an epidemic tips, when it is jolted out of equilibrium, it tips because something has happened, some change has occurred in one (or two or three) of those areas.[7]

As these innovators/leaders gradually met, became friends, and coalesced into a relational network over a ten-year period while doing contextual ministry in their various local contexts, their ideas became infectious. Gladwell describes the phenomenon I have observed as a social epidemic, using the term *the law of the few* to explain the process I have observed:

> Social epidemics work in exactly the same way. They are also driven by the efforts of a handful of exceptional people. . . . The Law of the Few says the answer is that one of these exceptional people found out about the trend, and through social connections and energy and enthusiasm and personality spread the word.[8]

The stories of Glen and Lea, Casey and Lora, and hundreds of others are occurring because an idea brought new understandings into their lives as Native followers of Jesus. This resulted in longed-for liberty, wholeness and a sense of Creator's affirmation as tribal/Indigenous people. These ideas were not a passing fad or novelty—they stuck. It is what Gladwell calls the "stickiness factor."[9]

> This idea of the importance of stickiness in tipping has enormous implications for the way we regard social epidemics as well. We tend to spend a lot of time thinking about how to make these messages more contagious—how to reach as many people as possible with our products or ideas. But the hard part of communication is often figuring out how to make sure a message doesn't go in one ear and out the other. Stickiness means that a message makes an impact. You can't get it out of your head. It sticks in your memory.[10]

Summary

All across the land these ideas about critical contextualization are "sticking." Not only are they not just a passing fad, they are growing exponentially. They are reaching critical mass and in the near future will "tip" to become a newly recognized, biblically legitimate and preferred way of carrying out the words and works of Jesus in First Nations/Indigenous communities in North America—and globally.

I close with some poignant remarks from my dear friend Adrian Jacobs, with whom I have walked on this road for twenty-some years:

> It is out of this seedbed of honesty, forgiveness, and humility that an Indigenous Christianity can grow—an Indigenous Christianity that seeks the peer respect of the treaty-making nature of Native people. This is a Christianity that seeks the least in its midst as having a legitimate voice. This is a Christianity that listens like a brother and fights like a warrior for the vulnerable in its midst. It is a Christianity that is not afraid to laugh at itself and at the pretensions of leadership. It is a Christianity that believes we are stronger as a group and that humbly relies on others for support and correction.
>
> The journey out of colonial abuse begins with the word "no." No, I will no longer be a peon in your game. No, my identity is not given to me by you. No, you will not think for me and tell me how I should feel.

We must embrace our history. To "do justly" we must tell our story and express all the pain of our history. You will hear our bright hopes and our painful deaths. Weep with us and sing with us. The pain will be so deep its only consolation is in our Creator. The great sin against our dignity is answered by a love that brings arrogant violence to its knees. This is the message of the blood of Jesus that speaks better things than that of Abel.[11]

DISCUSSION QUESTIONS

1. What long-term impact will these contextualization efforts have on the future of Christian missions among First Nations people in North America?

2. How can the challenges facing the Native church be overcome?

3. Propose a better word or phrase for "contextualization." Dr. Twiss mentions a new "way of doing story." What do you think he means by this?

4. Dr. Twiss describes Jesus as the first one to "do contextualization" during his life on earth. With Holy Spirit in us, how can we continue this sacred mission through our own stories?

EDITORS' ACKNOWLEDGMENTS

To our dear friend and sister Katherine Twiss: *Thank you*. We were deeply honored when you asked us to complete the work on this book after Richard's passing. We appreciate your prayers, encouragement and friendship. You allowed us full access to Richard's prior writings— we could not have done the work without your constant support.

Terry LeBlanc, Randy Woodley, Adrian Jacobs and Ray Aldred: Great job stepping up and writing a heartfelt foreword for this book.

Gary and Mary Ann Eastty of Wiconi International: Your help was invaluable.

Al Hsu, senior editor: *Thank you* for answering our many questions and providing much sound advice. We owe a debt of gratitude to you and your very helpful team at InterVarsity Press.

There are many others who helped in many ways. Be sure that we appreciate your efforts as well.

We believe it is fitting to include, on his behalf, part of the acknowledgment section from Dr. Twiss's formal dissertation. The segment follows:

I am humbled and so very deeply grateful to the Native North American men and women who shared the gift of their stories with me and allowed me to put them into words for others to read. Your stories, in fact, made it possible for me to receive a Doctoral degree.

I pray to Creator-Jesus that I can be a "pitiful human being" and trust in Creator's love and purpose for my life as I use these things in a good way for the betterment of the people and the pleasure of my *Ate Wakan Tanka*, "Father Great Spirit," in heaven.

Lila Pilamaya—"Thank you very much."

Richard Twiss, DMiss

Ray and Sue Martell

EDITORS' TRIBUTE TO RICHARD TWISS

Often, when working on this book, we would say that Richard would continue to speak through his written words. It has been a bittersweet journey, at first working together with our friend and then finishing the work after his passing.

Our feelings about our dear friend Richard Twiss are best summed up by the words of Henry Ward Beecher:

> When the sun goes below the horizon, he is not set; the heavens glow for a full hour after his departure. And when a great and good man sets, the sky of this world is luminous long after he is out of sight. Such a man cannot die out of this world. When he goes he leaves behind him much of himself. Being dead, he speaks.

Toksa ake, Richard—"See you later."
Ray and Sue Martell

APPENDIX A

Final Words on Indigenous Education and Theology

As we journey through the process of developing a Native Christian theology and an Indigenous style of theological education, we should learn from the previous generations who have gone before us in the faith—and build on the foundation they left for us.[1] There should be an ongoing conversation as we learn from others in the body of Christ, and as we observe the lessons Creator has placed in his creation.

I will compare the process of Indigenous theologizing with living systems theory, using its concept of "panarchy" as a starting point. The authors and contributors to *Panarchy: Understanding Transformations in Human and Natural Systems* each studied a large natural system such as a reef, savannah, or glacier, and they would meet periodically to compare notes.[2] C.S. Holling defines *panarchy* using the results of their research:

> "Panarchy" is the term we use to describe a concept that explains the evolving nature of complex adaptive systems. Panarchy is the hierarchical structure in which systems of nature (for example, forests, grasslands, lakes, rivers, and seas), and humans (for example, structures of governance, settlements, and cultures), as well as combined human-nature systems . . . are interlinked in never-ending adaptive cycles of growth, accumulation, restructuring, and renewal.[3]

Like a living system, theological reformation is a vital, unending reality. There is a growth process involved. For example, the sixteenth-century Protestant reformers sought freedom from religious oppression and pursued a new expression of the Christian faith. While they distanced themselves from Roman Catholicism, they nonetheless *built on what had gone before them*. While Catholicism became the *sustenance* nourishing the growth of the new reformation, it did not result in the demise of Roman Catholicism. Instead there was adaptation and improvement, and a *new* expression of Christian faith flourished. I suggest that Euro-American/Western Christianity is now becoming the *sustenance* used to cultivate and give way to new adaptations of Christian faith—inspired by Indigenous worldview perspectives—as part of the constant reemergence of Christ and the Kingdom.

In neocolonial (Western) theologizing, there is always a static hierarchy of biblical knowledge—never true collegiality or equality. Eurocentric theology presupposes superiority and condescension toward Christian theologies developed in Africa, Asia or Central and South America. Modern thought has attempted to assign theology as a "knowledge" culture over and against an Indigenous "wisdom" culture or tradition. We contend that there cannot be legitimate theologies developed without the collaboration of east/west, north/south and modern/postmodern or from the absence of the views originating within the Indigenous world.

Indigenous theologizing remains largely outside the confines of Western modernity and thus maintains its embrace of mystery and spirituality. It is free to flourish outside the reductionism of Western dualism and the rigidity of Western systemization of theology as science. Indigenous theology as a system of thought is experienced as fluid, organic, always developing and never static—always in tension between the divine and human—without the need for "absolutes."

Indigenous theologizing is undergoing a process of maturation. Today, many innovations exist that were not part of our theological landscape twenty-five years ago or before. We contend that the Protestant Reformation must *continue reforming*. The Reformation did not become fixed, static, or conclude with the death of Luther, Calvin, Wesley and so many others in the 1600s.

We *do not* feel compelled to separate ourselves from what has gone before, but instead to learn from our "mothers and fathers" because we are integrally connected to them within the stream of ever-evolving Christian thought. Ambiguity founded in the surety of Creator's revealed presence and providence—whether located in literate or oral knowledge traditions—serves as a basis for an Indigenous systematic theology. Unlike Western systems grounded in modernity and epistemological surety, our systems function as organic, relational, *living* systems— shared bodies of knowledge held in community.

When we see our organizations, institutions, projects and even our conversations as living systems, we gain new understanding as to what brings *life* to the system and where to intervene when there is a lack of vitality. Theologizing is a living relational system; it is a communal enterprise. I want to suggest that if we view theology as a living conversation—the intersection of human and divine exchange, an invitation to community, or a dialogic connecting point in creation between heaven and earth—we begin to rescue Western theology from rational enterprise and hegemony and set into motion a free-form, organic conversation between Creator and human and non-human creation.

This invitation to dialogue frees us from the perceived need to protect God from the assault of heresy, and therefore become defenders of "truth" on "God's side" against those whose theology threatens Western control. The Indigenous dialogic framework becomes a house, wherein participants gather *in the presence of* and *with* the Creator of heaven and earth— out of which is birthed a new vitality and communion.

In the traditional Indigenous "seven-generation continuum," we learn from the *previous* three generations, who then inform our *current* generation to help us prepare the way for the *next* three generations.

May this be good tobacco to put into your pipe to smoke and share with friends and see what new smoke rings you create together as a "community of enquirers"!

Hohecetuwe yelo,
"And that's all I have to say—that's the way it is."

APPENDIX B

What Should We Call You?

W hat is the acceptable name for "North American tribal people?" In contemporary writings by Native authors, there is no preferred name used when referring to the tribal people of North America. Native American, Native North American, Native, Indian, American Indian, First Nations, Indigenous People, Aboriginal, Alaska Native, Eskimo and Host People are the most commonly used.

Indian, American Indian, Native and Native American. Critical thinkers like James B. LaGrand, Vine Deloria Jr., George Tinker and a host of other prolific writers use these various names interchangeably in their writings and in the titles of their books: for example, *Indian Metropolis: Native Americans in Chicago; Native American Spirituality: The Past and Future of American Indian Sovereignty;* and *God is Red: A Native View of Religion.*[1] In keeping with current literature I use all of these names interchangeably, but primarily use Native, Native American and First Nations. Among innumerable Native-focused organizations, the range of names used is wide and varied.

The NCAI was founded in 1944 in response to termination and assimilation policies that the United States forced upon the tribal governments in contradiction of their treaty rights and status as sovereigns. NCAI stressed the need for unity and cooperation among tribal governments for the protection of their treaty and sovereign rights. Since 1944, the National Congress of American

Indians has been working to inform the public and Congress of the governmental rights of American Indians and Alaska Natives.[2]

First Nations. The name "First Nations" was first used among Canada's Native population but has become widely used among all Native peoples in North America especially, but in other parts of the world as well. The following book titles use "First Nations": *A Concise History of Canada's First Nations* by Olive Patricia Dickason and Moira Jean Calder; and *Benjamin Franklin, Pennsylvania, and the First Nations: The Treaties of 1736–62* by Susan Kalter.[3] The Assembly of First Nations (AFN) is a national advocacy organization representing First Nation citizens in Canada. Their role includes "facilitation and coordination of national and regional discussions and dialogue, advocacy efforts and campaigns, legal and policy analysis," and "communicating with governments." First Nations peoples are identified in the Canadian Constitution as one of the founding nations of Canada, along with England and France.[4]

Aboriginal. In Canada, the term *Aboriginal* is also widely used, but rarely in the United States. The following titles are examples of this usage: *Aboriginal Health in Canada: Historical, Cultural, and Epidemiological Perspectives* by James B. Waldram, D. Ann Herring and T. Kue Young; *Justice for Canada's Aboriginal Peoples* by Renée Dupuis and Robert Chodos; and *The Dawn of Canadian History: A Chronicle of Aboriginal Canada* by Stephen Leacock.[5] The Evangelical Fellowship of Canada established an Aboriginal Ministries Council to help "[bring] together Aboriginal Christian leaders from various Aboriginal communities across Canada. The Council act[s] as a bridge between the Aboriginal and non-Aboriginal Church, seeking to provide resources that will enhance communications and enrich the Church as a whole."[6]

Métis/Metis of Canada—"Half-Breeds." According to Wendy Beauchemin Peterson (PhD—ABD), a Red River Métis, the legal term used by the British and Canadian Governments for the offspring of mixed marriages between First Nations people and the early fur traders, colonists and settlers was "half-breed," as evidenced in five Beauchemin family land scripts from the 1870s (for example, one signed by Jean Baptiste Beauchemin on August 18, 1875 wherein he declares "I am a Half-breed head of a family").[7] Eventually the self-designation of Métis was officially accepted. Current literature includes *The Western Métis: Profile of a People*, edited by Patrick Douaud; D. N. Sprague's and R. P. Frye's *Genealogy of the First Métis Nation*; and John Weinstein's *Quiet Revolution West: The Rebirth of Métis Nationalism*.[8] Increasingly, scholars are replacing the Francophone form with the Anglicized "Metis" to refer to "mixed blood" people who are not direct descendants of the Red River Métis (the Red River designation is associated with the present city of Winnipeg, Manitoba, and its environs).

Eskimo—Inuit/Yupik/Inupiat. The term *Eskimo* has been the common universal name used by people in the United States and Canada to identify Yupik, Inuit and Inupiat peoples. Inuit are culturally similar to the other Indigenous peoples who inhabit the arctic regions of Greenland, Canada and the United States. Two of many book titles using these names are *Critical Inuit Studies: An Anthology of Contemporary Arctic Ethnography* by Pamela Stern and Lisa Stevenson (editors) and *The Eskimo: The Inuit and Yupik People* by Alice Osinski.[9]

Indigenous. "Indigenous" is another name commonly used in North America and around the world. These book titles reflect its usage: *The Native Americans: The Indigenous People of North America* by Colin F. Taylor; *Perversions of Justice: Indigenous Peoples and Anglo-American Law* by Ward Churchill; and *"Real" Indians and Others: Mixed-Blood Urban Native Peoples and Indigenous Nationhood* by Bonita Lawrence. The World Christian Gathering of Indigenous People was established in 1996 to address issues of relevance to Native peoples from a biblical perspective.[10]

Indian Country. Another frequently used phrase to speak of the national Native scene is "Indian Country." *Indian Country Today* is the name of the largest Native-owned and operated weekly periodical in the United States. There are numerous books with this phrase in the title. It is a term commonly used by Native folks to reference the universal struggles, cultural dynamics and serious issues faced by all Native people today.

GLOSSARY

Acculturation. The deliberate modification of culture that stripped Native people of their language, culture and customs.

Aggressive realism. The Anglo-European idea that nature, no matter how mysterious, grand or impossible, could and should be conquered for the good of humanity.

Contextualization. The process of framing the gospel message culturally as either a sacred story or a myth of divine proportions so that it makes sense to people "on the ground" where they live every day.

Counteractive syncretism. The blending or mixing of different core religious beliefs, which ultimately diminishes, fully resists or finally stops—"counteracts"—one's personal faith journey as a follower of Jesus and his ways.

Diffusion. Any process through which ideas spread.

Epistemology. The study of how we learn.

Eschatology. The study of the "end times" as described in the Christian Scriptures.

Ethnocentrism. The belief in the superiority of your own group (for example, nationality, race or creed).

Exegesis. The interpretation of text.

Hegemony. Authority or dominance over others.

Hermeneutics. The study of how to interpret texts, such as the Christian Scriptures.

Hymnody. A collection of hymns belonging to a certain group or culture.

Indian Country. A frequently used phrase referring to the Native scene in the United States and Canada.

Indigenization. A process by which local Indigenous members and leaders move away from Euro-American cultural expectations and begin defining faith within their spiritual and cosmic world.

Indigenous. Originating in a particular region.

Liminality. The state of being in-between or in transition.

Manifest Destiny. America's perceived "divine right," used to justify expansionism.

Missiology. The study of the church's mission history and activity.

Modernism. The idea that individuals can and should subdue nature using modern technology derived from scientific research.

Neocolonialism. Colonial attitudes and influence carried into modern times by some of today's modern Christian believers.

Pan-Indianism. A movement encouraging unity among Native Americans regardless of tribal origin or residential location.

Paternalism. A systemic attitude in which people are perpetually treated as children by those in authority.

Pedagogy. The profession or science of teaching.

Prophetic contextualization. Making Jesus known and living out that faith in partnership with what Creator is doing (contextualization by seeking and following Creator's leading).

Retraditionalization. A self-determined return to traditional Indigenous beliefs and practices.

Revolutionary paradigm. An innovative pattern; a breakthrough.

Smudging. A Native American purification ritual using smoke from the burning of sacred plants such as sage or sweet grass.

Sweat lodge. A dome-shaped structure used by some Native American tribes as a sacred place of divine encounter with the Creator.

Syncretism. A theological term that carries the idea of mixing religious beliefs together.

Tipping point. The point at which change is inevitable.

ABBREVIATIONS

AIM	American Indian Movement
BIA	Bureau of Indian Affairs
C&MA	Christian and Missionary Alliance (church)
CC & K	Christ, Culture and Kingdom Seminar
FNM	First Nations Monday
IBS	International Bible Society
IVCF	InterVarsity Christian Fellowship
MN1V	Many Nations One Voice celebrations
NAIITS	North American Institute for Indigenous Theological Studies (now referred to as NAIITS: an Indigenous Learning Community)
NANCC	North American Native Christian Council
NAMMY	Native American Music Award Association (the award itself)
NAYA	Native American Youth and Family Association, Portland, Oregon
NCAI	National Congress of American Indians
PK	Promise Keepers
TBN	Trinity Broadcasting Network
WCGIP	World Christian Gathering of Indigenous People
YWAM	Youth With a Mission

NOTES

CHAPTER 1: THE CREATOR'S PRESENCE AMONG NATIVE PEOPLE

[1]See Ps 131:2; Lk 13:34.

[2]See Ps 139:15; Rom 8:22; 1 Cor 15:47-49.

[3]Zeb Bradford Long and Douglas McMurry, *The Collapse of the Brass Heaven: Rebuilding Our Worldview to Embrace the Power of God* (Grand Rapids: Chosen Books, 1994), pp. 209-10.

[4]Ibid.

[5]Ibid.

[6]Washington Irving, "The Adventures of Captain Bonneville," in *Three Western Narratives* (New York: Literary Classics of the United States, 2004), p. 697.

[7]For a more detailed description of the events in this section, please refer to my previous book, *One Church, Many Tribes: Following Jesus the Way God Made You* (Ventura, CA: Regal Books, 2000).

[8]George G. Hunter III, *The Celtic Way of Evangelism: How Christianity Can Reach the West—Again* (Nashville, TN: Abingdon Press, 2000), pp. 40-44.

[9]"Winnipeg Church Nixes Native Dancing at Habitat for Humanity Event," CBC News, November 8, 2007, www.cbc.ca/news/canada/manitoba/winnipeg-church -nixes-native-dancing-at-habitat-for-humanity-event-1.690918.

[10]Evelyn Nieves, "Indian Reservation Reeling in Wave of Youth Suicides and Attempts," *New York Times* (June 9, 2007).

[11]David Wallace Adams, *Education for Extinction: American Indians and the Boarding School Experience, 1875–1928* (Lawrence, KS: University of Kansas Press, 1995).

[12]Francis Paul Prucha, *Documents of United States Indian Policy* (Lincoln, NE: University of Nebraska Press, 1990), pp. 141, 142, 242.

[13]G. E. Tinker, *Missionary Conquest: The Gospel and Native American Cultural Genocide* (Minneapolis: Fortress, 1993); George E. Tinker, *Spirit and Resistance: Political Theology and American Indian Liberation* (Minneapolis: Fortress, 2003); George E. Tinker, *American Indian Liberation: A Theology of Sovereignty* (Maryknoll, NY: Orbis Books, 2008); Philip Jenkins, *The Next Christendom: The Coming of Global Christianity* (New York: Oxford University Press, 2002); Philip Jenkins, *Dream Catchers: How Mainstream America Discovered Native Spirituality* (New York: Oxford University Press, 2004); Paul G. Hiebert, *Anthropological Insights for Missionaries* (Grand Rapids: Baker Books, 1987); Paul G. Hiebert, *Anthropological Reflections on Missiological Issues* (Grand Rapids: Baker Academic, 1994);

Paul G. Hiebert and Eloise Hiebert Meneses, *Incarnational Ministry: Planting Churches in Band, Tribal, Peasant and Urban Societies* (1995; repr., Grand Rapids: Baker Books, 1999); Paul G. Hiebert, Daniel Shaw, and Tite Tiénou, *Understanding Folk Religion: A Christian Response to Popular Beliefs and Practices* (Grand Rapids: Baker Books, 1999); and James Treat, *Around the Sacred Fire: Native Religious Activism in the Red Power Era: A Narrative Map of the Indian Ecumenical Conference* (New York: Palgrave Macmillan, 2003).

[14]Everett M. Rogers, *Diffusion of Innovations* (New York: Free Press, 2003).

[15]Craig Stephen Smith, *Boundary Lines: The Issue of Christ, Indigenous Worship, and Native American Culture* (Prince Albert, SK: Northern Canada Mission Distributors, 2000), a study commissioned by the Native American Association of the Christian and Missionary Alliance (2000); Nanci Des Gerlaise, *Muddy Waters: An Insider's View of North American Native Spirituality* (Eureka, MT: Lighthouse Trails, 2012); and CHIEF Ministries, Inc.

[16]Smith, *Boundary Lines* (2000); G. E. E. Lindquist, *The Red Man in the United States* (Clifton, NJ: A. M. Kelley, 1973); LeRoy Koopman, *Taking the Jesus Road: The Ministry of the Reformed Church in America Among Native Americans* (Grand Rapids: Eerdmans, 2005); Bonnie Sue Lewis, *Creating Christian Indians: Native Clergy in the Presbyterian Church* (Norman, OK: University of Oklahoma Press, 2003); and Homer Noley, *First White Frost: Native Americans and United Methodism* (Nashville, TN: Abingdon Press, 1991).

[17]Hilary Wyss, *Captivity and Christianity: Narrating Christian Indian Identity 1643-1829* (Capitol Hill, NC: University of North Carolina, 1998); Albert Borgmann, *Crossing the Postmodern Divide* (Chicago: University of Chicago Press, 1992); Ngũgĩ wa Thiong'o, *Decolonizing the Mind: The Politics of Language in African Literature* (Oxford, England: James Currey, 2009); Anders Stephanson, *Manifest Destiny: American Expansionism and the Empire of Right* (New York: Hill and Wang, 1995); and Jean Comaroff and John L. Comaroff, *Of Revelation and Revolution: Christianity, Colonialism, and Consciousness in South Africa* (Chicago: University of Chicago Press, 1991).

[18]Carl F. Starkloff, *A Theology of the In-Between: The Value of Syncretic Process* (Milwaukee, WI: Marquette University Press, 2002), p. 12.

[19]From a conversation with Dr. Twiss's friend, Harold Roscher.

[20]Peter van der Veer, "Syncretism, Multiculturalism and the Discourse of Tolerance," in *Syncretism/Anti-Syncretism: The Politics of Religious Synthesis*, ed. Charles Stewart and Rosiland Shaw (London, New York: Routledge, 1994), pp. 196-97.

[21]Christian Hope Indian Eskimo Fellowship (CHIEF), *A Biblical Position by Native Leaders on Native Spirituality*, April 2, 1998, p. 2.

[22]Smith, *Boundary Lines*, p. 1.

[23]van der Veer, "Syncretism," p. 196.

[24]Charles H. Kraft, *Anthropology for Christian Witness* (Maryknoll, NY: Orbis Books, 1996), p. 376.

[25]Ray Aldred, BTh, MDiv, PhD (cand.), is a NAIITS board member and assistant professor of theology at Ambrose University and Seminary, Calgary, Alberta, Canada, among other distinctions.

[26]Dean S. Gilliland, *The Word Among Us: Contextualizing Theology for Mission Today* (Dallas: Word Publishing, 1989), p. 13.

[27]Brian McLaren, *A New Kind of Christianity: Ten Questions That Are Transforming the Faith* (San Francisco: HarperOne, 2010), pp. 33-45.

[28]Charles H. Kraft, "Culture, Communication and Christianity" in *Readings in Missionary Anthropology II*, ed. William A. Smalley (1978; repr., Pasadena, CA: William Carey Library, 1986), pp. 490-491.

[29]Andrew F. Walls, *The Missionary Movement in Christian History: Studies in the Transmission of Faith* (Maryknoll, NY: Orbis Books, September 2004), pp. 223, 234-235.

[30]Lesslie Newbigin, *Foolishness to the Greeks: The Gospel and Western Culture* (London: SPCK, 1986), p. 4.

[31]William Reyburn, "The Missionary and Cultural Diffusion," in *Readings in Missionary Anthropology II*, ed. William A. Smalley (1978; repr., Pasadena, CA: William Carey Library, 1986), p. 510.

[32]Ibid., p. 513.

[33]Ibid., p. 515.

[34]Ibid., p. 518.

[35]Dale Kietzman and William A. Smalley, "The Missionary Role in Culture Change," in *Readings in Missionary Anthropology II*, ed. William A. Smalley (1978; repr., Pasadena, CA: William Carey Library, 1986), p. 524.

[36]Newbigin, *Foolishness to the Greeks*; Soong-Chan Rah, *The Next Evangelicalism: Releasing the Church from Western Cultural Captivity* (Downers Grove, IL: InterVarsity Press, 2009).

[37]Jim Chosa and Faith Chosa, *Thy Kingdom Come Thy Will Be Done In Earth: A First Nations Perspective on Strategic Keys for Territorial Deliverance and Transformation* (Yellowstone, MT: Day Chief Ministries, 2004); Smith, *Boundary Lines*; and Nanci Des Gerlaise, *Muddy Waters*.

[38]Rogers, *Diffusion of Innovations*, p. 12.

[39]Ibid., p. 35.

[40]Malcolm Gladwell, *The Tipping Point: How Little Things Can Make a Big Difference* (Boston: Little, Brown, 2002).

[41]Rogers, *Diffusion of Innovations*, p. 172.

[42]Ibid., p. 180.

[43]Ibid., p. 255.

[44]Tinker, *Missionary Conquest*, p. 118.

[45]Rogers, *Diffusion of Innovations*, p. 178.

[46]Ibid., pp. 369-370.

[47]Ibid., p. 49.

[48]Ibid.

[49]Dean Flemming, *Contextualization in the New Testament: Patterns for Theology and Mission* (Downers Grove, IL: InterVarsity Press, 2005), p. 15.

[50]Darrell L. Whiteman, "Contextualization: The Theory, The Gap, The Challenge," *International Bulletin of Missionary Research*, January 1997, p. 2.

[51]Ibid., pp. 2-4.

[52]Hiebert, *Anthropological Insights*, p. 108.

[53]Hiebert, *Anthropological Reflections*, p. 92.

[54]Hiebert, *Anthropological Insights*, p. 186.

[55]Hiebert, Shaw, and Tiénou, *Understanding Folk Religion*, p. 21.

[56]Samuel Escobar, *The New Global Mission: The Gospel From Everywhere to Everyone* (Downers Grove, IL: InterVarsity Press, 2003), p. 19.

[57]Ibid., p. 12.

[58]Ibid.

[59]Hiebert, Shaw, and Tiénou, *Understanding Folk Religion*, p. 384.

[60]Hiebert and Hiebert Meneses, *Incarnational Ministry*, p. 243.

[61]Ibid., p. 244.

[62] Hiebert, Shaw, and Tiénou, *Understanding Folk Religion*, pp. 254-255.

[63]Walls, *The Missionary Movement*, pp. 175-176.

[64]David J. Bosch, *Transforming Mission: Paradigm Shifts in Theology of Mission* (Maryknoll, NY: Orbis, 1997), pp. 450-57.

[65]William A. Smalley, ed., *Readings in Missionary Anthropology II* (1978; repr., Pasadena, CA: William Carey Library, 1986), p. 363.

[66]Charles H. Kraft, *Christianity in Culture: A Study in Dynamic Biblical Theologizing in Cross-Cultural Perspective* (Maryknoll, NY: Orbis Books, 2003), p. 320.

[67]Smalley, *Readings in Missionary Anthropology II*, p. 366.

[68]Ibid.

[69]The *Polished Arrow Directory*, founded in 2000, is maintained by Dee Toney. It is published every two years, free of charge to everyone listed in the directory. The 2011 edition lists approximately one thousand Native ministries, churches and other resources; www.polishedarrow.com.

[70]Beatrice Medicine and Sue Ellen Jacobs, eds., *Learning to Be an Anthropologist and Remaining "Native": Selected Writings* (Urbana, IL: University of Illinois Press, 2001), p. xxiv.

[71]Ibid., p. 5.

[72]Ibid., p. xxiv.

[73]Donald Lee Fixico, "Ethics and Responsibilities in Writing American Indian History," in *Natives and Academics: Researching and Writing About American Indians*, ed. Devon Mihesuah (Lincoln, NE: University of Nebraska Press, 1998), pp. 85-92.

[74]Ibid., p. 91.

[75]Karen Gayton Swisher, "Why Indian People Should Be the Ones to Write About Indian Education," in *Natives and Academics: Researching and Writing About American Indians*, ed. Devon Mihesuah (Lincoln, NE: University of Nebraska Press, 1998), p. 190.

[76]Linda Tuhiwai Smith, *Decolonizing Methodologies—Research and Indigenous People* (London: Zed Books, 1999), p. 1.

[77]Ibid.

[78]Ibid., p. 15.

[79]Susan Lobo and Kurt Peters, eds., *American Indians and the Urban Experience, Contemporary Native American Communities* (Walnut Creek, CA: Altamira Press, 2001), p. xiv.

[80]Ibid.

[81]Taiaiake Alfred, *Peace, Power, Righteousness: An Indigenous Manifesto* (New York: Oxford University Press, 1999), pp. 88-89.

[82]Ibid., p. 89.

CHAPTER 2: THE COLONIZATION, EVANGELIZATION AND ASSIMILATION OF FIRST NATIONS PEOPLE

[1]Scot McKnight, *A Community Called Atonement* (Nashville, TN: Abingdon Press, 2007), p. 44.

[2]Peter d'Errico, foreword to *Pagans in the Promised Land: Decoding the Doctrine of Christian Discovery*, by Steven T. Newcomb (Golden, CO: Fulcrum, 2008), p. ix.

[3]Lamin O. Sanneh, *Whose Religion is Christianity? The Gospel Beyond the West* (Grand Rapids: Eerdmans, 2003), p. 22.

[4]Tite Tiénou , "World Christianity and Theological Reflection," in *Globalizing Theology: Belief and Practice in an Era of World Christianity*, eds. Craig Ott and Harold A. Netland (Grand Rapids: Baker Academic, 2006), p. 38.

[5]Philip Jenkins, *The Next Christendom: The Coming of Global Christianity* (New York: Oxford University Press, 2002), pp. 1-2.

[6]d'Errico, foreword to *Pagans in the Promised Land*, p. ix.

[7]A. H. Mathias Zahniser, *Symbol and Ceremony: Making Disciples Across Cultures*, Innovations in Mission (Monrovia, CA: MARC, 1997), pp. 92-93.

[8]Susan Lobo and Kurt Peters, eds., *American Indians and the Urban Experience, Contemporary Native American Communities* (Walnut Creek, CA: Altamira Press, 2001), p. 85.

[9]Ibid.

[10]Ibid.

[11]According to the 2010 US Census, 22% of those people who self-identified as Native American, Alaska Native or "multiple-race Native" lived on "Native Indian areas" (reservations, trust lands, etc.). Those living "outside Native areas" (urban and rural) amounted to 78%.

[12]Lobo and Peters, *American Indians and the Urban Experience*, p. 85.

[13]Ibid., p. 86.

[14]Ibid., p. 88.

[15]Ibid., p. xiii.

[16]Ibid., p. 76.

[17]Lomawaima and McCarty, *"To Remain an Indian": Lessons in Democracy from a Century of Native American Education* (New York: Teachers College Press, 2006); Cobb, *Native Activism in Cold War America: The Struggle for Sovereignty* (Lawrence, KS: University Press of Kansas, 2008); Wyss, *Writing Indians: Literacy Christianity and Native Community in Early America* (Amherst, MA: University of Massachusetts Press, 2000); and Yong and Brown Zikmund, eds., *Remembering Jamestown: Hard Questions About Christian Mission* (Eugene, OR: Pickwick, 2010).

[18]Philip Jenkins, *Dream Catchers: How Mainstream America Discovered Native Spirituality* (New York: Oxford University Press, 2004), p. 44.

[19]Ibid.

[20]Ibid., p. 48.

[21]Ibid., p. 47.

[22]Ibid.. p. 48

[23]Ibid., p. 74.

[24]Kristina Bross, *Dry Bones and Indian Sermons: Praying Indians in Colonial America* (Ithaca, NY: Cornell University Press, 2004), pp. 3-4.

[25]Ibid., p. 29.

[26]Ibid., p. 31.

[27]Ibid., p. 149.

[28]George E. Tinker, *Missionary Conquest: The Gospel and Native American Cultural Genocide* (Minneapolis: Fortress, 1993), p. 3.

[29]Ibid., p. 5

[30]Ibid., p. 6.

[31]Ibid.

[32]Ibid., p. 16.

[33]Ibid., p. 118.

[34]Jim Chosa and Faith Chosa, *Thy Kingdom Come Thy Will Be Done In Earth: A First Nations Perspective on Strategic Keys for Territorial Deliverance and Transformation* (Yellowstone, MT: Day Chief Ministries, 2004), appendix.

[35]Nanci Des Gerlaise, *Muddy Waters: An Insider's View of North American Native Spirituality* (Eureka, MT: Lighthouse Trails, 2012), pp. 135-36.

[36]Tinker, *Missionary Conquest*, p. 6.

[37]Wyss, *Writing Indians*, p. 92.

[38]Ibid., p. 67.

[39]Ibid., p. 70.

[40]Ibid., p. 89.

[41]Paul G. Hiebert, *Anthropological Reflections on Missiological Issues* (Grand Rapids: Baker Academic, 1994), p. 54.

[42]Ibid., 54-55.

[43]Albert Borgmann, *Crossing the Postmodern Divide* (Chicago: University of Chicago Press, 1992), pp. 40-41.

[44]Ibid., p. 22.

[45]Ibid., p. 23.

[46]Ibid., p. 25.

[47]Ibid., p. 27.

[48]Ibid., p. 35.

[49]Peter L. Berger and Thomas Luckmann, *The Social Construction of Reality: A Treatise in the Sociology of Knowledge* (Garden City, NY: Anchor Books, 1967), p. 104.

[50]Ibid., p. 105.

[51]Ibid., p. 106.

[52]Ibid., p. 107.

[53]Wyss, *Writing Indians*, p. 93.

[54]Jean Comaroff and John L. Comaroff, *Of Revelation and Revolution: Christianity, Colonialism, and Consciousness in South Africa* (Chicago: University of Chicago Press, 1991), pp. 93-95.

[55]Ibid., pp. 24-26.

[56]Ibid., p. 4.

[57]Ngũgĩ wa Thiong'o, *Decolonizing the Mind: The Politics of Language in African Literature* (Oxford, England: James Currey, 2009), p. 3.

[58]Ibid., p. 16.

[59]Comaroff and Comaroff, *Of Revelation and Revolution*, p. 26.

[60]John S. Mbiti, *African Religions and Philosophy*, rev. ed. (1989; repr., Portsmouth, NH: Heinemann, 1999), p. 212.

[61]Comaroff and Comaroff, *Of Revelation and Revolution*, pp. 244-245.

[62]Ibid., p. 309.

[63]Steven T. Newcomb, *Pagans in the Promised Land: Decoding the Doctrine of Christian Discovery* (Golden, CO: Fulcrum, 2008), p. 83.

[64]Ibid.

[65]Robert J. Miller, *Native America, Discovered and Conquered: Thomas Jefferson, Lewis and Clark and Manifest Destiny* (Lincoln, NE: University of Nebraska Press, 2008), pp. 17-18.

[66]Ibid., p. 19.

[67]Ibid.

[68]Ibid., p. 21.

[69]Ibid., p. 19.

[70]Ibid., p. 37.

[71]John O'Sullivan, "The True Title," quoted in Anders Stephanson, *Manifest Destiny: American Expansion and the Empire of Right* (New York: Hill and Wang, 1995), p. xiii.

[72]Stephanson, *Manifest Destiny*, p. xi.

[73]Miller, *Native America*, pp. 118-19.

[74]Ibid., p. 156.

[75]Stephanson, *Manifest Destiny*, p. xiv.

[76]Ibid.

[77]Ibid.

[78]Ibid., p. 6.

[79]Ibid.

[80]Ibid., p. 27.

[81]Anthony F. C. Wallace, *Jefferson and the Indians: The Tragic Fate of the First Nations* (Cambridge, MA: Belknap Press of Harvard University Press, 1999); Miller, *Native America*; Newcomb, *Pagans in the Promised Land*; and Bernd C. Peyer, *The Tutor'd Mind: Indian Missionary-Writers in Antebellum America* (Amherst, MA: University of Massachusetts Press, 1997).

[82]Newcomb, *Pagans in the Promised Land*, p. xv.

[83]Stephanson, *Manifest Destiny*, p. 8.

[84]Bross, *Dry Bones*, p. 186.

[85]Ibid., p. 187.

[86]Francis Paul Prucha, *Documents of United States Indian Policy* (Lincoln, NE: University of Nebraska Press, 1990), p. 141-42.

[87]Ibid., p. 157.

[88]Newcomb, *Pagans in the Promised Land*, p. 13.

[89]Ibid., pp. 13-14.

[90]Randy Woodley, "A View of the Native North American Contextual Movement and Its Undecided Future," *Journal of the North American Institute for Indigenous Theological Studies* 4 (2006): 103.

Chapter 3: Sweating with Jesus

[1]D. Jean Clandinin and F. Michael Connelly, *Narrative Inquiry: Experience and Story in Qualitative Research* (San Francisco: Jossey-Bass, 2000), p. 25.

[2]Elizabeth Cook-Lynn, "American Indian Intellectualism and the New Indian Story," in *Natives and Academics: Researching and Writing About American Indians*, ed. Devon A. Mihesuah (Lincoln: University of Nebraska Press, 1998), p. 111.

[3]This refers to the "Theory of Revitalization," a paper written in 1956 by Anthony F. C. Wallace, illustrating how cultures bring about change within themselves.

[4]Donald Lee Fixico, "Ethics and Responsibilities in Writing American Indian History," in *Natives and Academics: Researching and Writing About American Indians*, ed. Devon Mihesuah (Lincoln, NE: University of Nebraska Press, 1998), p. 88.

[5]Cook-Lynn, "American Indian Intellectualism," p. 111.

[6]Babacar Fall, "Orality and Life Histories: Rethinking the Social and Political History of Senegal," *Africa Today* 50, no. 2 (2003): 55.

[7]Ibid.

[8]Robert Atkinson, *The Life Story Interview* (Thousand Oaks, CA: Sage, 1998), p. v.

[9]Ibid., pp. 10-11.

[10]Ibid., p. 76.

Chapter 4: A View from the Hill

[1]Everett M. Rogers, *Diffusion of Innovations* (New York: Free Press, 1983), p. 11.

[2]Dean Flemming, *Contextualization in the New Testament: Patterns for Theology and Mission* (Downers Grove, IL: InterVarsity Press, 2005), p. 20.

[3]Ibid.

[4]Rogers, *Diffusion of Innovations*, p. 12.

[5]Ibid., 35.

[6]Randy Woodley, "A View of the Native North American Contextual Movement and Its Undecided Future," *Journal of the North American Institute for Indigenous Theological Studies* 4 (2006): 106.

[7]Rogers, *Diffusion of Innovations*, p. 46.

[8]Ibid.

[9]Ibid.

[10]Ibid., pp. 316-18.

[11]Ibid., p. 305.

[12]Ibid., p. 36.

[13]Raymond A. Bucko, *The Lakota Ritual of the Sweat Lodge: History and Contemporary Practice* (Lincoln, NE: Bison Books, University of Nebraska Press, 1999), p. 12.

[14]Ibid., p. 30.

[15]Ibid.

[16]Ibid., pp. 32-36.

[17]A. H. Mathias Zahniser, *Symbol and Ceremony: Making Disciples Across Cultures*, Innovations in Mission (Monrovia, CA: MARC, 1997), p. 84.

[18]K. A. Dickson, "Christian and African Traditional Ceremonies," in *Readings in Missionary Anthropology II*, ed. William Smalley (Pasadena, CA: William Carey Library, 1978), p. 434.

[19]Richard Twiss, "Making Jesus Known in Knowable Ways," *Mission Frontiers* (September 1, 2010), www.missionfrontiers.org/issue/article/making-jesus-known-in-knowable-ways. Accessed December 21, 2014.

[20]Flemming, *Contextualization in the New Testament*, p. 297.

[21]Philip Jenkins, *Dream Catchers: How Mainstream America Discovered Native Spirituality* (New York: Oxford University Press, 2004), p. 44.

[22] Jim Chosa and Faith Chosa, *Thy Kingdom Come Thy Will Be Done In Earth: A First Nations Perspective on Strategic Keys for Territorial Deliverance and Transformation* (Yellowstone, MT: Day Chief Ministries, 2004), p. 244.

[23]Tara Browner, *Heartbeat of the People: Music and Dance of the Northern Powwow* (Chicago: University of Illinois Press, 2002), p. 35.

[24]Rogers, *Diffusion of Innovations*, p. 116.

[25]R. D. Theisz, *Sharing the Gift of Lakota Song* (Ranchos de Taos, NM: Dog Soldier Press, 2003), p. 2.

[26]Ben Black Bear and R. D. Theisz, *Songs and Dances of the Lakota: Cokatakiya Waci Uwo! Come Out to the Center and Dance!* (Aberdeen, SD: North Plains Press, 1976), p. 25.

[27]Clyde Ellis, Luke Eric Lassiter, and Gary H. Dunham, *Powwow* (Lincoln, NE: University of Nebraska Press, 2005), pp. 20-21.

[28]Charles H. Kraft, *Anthropology for Christian Witness* (Maryknoll, NY: Orbis Books, 1996), p. 377.

[29]George E. Tinker, *American Indian Liberation: A Theology of Sovereignty* (Maryknoll, NY: Orbis Books, 2008), p. 85.

[30]Browner, *Heartbeat of the People*, p. 3.

[31]Charles H. Burke, "Segments from the Circular No. 1665 and Supplement to Circular No. 1665," Department of the Interior Office of Indian Affairs, April 26, 1921 and February 14, 1923. www.webpages.uidaho.edu/~rfrey/PDF/329/IndianDances.pdf. Accessed December 21, 2014.

[32]Charles H. Kraft, *Christianity in Culture: A Study in Dynamic Biblical Theologizing in Cross-Cultural Perspective* (Maryknoll, NY: Orbis Books, 2003), p. 311.

[33]Paul G. Hiebert, *Anthropological Reflections on Missiological Issues* (Grand Rapids: Baker Academic, 1994), p. 46.

[34]Kraft, *Christianity in Culture*, pp. 303, 309.

[35]Hiebert, *Anthropological Reflections*, p. 310.

[36]Ibid.

[37]Jenkins, *Dream Catchers*, p. 10.

[38]Editors' note: Dr. Twiss served as board chair until his passing in February 2013.

[39]The ninth symposium was held at Tyndale University College and Seminary, Toronto, Ontario, in June 2013. The tenth symposium was held at George Fox Seminary and University, Newberg, Oregon, in June 2014.

[40]Stephen Neill, *A History of Christian Missions*, The Pelican History of the Church, vol. 6 (Baltimore, MD: Penguin, 1990), p. 399.

[41]Ibid.

[42]This did happen in June 2013.

[43]Richard Twiss, *One Church, Many Tribes: Following Jesus the Way God Made You* (Ventura, CA: Regal Books, 2000).

[44]Richard L. Twiss, *Christ, Culture, and Kingdom Seminar Study Guide: Presenting Biblical Principles for Native Ministry that Honor God, His People, and His Creation* (1996; repr., Richard L. Twiss, 2002).

[45]Richard L. Twiss, *Dancing Our Prayers* (Richard L. Twiss, 1998).

[46]Randy Woodley, *Living in Color: Embracing God's Passion for Ethnic Diversity* (Downers Grove, IL: InterVarsity Press, 2004); Woodley, *Mixed Blood, Not Mixed Up: Finding God-given Identity in a Multi-cultural World* (Scotland, PA: Healing the Land, 2004); Woodley, *When Going to Church is Sin and Other Essays on Native American Christian Missions* (Scotland, PA: Healing the Land, 2007); and Woodley, *Shalom and the Community of Creation: An Indigenous Vision* (Grand Rapids: Eerdmans, 2012).

[47]Adrian Jacobs, *Aboriginal Christianity: The Way it was Meant to Be* (Adrian Jacobs, 1998); Jacobs, *Pagan Prophets and Heathen Believers: Native American Believers in the Creator of the Bible* (Adrian Jacobs, 1999); and Jacobs, *Sacred Clowns* (Adrian Jacobs).

[48]Terry LeBlanc, ed., My People International VBS Curriculum, 5 vols.: *Creator Creates the World, Our Relationship with the Creator, Creator's Promises, Our Creator Saves Us,* and *Building Together* (Evansburg, Alberta: My People International, 2000).

[49]Neill, *A History of Christian Missions*, p. 297.

[50]Qaumaniq Suuqiina and Dr. Iglahliq Suuqiina, *Warfare by Honor: The Restoration of Honor: A Protocol Handbook* (Scotland, PA: Healing the Land, 2007); and Dr. Iglahliq Suuqiina, *Can You Feel the Mountains Tremble? A Healing the Land Handbook* (Dr. Iglahliq Suuqiina, 2004).

[51]Rogers, *Diffusion of Innovations*, p. 27.

[52]All of the articles referenced can be downloaded at no cost at www.missionfrontiers .org.

[53]*The Jesus Way New Testament*, New International Reader's Version (Colorado Springs, CO: IBS, 1995), p. A4.

[54]Rogers, *Diffusion of Innovations*, p. 12.

CHAPTER 5: FROM COLONIZATION TO CONTEXTUALIZATION

[1]Evan Pritchard, *Native American Stories of the Sacred: Annotated and Explained* (Woodstock, VT: Skylight Paths, 2005), p. xxi.

[2]Bernd C. Peyer, *The Tutor'd Mind: Indian Missionary-Writers in Antebellum America* (Amherst, MA: University of Massachusetts Press), p. 1.

[3]Ibid., p. 13.

[4]Malcolm McFee, "The 150% Man, A Product of Blackfeet Acculturation," *American Anthropologist, New Series* 70, no. 6 (December 1968): 1001, www.jstor.org /stable/669511.

[5]Everett M. Rogers, *Diffusion of Innovations* (New York: Free Press, 2003), pp. 48-49.

[6]Ibid.

[7]Ibid., p. 55.

[8]Malcolm Gladwell, *The Tipping Point: How Little Things Can Make a Big Difference* (Boston: Little, Brown, 2002), p. 7.

[9]Ibid., pp. 9-12.

[10]Eugene Nida, *Customs and Cultures* (Pasadena, CA: William Carey Library, 1975).

[11]Charles H. Kraft, *Appropriate Christianity* (Pasadena, CA: William Carey Library, 2005), pp. 10-11.

[12]Ibid., pp. 4-5.

[13]Ibid., p. 12.

[14]David R. Scates, *Why Navajo Churches Are Growing: The Cultural Dynamics of Navajo Religious Change* (Grand Junction, CO: Navajo Christian Churches, 1981).

[15]Ibid.

[16]Lesslie Newbigin, *Foolishness to the Greeks: The Gospel and Western Culture* (London: SPCK, 1986), p. 4.

[17]Tina Norris, Paula L. Vines and Elizabeth M. Hoeffel, "The American Indian and Alaska Native Population: 2010," United States Census Bureau Special Reports, January 2012, p. 13.

[18]Dean Flemming, *Contextualization in the New Testament: Patterns for Theology and Mission* (Downers Grove, IL: InterVarsity Press, 2005), p. 306.

[19]Ibid., p. 309.

[20]William A. Smalley, ed., *Readings in Missionary Anthropology II* (1978; repr., Pasadena, CA: William Carey Library, 1986), p. 370.

[21]Stephen Neill, *A History of Christian Missions*, The Pelican History of the Church, vol. 6 (Baltimore, MD: Penguin, 1990), p. 396.

[22]Charles H. Kraft, *Christianity in Culture: A Study in Dynamic Biblical Theologizing in Cross-Cultural Perspective* (Maryknoll, NY: Orbis Books, 2003), p. 19.

[23]Neill, *History of Christian Missions*, pp. 397-98.

[24]Craig Stephen Smith, *Whiteman's Gospel* (Winnipeg, MB: Indian Life Books, 1998), p. 126.

[25]Craig Stephen Smith, *Boundary Lines: The Issue of Christ, Indigenous Worship, and Native American Culture*, a study commissioned by the Native American Association of the Christian and Missionary Alliance (2000), p. 34.

[26]CHIEF stands for Christian Hope Indian Eskimo Fellowship. See www.chief.org.

[27]Craig Stephen Smith, *Boundary Lines*, p. 2.

[28]Charles Stewart and Rosalind Shaw, *Syncretism/Anti-syncretism: The Politics of Religious Synthesis* (New York: Routledge, 1994), p. 1.

[29]Paul G. Hiebert, *Anthropological Insights for Missionaries* (Grand Rapids: Baker Book House, 1987), p. 109.

[30]Neill, *History of Christian Missions*, p. 398.

[31]David J. Hesselgrave and Edward Rommen, *Contextualization: Meanings, Methods, and Models* (Pasadena, CA: William Carey Library, 1989), p. 150.

[32]Flemming, *Contextualization in the New Testament*, p. 298.

[33]Ibid., p. 20.

[34]Smalley, ed., *Readings in Missionary Anthropology II*, p. 366.

[35]Ibid., p. 369.

[36]Ibid., p. 370.

[37]Kraft, *Christianity in Culture*, pp. 318, 321.

[38]The church has struggled to maintain its momentum and has mostly returned to its Pentecostal roots in terms of church services. Members continue to participate in various cultural and ceremonial ways. Theresa passed on in 2010.

[39]Kraft, *Christianity in Culture*, p. 315.

[40]Smalley, ed., *Readings in Missionary Anthropology II*, p. 367.

[41]Susan Lobo and Kurt Peters, eds., *American Indians and the Urban Experience, Contemporary Native American Communities* (Walnut Creek, CA: Altamira Press, 2001), p. xiii.

CHAPTER 6: LOOKING DOWN THE ROAD

[1]Lamin O. Sanneh, *Whose Religion is Christianity? The Gospel Beyond the West* (Grand Rapids: Eerdmans, 2003), p. 24.

[2]Ibid.

[3]Amia Lieblich, Rivka Tuval-Mashiach, and Tamar Zilber, *Narrative Research: Reading Analysis, and Interpretation* (Thousand Oaks, CA: Sage, 1998), p. 168.

[4]Everett M. Rogers, *Diffusion of Innovations* (New York: Free Press, 2003), p. 180.

[5]Malcolm McFee, "The 150% Man, A Product of Blackfeet Acculturation," *American Anthropologist, New Series* 70, no. 6 (December 1968): 1001.

[6]Robert Atkinson, *The Life Story Interview* (Thousand Oaks, CA: Sage, 1998), p. 14.

[7]Malcolm Gladwell, *The Tipping Point: How Little Things Can Make a Big Difference* (Boston: Little, Brown, 2002), p. 18.

[8]Ibid., pp. 21-22.

⁹Ibid., pp. 24-25.

¹⁰Ibid.

¹¹Adrian Jacobs, "A History of Slaughter: Embracing Our Martyrdom at the Margins of Encounter," *Journal of the North American Institute for Indigenous Theological Studies* 4 (2006): 123-25.

APPENDIX A

¹Editors' note: This appendix is borrowed courtesy of Wendy Peterson, the editor of NAIITS Journal #10 and Terry LeBlanc, director, NAIITS: An Indigenous Learning Community. The appendix is an excerpt from a paper presented by Dr. Richard Twiss at the 2012 NAIITS Symposium.

²L. H. Gunderson, C. S. Holling, et al, eds., *Panarchy: Understanding Transformations in Human and Natural Systems* (Washington, DC: Island Press, 2002).

³C. S. Holling, "Understanding the Complexity of Economic, Ecological, and Social Systems," in *Ecosystems* (2001), 4:392.

APPENDIX B

¹James B. LaGrand, *Indian Metropolis: Native Americans in Chicago, 1945–1975* (Chicago: University of Illinois Press, 2002); Vine Deloria Jr. and C. M. Lytle, *The Nations Within: The Past and Future of American Indian Sovereignty* (Austin, TX: Pantheon Books, 1984); Vine Deloria Jr., *God is Red: A Native View of Religion* (Golden, CO: Fulcrum, 2003); and Tinker, *Missionary Conquest*.

²National Congress of American Indians (NCAI), www.ncai.org.

³Dickason and Calder, *A Concise History of Canada's First Nations* (London: Oxford University Press, 2010); and Susan Kalter, *Benjamin Franklin, Pennsylvania, and the First Nations: The Treaties of 1736–62* (Chicago: University of Illinois Press, 2006).

⁴Assembly of First Nations (AFN), www.afn.ca.

⁵James B. Waldram, D. Ann Herring, and T. Kue Young, *Aboriginal Health in Canada: Historical, Cultural, and Epidemiological Perspectives* (Toronto: University of Toronto Press, 2006); Renée Dupuis and Robert Chodos, *Justice for Canada's Aboriginal Peoples* (Holt, MI: Lorimer Press, 2002); and Stephen Leacock, *The Dawn of Canadian History: A Chronicle of Aboriginal Canada* (Nabu Press, 2010).

⁶Evangelical Fellowship of Canada, www.evangelicalfellowship.ca/page.aspx?pid=325.

⁷This was from a conversation Richard Twiss had with Wendy Beauchemin Peterson, editor, *NAIITS journals*. Permission has been granted.

⁸Patrick Douaud, ed., *The Western Métis: Profile of a People*, Canadian Plains Studies (CPS) (Regina, Saskatchewan: Canadian Plains Research Center, 2007); D. N. Sprague, *The Genealogy of the First Métis Nation*, ed. R. P. Frye (Winnipeg, MB:

Pemmican, 1983); and John Weinstein, *Quiet Revolution West: The Rebirth of Métis Nationalism* (Markham, Ontario: Fifth House, 2007).

[9]Pamela Stern and Lisa Stevenson, eds., *Critical Inuit Studies: An Anthology of Contemporary Arctic Ethnography* (Lincoln, NE: University of Nebraska Press, 2006); and Alice Osinski, *The Eskimo: The Inuit and Yupik People* (Chicago: Children's Press, 1985).

[10]Colin F. Taylor, *The Native Americans: The Indigenous People of North America* (Philadelphia: Courage Books, 2002); Ward Churchill, *Perversions of Justice: Indigenous Peoples and Anglo-American Law* (San Francisco: City Lights, 2003); and Bonita Lawrence, *"Real" Indians and Others: Mixed-Blood Urban Native Peoples and Indigenous Nationhood* (Lincoln: University of Nebraska Press, 2004).

BIBLIOGRAPHY

Adams, David Wallace. *Education for Extinction: American Indians and the Boarding School Experience, 1875–1928.* Lawrence, KS: University of Kansas Press, 1995.

Aldred, Ray. "The Resurrection of Story." *Journal of the North American Institute of Indigenous Theological Studies* 2 (2004): 5-14.

Alfred, Taiaiake. *Peace, Power, Righteousness: An Indigenous Manifesto.* New York: Oxford University Press, 1999.

———. "Warrior Scholarship, Seeing the University as a Ground of Contention." In *Indigenizing the Academy: Transforming Scholarship and Empowering Communities, Contemporary Indigenous Issues,* edited by Devon Abbott Mihesuah and Angela Cavender Wilson. Lincoln, NE: University of Nebraska Press, 2004.

Atkinson, Robert. *The Life Story Interview.* Thousand Oaks, CA: Sage, 1998.

Beaver, R. Pierce, ed. *The Native American Christian Community: A Directory of Indian, Aleut, and Eskimo Churches.* Monrovia, CA: Marc, 1979.

Berger, Peter L., and Thomas Luckmann. *The Social Construction of Reality: A Treatise in the Sociology of Knowledge.* Garden City, NY: Anchor Books, 1967.

Bevans, Stephan B. *Models of Contextual Theology.* Maryknoll, NY: Orbis Books, 2004.

Black Bear, Ben, and R. D. Theisz. *Songs and Dances of the Lakota: Cokatakiya Waci Uwo! Come Out to the Center and Dance!* Aberdeen, SD: North Plains Press, 1976.

Bonk, Jon. *Missions and Money: Affluence as a Western Missionary Problem.* Maryknoll, NY: Orbis Books, 1991.

Borgmann, Albert. *Crossing the Postmodern Divide.* Chicago: University of Chicago Press, 1996.

Bosch, David. J. *Transforming Mission: Paradigm Shifts in Theology of Mission.* Maryknoll, NY: Orbis, 1997.

Boyd, Robert. *People of the Dalles: The Indians of the Wascopam Missions: A Historical Ethnography Based on the Papers of the Free Methodist Missionaries.* Lincoln, NE: University of Nebraska Press, 1996.

Bross, Kristina. *Dry Bones and Indian Sermons: Praying Indians in Colonial America.* Ithaca, NY: Cornell University Press, 2004.

Browner, Tara. *Heartbeat of the People: Music and Dance of the Northern Powwow.* Chicago: University of Illinois Press, 2002.

Bucko, Raymond A. *The Lakota Ritual of the Sweat Lodge: History and Contemporary Practice.* Lincoln, NE: Bison Books, 1999.

Burke, Charles H. "Segments from the Circular No. 1665 and Supplement to Circular No. 1665." Department of the Interior Office of Indian Affairs. April 26, 1921, and February 14, 1923.

CBC News Network. "Winnipeg Church Nixes Native Dancing at Habitat for Humanity Event." November 12, 2007.

Chosa, Jim, and Faith Chosa. *Thy Kingdom Come Thy Will Be Done in Earth: A First Nations Perspective on Strategic Keys for Territorial Deliverance and Transformation.* Yellowstone, MT: Day Chief Ministries, 2004.

Christian Hope Indian Eskimo Fellowship (CHIEF). *A Biblical Position by Native Leaders on Native Spirituality.* Phoenix, AZ: Christian Hope Indian Eskimo Fellowship (CHIEF), 1998.

Churchill, Ward. *Perversions of Justice: Indigenous Peoples and Anglo-American Law.* San Francisco: City Lights, 2003.

Clandinin, Jean D., and F. Michael Connelly. *Narrative Inquiry: Experience and Story in Qualitative Research.* San Francisco: Jossey-Bass, 2000.

Cobb, Daniel M. *Native Activism in Cold War America: The Struggle for Sovereignty.* Lawrence, KS: University Press of Kansas, 2008.

Comaroff, Jean, and John L. Comaroff. *Of Revelation and Revolution: Christianity, Colonialism, and Consciousness in South Africa.* Chicago: University of Chicago Press, 1991.

Cook-Lynn, Elizabeth. "American Indian Intellectualism and the New Indian Story." In *Natives and Academics: Researching and Writing About American Indians,* edited by Devon A. Mihesuah, pp. 111-38. Lincoln, NE: University of Nebraska Press, 1998.

Cresswell, John W. *Research Design: Qualitative, Quantitative, and Mixed Method Approaches.* 2nd ed. Thousand Oaks, CA: Sage, 2003.

Deloria, V., and C. M. Lytle. *The Nations Within: The Past and Future of American Indian Sovereignty.* New York: Pantheon Books, 1984.

Deloria, Vine. *God is Red: A Native View of Religion.* Golden, CO: Fulcrum, 2003.

d'Errico, Peter. Forward to *Pagans in the Promised Land: Decoding the Doctrine of Christian Discovery,* by Steven T. Newcomb, p. ix. Golden, CO: Fulcrum, 2008.

Des Gerlaise, Nanci. *Muddy Waters: An Insider's View of North American Native Spirituality*. Eureka, MT: Lighthouse Trails, 2012.

Dickason, Olive Patricia, and Moira Jean Calder. *A Concise History of Canada's First Nations*. London: Oxford University Press, 2010.

Dickson, K. A. "Christian and African Traditional Ceremonies." In *Readings in Missionary Anthropology II*, edited by William Smalley. Pasadena, CA: William Carey Library, 1978.

Douaud, Patrick, ed. *The Western Métis: Profile of a People*. Canadian Plains Studies (CPS). Regina, Saskatchewan: Canadian Plains Research Center, 2007.

Drury, Clifford Merrill. *The Diaries and Letters of Henry Harmon Spalding and Asa Bowen Smith Relating to Nez Perce Mission*. Glendale, CA: The Arthur H. Clark Co., 1958.

Dupuis, Renée, and Robert Chodos. *Justice for Canada's Aboriginal Peoples*. Holt, MI: Lorimer Press, 2002.

Ellis, Clyde, Luke Eric Lassiter, and Gary H. Dunham. *Powwow*. Lincoln, NE: University of Nebraska Press, 2005.

Escobar, Samuel. *The New Global Mission: The Gospel from Everywhere to Everyone*. Downers Grove, IL: InterVarsity Press, 2003.

Fall, Babacar. "Orality and Life Histories: Rethinking the Social and Political History of Senegal." *Africa Today*, Fall/Winter 2003, pp. 55-65.

Fixico, Donald Lee. *The American Indian Mind in a Linear World: American Indian Studies and Traditional Knowledge*. New York: Routledge, 2003.

———. "Ethics and Responsibilities in Writing American Indian History." In *Natives and Academics: Researching and Writing About American Indians*, edited by Devon Mihesuah. Lincoln, NE: University of Nebraska Press, 1998.

Flemming, Dean. *Contextualization in the New Testament: Patterns for Theology and Mission*. Downers Grove, IL: InterVarsity Press, 2005.

Gilliland, Dean S., ed. *The Word Among Us: Contextualizing Theology for Mission Today*. Dallas: Word, 1989.

Gladwell, Malcolm. *The Tipping Point: How Little Things Can Make a Big Difference*. Boston: Little, Brown, 2002.

Grady, J. Lee. "Native Americans Use Culture for Christ." *Charisma Magazine*, June 30, 2000, www.charismamag.com/site-archives/134-peopleevents/people-events/63-native-americans-use-culture-for-christ.

Grenz, Stanley J., David Guretzki, and Cherith Fee Nordling. *Pocket Dictionary of Theological Terms*. Downers Grove, IL: InterVarsity Press, 1999.

Hesselgrave, David J., and Edward Rommen. *Contextualization: Meanings,*

Methods, and Models. Pasadena, CA: William Carey Library, 1989.

Hiebert, P. G., Daniel Shaw, and Tite Tiénou. *Understanding Folk Religion: A Christian Response to Popular Beliefs and Practices*. Grand Rapids: Baker Books, 1999.

Hiebert, Paul G., and Eloise Hiebert Meneses. *Incarnational Ministry: Planting Churches in Band, Tribal, Peasant, and Urban Societies*. 1995. Reprint, Grand Rapids: Baker Books, 1999.

Hiebert, Paul G. *Anthropological Insights for Missionaries*. Grand Rapids: Baker Book House, 1987.

———. *Anthropological Reflections on Missiological Issues*. Grand Rapids: Baker Academic, 1994.

Hunter III, George G. *The Celtic Way of Evangelism: How Christianity Can Reach the West—Again*. Nashville, TN: Abingdon Press, 2000.

International Bible Society. *The Jesus Way New Testament*. Colorado Springs, CO: International Bible Society, 1995.

Irwin, Eunice. "The Status of Syncretism in Missiological Studies and a Modest Proposal for the 21st Century from the Perspective of Fourth World Peoples." Unpublished Paper sent via email, n.d.

Irving, Washington. "The Adventures of Captain Bonneville" in *Three Western Narratives*. New York: Literary Classics of the United States, 2004.

Irwin, Lee. *Native American Spirituality: A Critical Reader*. Lincoln, NE: University of Nebraska Press, 2000.

Jacobs, Adrian. *Aboriginal Christianity: The Way It Was Meant to Be*. Adrian Jacobs, 1998.

———. "A History of Slaughter: Embracing Our Martyrdom at the Margins of Encounter." Edited by Wendy Peterson. *Journal of the North American Institute for Indigenous Theological Studies* 4 (2006).

———. *Pagan Prophets and Heathen Believers: Native American Believers in the God of the Bible*. Adrian Jacobs, 1999.

———. *Sacred Clowns*. Adrian Jacobs, n.d.

Jenkins, Philip. *Dream Catchers: How Mainstream America Discovered Native Spirituality*. Oxford, New York: Oxford University Press, 2004.

———. *The Next Christendom: The Coming of Global Christianity*. Oxford, New York: Oxford University Press, 2002.

Jessett, Thomas E. *Chief Spokane Garry—Statesman, and Friend of the Whiteman*. Minneapolis: Denison and Company, 1960.

Kalter, Susan. *Benjamin Franklin, Pennsylvania, and the First Nations: The*

Treaties of 1736–62. Chicago: University of Illinois Press, 2006.

Keitzman, Dale, and William A. Smalley. "The Missionary Role in Culture Change." In *Readings in Missionary Anthropology II*, edited by William A. Smalley, pp. 524-29. 1978. Reprint, Pasadena, CA: William Carey Library, 1986.

Kidwell, Clare Sue, Homer Noley, and George E. Tinker. *A Native American Theology.* Maryknoll, NY: Orbis Books, 2004.

Koopman, LeRoy. *Taking the Jesus Road: The Ministry of the Reformed Church in America Among Native Americans.* Grand Rapids: Eerdmans, 2005.

Kraft, Charles H. *Anthropology for Christian Witness.* Maryknoll, NY: Orbis Books, 1996.

———. *Appropriate Christianity.* Pasadena, CA: William Carey Library, 2005.

———. *Christianity in Culture: A Study in Dynamic Biblical Theologizing in Cross-Cultural Perspective.* Maryknoll, NY: Orbis Books, 2003.

———. "Culture, Communication and Christianity." In *Readings in Missionary Anthropology II*, edited by William A. Smalley, pp. 486-94. 1978. Reprint, Pasadena, CA: William Carey Library, 1986.

LaGrand, James B. *Indian Metropolis: Native Americans in Chicago, 1945–75.* Urbana, IL: University of Illinois Press, 2002.

Lawrence, Bonita. *"Real" Indians and Others: Mixed-Blood Urban Native Peoples and Indigenous Nationhood.* Lincoln, NE: University of Nebraska Press, 2004.

Leacock, Stephen. *The Dawn of Canadian History: A Chronicle of Aboriginal Canada.* Nabu Press, 2010.

LeBlanc, Terry, ed. My People International VBS Curriculum. 5 vols: *Creator Saves the World, Our Relationship with the Creator, Creator's Promises, Our Creator Saves Us*, and *Building Together.* Evansburg, Alberta: My People International, 2000.

Lewis, Bonnie Sue. *Creating Christian Indians: Native Clergy in the Presbyterian Church.* Norman, OK: University of Oklahoma Press, 2003.

Lieblich, Amia, Rivka Tuval-Mashiach and Tamar Zilber. *Narrative Research: Reading, Analysis, and Interpretation.* Thousand Oaks, CA: Sage, 1998.

Lindquist, G. E. E. *The Red Man in the United States.* Clifton, NJ: A. M. Kelley, 1973.

Lobo, Susan, and Kurt Peters, eds. *American Indians and the Urban Experience.* Vol. 5 of *Contemporary Native American Communities.* Walnut Creek, CA: Altamira Press, 2001.

Lomawaima, K. Tsianina, and Teresa L. McCarty. *To Remain Indian: Lessons in Democracy from a Century of Native American Education.* New York: Teachers College Press, 2006.

Long, Zeb Bradford, and Douglas McMurry. *The Collapse of the Brass Heaven: Rebuilding Our Worldview to Embrace the Power of God.* Grand Rapids: Chosen Books, 1994.

Mbiti, John S. *African Religions and Philosophy.* Portsmouth, NH: Heinemann, 1999.

McFee, Malcolm. "The 150% Man, A Product of Blackfeet Acculturation." *American Anthropologist, New Series,* 70, no. 6 (December 1968): 1096-1107.

McKnight, Scot. *A Community Called Atonement.* Nashville, TN: Abingdon Press, 2007.

McLaren, Brian. *A New Kind of Christianity: Ten Questions That Are Transforming the Faith.* San Francisco: HarperOne, 2010.

Medicine, Beatrice, and Sue Ellen Jacobs, eds. *Learning to Be an Anthropologist and Remaining "Native": Selected Writings.* Urbana: University of Illinois Press, 2001.

Mihesuah, Devon A. *Natives and Academics: Researching and Writing About American Indians.* 1st ed. Lincoln, NE: University of Nebraska Press, 1998.

Miller, Robert J. *Native America, Discovered and Conquered: Thomas Jefferson, Lewis and Clark, and Manifest Destiny.* Lincoln, NE: University of Nebraska Press, 2000.

Mish, Frederick C., ed. *Merriam-Webster Collegiate Dictionary.* Springfield, MA: Merriam-Webster, 1993.

Morgan, Lewis Henry. *Ancient Society; Or, Researches in the Lines of Human Progress from Savagery, Through Barbarism to Civilization.* New York: Holt and Company, 1877.

Neill, Stephan. *A History of Christian Missions: The Pelican History of the Church.* Vol. 6. Baltimore, MD: Penguin Books, 1990.

Newbigin, Lesslie. *Foolishness to the Greeks: The Gospel and Western Culture.* London: SPCK, 1986.

Newcomb, Steven T. *Pagans in the Promised Land: Decoding the Doctrine of Christian Discovery.* Goldon, CO: Fulcrum, 2008.

Nicholls, Bruce, and Charles F. Kraft. "Anglo America." In *Contextualization: Meanings, Methods, and Models,* by David J. Hesselgrave and Edward Rommen. Grand Rapids: Baker Book House, 1989.

Nida, Eugene. *Customs and Cultures.* Pasadena, CA: William Carey Library, 1975.

Nieves, Evelyn. "Indian Reservation Reeling in Wave of Youth Suicides and Attempts." *New York Times,* June 9, 2007.

Noley, Homer. *First White Frost: Native Americans and United Methodism.* Nashville, TN: Abingdon Press, 1991.

Osinski, Alice. *The Eskimo: The Inuit and Yupik People.* Chicago: Children's Press, 1985.

Peterson, Eugene H. *The Message: The Bible in Contemporary Language.* Colorado Springs, CO: NavPress, 2005.

Peyer, Bernd C. *The Tutor'd Mind: Indian Missionary-Writers in Antebellum America.* Amherst, MA: University of Massachusetts Press, 1997.

Pratt, Richard H. *The Official Report of the Nineteenth Annual Conference of Charities and Correction,* 1892, pp. 46-59. Reprinted in "The Advantages of Mingling Indians with Whites." In *Americanizing the American Indians: Writings by the "Friends of the Indian,"* 1880-1900. Cambridge, MA: Harvard University Press, 1973.

Pritchard, Evan. *Native American Stories of the Sacred: Annotated and Explained.* Woodstock, VT: Skylight Paths, 2005.

Prucha, Francis Paul. *Documents of United States Indian Policy.* Lincoln, NE: University of Nebraska Press, 1990.

Rah, Soong-Chan. *The Next Evangelicalism: Releasing the Church from Western Cultural Captivity.* Downers Grove, IL: InterVarsity Press, 2009.

Reyburn, William. "The Missionary and Cultural Diffusion." In *Readings in Missionary Anthropology II,* edited by William A. Smalley, pp. 510-23. 1976. Reprint, Pasadena, CA: William Carey Library, 1986.

Rogers, Everett M. *Diffusion of Innovations, Fifth Edition.* New York: Free Press, 1983.

Sanneh, Lamin O. *Whose Religion is Christianity? The Gospel Beyond the West.* Grand Rapids: Eerdmans, 2003.

Scates, David R. *Why Navajo Churches Are Growing: The Cultural Dynamics of Navajo Religious Change.* Grand Junction, CO: Navajo Christian Churches, 1981.

Stewart, Charles, and Rosalind Shaw. *Syncretism/Anti-Syncretism: The Politics of Religious Synthesis.* New York: Routledge, 1994.

Smalley, William A., ed. *Readings in Missionary Anthropology II.* 1978. Reprint, Pasadena, CA: William Carey Library, 1986.

Smith, Andrea, "Soul Wound: The Legacy of Native American Schools." *Amnesty International Magazine* (March 26, 2007), www.amnestyusa.org/node/87342.

Smith, Craig Stephan. *Boundary Lines: The Issue of Christ, Indigenous Worship, and Native American Culture.* Prince Albert, SK: Northern Canada Mission Distributors, 2000.

———. *Whiteman's Gospel.* Winnipeg, MB: Indian Life Books, 1998.

Smith, Linda Tuhiwai. *Decolonizing Methodologies: Research and Indigenous People.* London: Zed Books, 1999.

Sprague, D. N., and R. P. Frye, eds. *The Geneology of the First Métis Nation.* Winnipeg, MB: Pemmican, 1983.

Starkloff, Carl F. *A Theology of the In-Between: The Value of Syncretic Process.* Milwaukee, WI: Marquette University Press, 2002.

Stephanson, Anders. *Manifest Destiny: American Expansionism and the Empire of Right.* New York: Hill and Wang, 1995.

Stern, Pamela, and Lisa Stevenson, eds. *Critical Inuit Studies: An Anthology of Contemporary Arctic Ethnography.* Lincoln, NE: University of Nebraska Press, 2006.

Storti, Craig. *The Art of Crossing Cultures.* Yarmouth, ME: Intercultural Press, 2001.

Strauss, Anselm, and Juliet Corbin. *Basics of Qualitative Research: Techniques and Procedures for Developing Grounded Theory.* Thousand Oaks, CA: Sage, 1998.

Suuqiina, Dr. Iglahliq. *Can You Feel the Mountains Tremble? A Healing the Land Handbook.* Portland, TN: Inuit Ministries International, 2004.

Suuqiina, Qaumaniq, and Dr. Iglahliq Suuqiina. *Warfare by Honor: The Restoration of Honor: A Protocol Handbook.* Scotland, PA: Healing the Land, 2007.

Swisher, Karen Gayton. "Why Indian People Should Be The Ones to Write About Indian Education." In *Natives and Academics: Researching and Writing About American Indians*, edited by Devon Mishesuah. Lincoln, NE: University of Nebraska Press, 1998.

Taber, Charles R. "The Limits of Indigenization in Theology." *Missiology: An International Review*, January 1978.

Taylor, Colin F. *The Native Americans: The Indigenous People of North America.* Philadelphia, PA: Courage Books, 2002.

Theisz, R. D. *Sharing the Gift of Lakota Song.* Ranchos de Taos, NM: Dog Soldier Press, 2003.

Thiong'o, Ngũgĩ wa. *Decolonizing the Mind: The Politics of Language in African Literature.* Oxford, England: James Currey Publishers, 2009.

Tiénou, Tite. "World Christianity and Theological Reflection." In *Globalizing Theology: Belief and Practice in an Era of World Christianity*, edited by Craig Ott and Harold A. Netland. Grand Rapids: Baker Academic, 2006.

Tinker, G. E. *American Indian Liberation: A Theology of Sovereignty.* Maryknoll, New York: Orbis Books, 2008.

———. *Missionary Conquest: The Gospel and Native American Cultural Genocide.* Minneapolis: Fortress, 1993.

———. *Spirit and Resistance: Political Theology and American Indian Liberation.* Minneapolis: Fortress, 2003.

Tippett, Alan R. "Christopaganism or Indigenous Christianity?" In *Christopaganism or Indigenous Christianity?*, edited by Tetsunao Yamamori and Charles Taber. Pasadena, CA: William Carey Library, 1975.

Treat, James. *Around the Sacred Fire: Native Religious Activism in the Red Power Era: A Narrative Map of the Indian Ecumenical Conference.* New York: Palgrave Macmillan, 2003.

Twiss, Richard L. *Christ, Culture and Kingdom Seminar Study Guide: Presenting Biblical Principles for Native Ministry that Honor God, His People and His Creation.* Richard L. Twiss, 1996.

———. *Dancing Our Prayers: Perspectives on Syncretism, Critical Contextualization and Cultural Practices in First Nations Ministry.* Richard L. Twiss, 1998.

———. "Making Jesus Known in Knowable Ways." *Mission Frontiers,* September 2010, www.missionfrontiers.org/issue/article/making-jesus-known-in-knowable -ways.

———. *One Church, Many Tribes: Following Jesus the Way God Made You.* Ventura, CA: Regal Books, 2000.

———. "Rescuing Theology from the Cowboys: An Emerging Indigenous Expression of the Jesus Way in North America." Edited by Wendy Peterson. *The North American Institute for Indigenous Theological Studies* 10 (2014): 5-45.

United States Census 2000. "We the People: American Indians and Alaska Natives in the United States." Special Reports, February 2006, p. 2.

United States Census 2010. "The American Indian and Alaska Native Population: 2010." Special Reports, January 2012, p. 13.

van der Veer, Peter. "Syncretism, Multiculturalism and the Discourse of Tolerance." In *Syncretism/Anti-Syncretism: The Politics of Religious Synthesis*, edited by Charles Stewart and Rosiland Shaw. New York: Routledge, 1994.

van Gennep, Arnold. *The Rites of Passage.* 2nd edition, First edition in German, 1909. Chicago: University of Chicago Press, 1960.

Waldman, Carl. *Atlas of the North American Indian.* New York: Checkmark Books, 2000.

Waldram, James B., D. Ann Herring, and T. Kue Young. *Aboriginal Health in Canada: Historical, Cultural, and Epidemiological Perspectives.* Toronto, Ontario: University of Toronto Press, 2006.

Wallace, Anthony F. C. *Jefferson and the Indians: The Tragic Fate of the First Nations*. Cambridge, MA: The Belknap Press of Harvard University Press, 1999.

Walls, Andrew F. *The Missionary Movement in Christian History: Studies in the Transmission of Faith*. Maryknoll, NY: Orbis Books, 2004.

Weinstein, John. *Quiet Revolution West: The Rebirth of Métis Nationalism*. Markham, Ontario: Fifth House, 2007.

Whiteman, Darrell. *Anthropology and Mission: The Incarnational Connection*. Chicago: CCGM Publications, 2003.

———. "Contextualization: The Theory, the Gap, the Challenge." *International Bulletin of Missionary Research*, January 1997, p. 2.

Woodley, Randy. *Living in Color: Embracing God's Passion for Ethnic Diversity*. Downers Grove, IL: InterVarsity Press, 2004.

———. *Mixed Blood, Not Mixed Up: Finding God-given Identity in a Multi-cultural World*. Scotland, PA: Healing the Land, 2005.

———. *Shalom and the Community of Creation: An Indigenous Vision*. Grand Rapids: Eerdmans, 2012.

———. "A View of the Native North American Contextual Movement and Its Undecided Future." *Journal of the North American Institute for Indigenous Theological Studies* 4 (2006).

———. *When Going to Church Is Sin and Other Essays on Native American Missions*. Scotland, PA: Healing the Land, 2007.

Wyss, Hilary. *Captivity and Christianity: Narrating Christian Indian Identity 1643–1829*. Capitol Hill, NC: University of North Carolina, 1998.

———. *Writing Indians: Literacy, Christianity and Native Community in Early America*. Amherst, MA: University of Massachusetts Press, 2000.

Yamamori, T., and C. R. Taber, ed. *Christopaganism or Indigenous Christianity?* South Pasadena, CA: William Carey Library, 1975.

Yin, Robert K. *Case Study Research: Design and Methods*. Thousand Oaks, CA: Sage, 2003.

Yong, Amos, and Barbara Brown Zikmund, eds. *Remembering Jamestown: Hard Questions About Christian Mission*. Eugene, OR: Pickwick Publications, 2010.

Zahniser, A. H. Mathias. *Symbol and Ceremony: Making Disciples Across Cultures, Innovations in Mission*. 6th ed. Monrovia, CA: Marc, 1997.

WICONI INTERNATIONAL

Removing Barriers, Building Bridges

Learn more about Wiconi International's ongoing ministry:

Wiconi International
P.O. Box 5246
Vancouver, WA 98668
www.wiconi.com
Email: office@wiconi.com
Phone: 360-546-1867